# THE AMERICAN UNIVERSITY IN SUMMER

# The American University

BY

CLARENCE A. SCHOENFELD

WITH

DONALD N. ZILLMAN

FOREWORD BY JOHN GUY FOWLKES

in Summer

1967

MADISON, MILWAUKEE, AND LONDON

THE UNIVERSITY OF WISCONSIN PRESS

BOOKS BY CLARENCE A. SCHOENFELD

*The University and Its Publics*
*Effective Feature Writing*
*Publicity Media and Methods*
*The Shape of Summer Sessions to Come (editor)*
*Year-Round Education (with Neil Schmitz)*
*University Extension (with T. J. Shannon)*
*Wisconsin Sideroads to Somewhere*
*Cabins, Conservation, and Fun*

*Published by the University of Wisconsin Press*
*Madison, Milwaukee, and London*
*U.S.A.: Box 1379, Madison, Wisconsin 53701*
*U.K.: 26–28 Hallam Street, London, W. 1*
*Copyright © 1967 by the Regents of the*
*University of Wisconsin*
*All rights reserved*
*Printed in the United States of America*
*by The Heffernan Press, Inc., Worcester, Massachusetts*
*Library of Congress Catalog Card*
*Number 67-25941*

Here is the ghost
Of a summer that lived for us,
Here is a promise
Of summer to be.

WM. LEWIS HENLEY
*Rhymes and Rhythms*

# Foreword

## THE UNIVERSITY SUMMER TERM— MUDDLE OR MODEL?

JOHN GUY FOWLKES

Anderson Professor of Educational Administration
The University of Wisconsin

TIME WAS when most colleges and universities in the United States did not offer any substantial curricular program during the period between approximately June 15 and September 15. Among those institutions in which "summer sessions" were held, the breadth and depth, and therefore the balance, of the curriculum made available was seriously inadequate in contrast to the programs provided during the so-called academic year. Summer sessions were more important to teachers colleges, or to the division responsible for the preparation of teachers in the larger universities. For a long time the stimulus for holding a summer session was the increasingly large number of elementary and secondary school teachers and administrators who in many instances had not finished even the baccalaureate degree, and who therefore were in no few instances required by legal certification provisions to pursue continuing education. The length of these summer sessions varied, and course offerings were determined by the funds which it was estimated would be available, since the major source of revenue was student fees. On many campuses, at least, a number if not the majority of the abler members of the faculty would not make themselves available for summer session work.

This situation by no means holds true today. Summer sessions were held in some 1,300 institutions of higher learning during the summer of 1966, with a total enrollment of approximately a million students. Impressive as these figures are, the marked increase in educational opportunities made available in summer sessions is even more impressive. Where, only a few years past, on many college and university campuses academic programs were made available by only a small portion of all schools and departments, at present even among the largest institutions it is seldom that substantial participation in summer sessions by all of the regular organized units offering work during the academic year is not found. Equally important is an increasingly wide participation by the most illustrious and scholarly professorial staff in the summer session programs.

One of the major factors in this marked expansion of summer sessions in our colleges and universities was the impact of World Wars I and II. To a limited degree, and in a relatively small number of specialized areas, universities and colleges made significant contributions toward the preparation of military personnel during World War I. During World War II the role of institutions of higher learning in this respect was nothing short of gigantic. Traditional academic calendars were thrown to the winds during the 1940's. At one major university, during a fifteen-week period there were thirty-nine different lengths of academic calendars for as many specialized groups of students. In addition to the national impact of the World War II experience, the lay public increasingly asked, "Why can't colleges and universities work a full twelve-month year along with those who provide the funds for the establishment and operation of such institutions of higher learning?" Also, and probably more significant philosophically, the question was raised more and more often as to why one should be forced to spend four years earning a baccalaureate degree when it would be possible for some to earn such a degree in three years, or, in a small number of cases, even two or two-and-a-half years. At the same time, the query appropriately arose as to why some fine individuals who require five or indeed six years to earn a baccalaureate degree should not be encouraged to do so, and both institutional and individual calendars of study be organized in terms of the total calendar year and the total needs of society.

The status of summer sessions with respect to organization and administrative, instructional, and supporting staffs still leaves much to be desired in many instances. Commonly, some summer sessions are required to be "self-supporting"—namely, staff salaries are determined by numbers of students drawn rather than on the judicious basis of work assignments in terms of social need, as is the case in the academic year. Not infrequently, budgets for summer sessions do not make adequate provision for the essential equipment and supplies which are taken as a matter of course in the budgets of the regular academic session. Despite such handicaps, however, the college and university summer session is now an institution of no small significance or proportion. Institutes, workshops, and month-long special seminars are commonplace among even the commonly designated superior educational institutions. In one such institution a special organization known as the School for Banking has been held for thirty years, and regularly enrolls distinguished bankers from the north, south, east, and west, including representatives of the larger cities and the largest banks. It has been clearly demonstrated in summer sessions that the sacred cow of academic credit may appropriately and validly be granted for much shorter periods of time than the traditional academic quarters or semesters. It has also been demonstrated that complete concentration upon a research project, whether it be the basis of a thesis or not, in many cases appears to produce more progress during summer sessions than is sometimes, if not often, the case during the regular year. As is easily understood, summer sessions increasingly have provided opportunity for both the amount and quality of sustained research carried on in the natural sciences, much of which simply cannot be implemented during any other period of the year.

Increasingly, it is observed that summer sessions reflect imaginative effort in the field of the fine arts. This is especially true with respect to instrumental and vocal music as well as the dramatic arts. Paralleling conspicuous achievement in these fields during the summer sessions is an increasingly larger offering in graphic arts. In many instances these summer programs in the arts are conducted for personal satisfaction and learning rather than for academic credit, although a substantial offering of academic credit work in the aesthetic fields is, of course, commonplace.

If there has been any no-man's land in the literature of American higher education, it has been on the subject of the summer term. What little has been written is as apt to be misleading as illuminating. This book brings clarity and understanding to a comprehensive discussion of that striking aspect of American educational enterprise: "the vast summer structure of our great universities." Conceived in a Chautauqua tent, adopted hesitantly by the campus, the summer term has now come of age as a significant yet special increment of the university's year-round program of teaching, research, and educational service. Will this new-found respectability and success spoil the summer session? The authors of this book suggest the answer may lie in the fact that the "regular year" and the summer term are each taking on the characteristics of the other, and the two together will stand or fall in terms of their mutual ability to surmount some fundamental stresses playing upon all of American higher education today. By lending focus and interpretation to new summer term concepts and dimensions, *The American University in Summer* becomes essential reading for any educator or layman seeking to understand the American higher education scene in the Sixties.

This work presents in an exciting as well as a scholarly and stimulating fashion a portrayal on a wide front of the trials, tribulations, strengths, weaknesses, and solid contributions of summer sessions. The administrative boards and officers responsible for academic calendars would do well to read and ponder this volume. It seems clear that summer sessions should be recognized as just as essential units of the academic organization as the regular academic year. It also seems highly possible, if not probable, that the activities of institutions of higher learning during the regular academic year might well be operated more effectively if they could be patterned more closely after the summer session model.

Reading this volume will be pleasant as well as informative. The opportunity to have been associated with the author over a long period of years in a wide variety of connections is prized, as is the privilege to present this prefatory note to all those interested in summer sessions.

The senior author has been associated with the administration of American higher education since 1948. At the University of Wisconsin he has been successively Assistant to the President, Associate Director of the News Service, Assistant to the Dean of Extension, Associate Director of Summer Sessions, and Assistant to the Chancellor of the University Center System. He is now Director of Summer Sessions for the Madison campus. By profession a journalist, Schoenfeld has been Chairman of the Extension Department of Journalism at Wisconsin. He is now Professor of Journalism and Wildlife Ecology, and Coordinator of the University's Conservation Education Program. In recent years he has served as a communications consultant to the Ford Foundation, the Carnegie Corporation, and the Continental Army Command.

Schoenfeld has made a specialty of interpreting higher education through numerous technical and popular articles and in his books, *The University and Its Publics*, *The Shape of Summer Sessions to Come*, *Year-Round Education*, and *University Extension*. He is also the author of two journalism texts, *Effective Feature Writing*, and *Publicity Media and Methods*; and two conservation readers, *Wisconsin Sideroads to Somewhere*, and *Cabins, Conservation, and Fun*. Before joining the University of Wisconsin faculty, Professor Schoenfeld was a newspaper editor, magazine writer, and public relations counsel. A veteran of World War II, he was recalled during the Korean Conflict to serve as a public information officer on the staff of General Mark Clark.

He is now a Lieutenant Colonel of Infantry in the Army Reserves.

The junior collaborator brings to *The American University in Summer* the perspective of a student in the "multiversity." As a college junior he was a member of the University of Wisconsin's undefeated "College Bowl" team. As a senior majoring in history he won membership in Phi Kappa Phi. He is now pursuing professional studies in law. Zillman was weaned on university administrative problems, his father having been a member of the University of Wisconsin staff since 1944.

The essential message of this book is quite clear: The American university in summer can be a muddle of unresolved functions and policies, or it can be a model, daring to present, establish, and maintain new arrangements—for students on the one hand and for faculty on the other—which, upon observation, will be adapted and adopted for the rest of the year. I have had the privilege of being associated with university summer sessions for many years—as a teacher-student, as a professor of education, as the dean of a school of education, and as the director of a major summer session. I believe this book presents for the first time an exhaustive consideration of the surprising scope and significance of the American university summer term, and a dispassionate evaluation of its problems and possibilities.

# Preface

THE DIVERSITY of American higher education is one of its signal strengths—and the despair of its analysts. Depending to an extent on what and how you count, there are today something over two thousand institutions engaged in post-high school collegiate education throughout the fifty states of this country. They can be found in city inner cores, in suburban complexes, in quaint villages, and in the open country, and they range in size from less than five hundred to more than fifty thousand students. They vary as much in their traditions, resources, and goals as in the composition of their student and faculty communities; the ethos of some unchanged for generations, of others as changing as the headlines; their administrators chosen sometimes for their nonconformity and sometimes for their compatability, depending on the desired posture of the institution. This multiplicity of academic forms, functions, and formulae has given the country a marvelously flexible system of higher education, whose genius is, in fact, that "it is not a *system*. It is diverse, flexible, and experimental. Its methods are not drawn from a single mold."[1]

The same multiplicity, of course, makes extremely hazardous any sweeping, synthetic view of the scope and nature of American higher education. Yet, perhaps somewhat surprisingly, there are also a great many similarities among our colleges and universities—enough, at least, to make it possible and desirable to generalize broadly about shared principles and policies, and to reach some tentative conclusions about common problems and prospects. And this, with respect to the university in summer, is what we shall attempt to do in this book. While admitting that, of all aspects of university life, the summer term may be least susceptible to definition, description, and delineation, we nonetheless assay here an overview of the American university in summer, in an effort to lend focus and interpretation to a striking aspect of American educational enterprise, one whose growing significance is exceeded only by its present paucity of systematic recognition.

Three points we must make clear at the outset: First, when we speak of the summer school or the summer session, we do not think of it as it is sometimes narrowly conceived. Rather, we are considering here the entire range of university enterprise in summer, whether it be technically under the aegis of the summer session per se or not. Second, while we make passing reference to the relatively minor summer operations of colleges, our focus is on what Minnesota's Dean E. W. Ziebarth calls "the vast summer structure of our universities."[2] And third, this is not strictly a research monograph. There is a growing body of objective data and subjective analysis on the American university in summer, but no book that represents a comprehensive collation of summer posture, principles, policies, problems, and prospects. As Norman Burns has said, very often the things about higher education that can be enumerated or counted are things that aren't very im-

[1] Herman B. Wells, "Branches for Opportunity," *American Education*, February 1966, p. 8.

[2] John E. Stecklein, Mary Corcoran, and E. W. Ziebarth, *The Summer Session: Its Role in the University of Minnesota Program* (Minneapolis: University of Minnesota Bureau of Institutional Research, 1958), p. 3.

portant.[3] Thus, while this book introduces some new data, it attempts in particular a synthesis of many previous studies of the summer session, and it does not eschew making value judgments based on experience.

A further limitation in our tactic is dictated by previous publications of the senior author dealing with university public relations and public service.[4] While we must necessarily touch on these subjects where they have important links with university summer enterprise, we do not treat them in detail here. Nor do we duplicate the extended debate about "year-round education" to be found in a previous book by that name.[5] Where we have found it useful to reiterate certain points made earlier, however, we have on occasion reproduced or paraphrased short sections or passages from two of these publications. We would therefore like to thank both Harper & Row and The Center for Applied Research in Education for their permission to use this material.

While we have tried mightily to lend national scope to this treatise, it is inevitable that there will be a disproportionate number of references to those institutions whose summer administrators have been most diligent in documenting their activities and aims. To them we are deeply grateful: Dean E. W. Ziebarth of the University of Minnesota, Associate Provost Royden Dangerfield of the University of Illinois, Director Robert Richey of Indiana University, Dean Frank Burrin of Purdue University, Dean Harold Dorr of the University of Michigan, Dean George Smith of Kansas University, Dean Clodus Smith of the University of Maryland, Director Thomas Crooks of Harvard University, and Dean John R. Little of the University of Colorado. We are particularly grateful to Dr. Harold Haswell of the United States Office of Education for his monumental national surveys.

It is perhaps most inevitable of all that University of Wisconsin

[3] "Methodology in the Study of Higher Educational Administration," *Review of Educational Research,* XXII (4), 379.

[4] Clarence A. Schoenfeld, *The University and Its Publics* (New York: Harper, 1954); Clarence A. Schoenfeld and Theodore J. Shannon, *University Extension* (New York: Center for Applied Research in Education, 1965).

[5] Clarence A. Schoenfeld and Neil Schmitz, *Year-Round Education* (Madison: Dembar Educational Research Services, 1964).

data will bulk large in these pages. For this we make no apologies. The University of Wisconsin is, in the words of its faculty Functions and Policies Committee, "a great and noble institution." It was one of the first to foster summer work; its summer session today is one of the ten largest in the country. And we are there, where we can see the growing summer endeavor in all its dimensions and where we can draw insight and inspiration from colleagues with a real sense of the scope and significance of summer enterprise: Robert Doremus, Associate Dean of the College of Letters and Science; Wilson Thiede, Professor of Education; Robben W. Fleming, former Chancellor, Madison Campus; L. H. Adolfson, Chancellor, University Center System; Donald R. McNeil, Chancellor, University Extension; John Guy Fowlkes, Anderson Professor of Education; L. Joseph Lins, former Director of Institutional Studies; Assistant Chancellors (Madison Campus) Robert Atwell and James Cleary; and Assistant Vice-President Edward Horkan.

CLARENCE A. SCHOENFELD
DONALD N. ZILLMAN

*Madison, Wisconsin*
*March 1967*

# Contents

THE AMERICAN UNIVERSITY IN SUMMER

# 1

## The Year-Round Posture
## of American Higher Education

WHEN WE EXAMINE the American university in summer, what we see depends both on what we are looking for and on how we look for it. If we are determined to criticize university summer enterprise, we may limit our perspective to its surfaces and conclude that summer sessions are no more than appendages to the "regular" academic year. Indeed, we may say, they cannot possibly meet normal university standards, for they compress and abbreviate material into a few weeks; they attract either remedial students or playboys; their curricular offerings and enrollments are sharply limited; and their overall program lacks cohesiveness and integration.[1] On the other hand, if we wish to

[1] See W. Hugh Strickler, "The College Calendar," in Samuel Baskin, ed., *Higher Education: Some Newer Developments* (New York: McGraw-Hill, 1965), pp. 224–231.

extol the summer university, we may broaden our perspective to include the manifold aspects of its campus life and the close articulation of this life with the work and goals of the regular year. We may then envision our great universities and colleges smoothly extending into the summer all the normal functions of the academic year, and we may conclude that just because the temperature goes up intellectual activity does not take a holiday.[2]

Both of these views contain elements of truth; yet each is essentially inaccurate, or at best incomplete, in that it sees the summer enterprise only in the light of so-called "regular-year" operations, without recognizing what is unique and distinctive about it. For the university in summer is, indeed, a peculiar institution; it can be understood only in terms of its unique organization, functions, capabilities, traditions, and goals. Its essential premise is the fruitful adaptation of the old American spirit of lifelong learning to the new American leisure. It adds to this an attitude of experimentalism and eclecticism. And the result is an institution that combines and balances a responsibility to academic traditions and standards with a responsiveness to public needs. Thus, while the summer university, through teaching, research, and educational services, does extend the regular work of the institution throughout the year, it adds to this work special thrusts of its own. And in analyzing its operations we must therefore maintain something of a double perspective, attempting to understand and identify what is unique, while at the same time keeping in mind that the "summer session" or "summer school" per se represents only a portion of total university enterprise in summer.

The summer university is big and it is important. Where once summer enterprise may have been something of an appendage to the academic calendar, today's university summer terms are an essential part of America's growth industry, education. Education employs 1,600,000 people at an annual investment of $12 billion; the auto industry employs only 500,000 for $5.4 million,

[2] See John E. Stecklein, Mary Corcoran, and E. W. Ziebarth, *The Summer Session: Its Role in the University of Minnesota Program* (Minneapolis: University of Minnesota Bureau of Institutional Research, 1958), pp. 6, 187.

steel 700,000 at $6.6, aerospace 1,300,000 at $8.6. At the top of the educational pyramid are our universities. While we may spend more for tobacco, or liquor, or recreation than we do for higher education, university enterprise in the United States today is still a wonder of the western world. Our universities are asked to be a font of technicians, a patron of the arts, a cradle of philosophers, a wellspring of sapient citizens, a bulwark of national defense, a replacement pool of professionals, a promoter of sports, an engine of democracy, a source of new ideas, a custodian of old traditions—where every man or woman has an equal right to achieve inequality. Increasingly our universities are asked to perform these functions the year around. Enter, hence, the summer term, its roots in the evangelism of another day, its present a response to popular pressures, its future as wide as the sky.

Education now represents 5.4 per cent of the gross national product and will grow to 6.1 per cent in the next seven years. This development is attracting big business: Raytheon, for example, recently bought D. C. Heath, a textbook firm. The time may have arrived when all large industries will have to have a vice-president just to keep an eye on this expanding segment of the economy[3]—and an assistant vice-president to keep track of university summer endeavors.

Total opening fall enrollment in college and university courses creditable toward a bachelor's or higher degree increased from 2.5 million in 1954 to 5.0 million in 1964 and is expected to climb to 8.7 million by 1974. These figures include all full-time and part-time, resident and extension, graduate and undergraduate enrollment in degree-credit courses in four-year institutions and in junior colleges. They exclude college enrollment in courses which do not carry degree credit. Full-time fall enrollment for degree credit in all institutions of higher education increased from an estimated 1,721,000 in 1954 to 3,418,000 in 1964 and is expected to reach 5,924,000 by 1974.[4] Even assuming that summer term enrollments will continue to run only about

[3] *Advertising Age*, February 7, 1966, p. 2.
[4] Kenneth Simon and Marie Fullham, *Projections of Educational Statistics to 1974–75* (Washington: U.S. Office of Education, 1965), pp. 2–3.

40 per cent of fall totals, we can project a summer student body of 2,400,000 by 1974, which is considerably greater than *fall* enrollments of ten years ago. Thus, even excluding the research and public service aspects of university summer work, the enterprise is hardly an insignificant one.

## THE SUMMER UNIVERSITY BACKGROUND

The American university as we know it is the direct product of three separate yet complementary academic backgrounds: the Crown academy, with its emphasis on prescribed liberal instruction; the German university, with its emphasis on research and advanced study; and the land-grant college, with its emphasis on vocational training and community service. This inheritance, as we shall see, has dictated the evolution of the summer term and is most clearly evident today in the activities of the university in summer. Yet while its roots may reach to nineteenth-century Europe, the summer university is essentially a twentieth-century American invention.

With the advent of the twentieth century, Americans witnessed the removal of many ancient landmarks. Under the impact of modern science and technology, of modern government, and of modern geography, old beliefs, attitudes, and institutions gave way, to be replaced by new conditions, ideas, and ideals characterized by their variety and flux. And since a university is not something apart from the social order to which it belongs, it was inevitable that the universities should reflect the change. Since 1890, therefore, the American educator has been coping with the task of making a new university for a new society.

For the two hundred years prior to 1885, American higher education had been, in the main, created and sustained, inspired and controlled, by religious groups, in a climate that was largely church-centered. Out of this fairly well-established culture the American college had developed a required curriculum and an assured method of teaching, in a community bounded by conventional campus walls. The university of this period was virtually a direct transplant of European institutions, concerned almost exclusively with the conservation of the classics. While this type of institution was adapted to the aristocratic society of the continent, it was not at all suited to serve the needs of a muscular young democracy; so with the shift to secular control in a state-centered climate, with the disintegration of the older life, the older scheme of knowledge, and the older social stratifications, came a consequent change in the older concept of university functions and policies.[5]

In the gradual adjustment of the American university to the American environment, we may discern seven reasonably distinct steps:

1. The first was the establishment and subsequent flourishing of the land-grant college under the Morrill Act—a public proclamation that higher education in the United States was not for the elite alone but for "the liberal and practical education of the [agricultural and] industrial classes of the several pursuits and professions in life." Only recently the National Manpower Council termed the Act "the most important single governmental step in connection with the training of scientific and professional personnel."

2. The adoption of the elective system opened the way for a proliferation of courses, which in turn attracted unprecedented numbers of young people to college. Harvard led the way in widening the classical curriculum to include what is now a bewildering array of sciences and social studies, and other institutions quickly followed.

3. The development of graduate schools—with their emphasis on productive scholarship and scientific research—caused the universities to become not only imparters but producers of knowledge.

4. With the establishment of numerous professional schools, some in connection with existing universities, others independently, schools of law, medicine, architecture, engineering, education, journalism, business, and so on began to turn out men who soon demonstrated the superiority of professional training over experience.

[5] Alexander Meiklejohn, *The Experimental College* (New York: Harper, 1932), p. xi.

5. This was followed by the rise of the "utilitarian" university, in which programs of adult education, public service, and extension made the skills and resources of the campus available and applicable to the people and their problems. And such public involvement in university activities carried back to the campus the impulses and aspirations of American society.

6. An increasing awareness of the importance of higher education for both the individual and the nation led to greater financial support of higher education from both private and public sources (federal grants, state appropriations, and philanthropy). This in turn led to an accelerated expansion of campus resources, skills, and enrollments.

7. Finally came the utilization of the summer months to strengthen and extend the impact of the other steps in the adjustment of the American university to American society.

NINETEENTH-CENTURY ORIGINS

To assume such an orderly progression of events, however, is somewhat misleading; for the modern summer university could not have become what it is without its kaleidoscopic background of early "experiments" in summer education. These, as we shall see, were frequently dominated by the public service motive, which had achieved a certain thrust even before it was institutionalized under the Morrill Act.

As early as 1789, members of a Sunday Society in Birmingham, England, organized regular courses of lectures on mechanics for factory workers, and later put together an artisans' library. About 1800 a Glasgow teacher organized a mechanics class for local machine shop workers. When he moved to London he formed similar classes there, and out of these grew, in 1823, the London Mechanics Institution. Similar centers spread rapidly throughout England. In 1857 Oxford University introduced a system of local examinations to lend stature to the mechanics' institutes, three hundred of which had now formed a national union. Ten years later a Cambridge fellow, James Stuart, originated the English university system of extension lectures when he accepted an invitation to make a series of appearances in cities of northern

England. In 1908 a Crown committee took a look at university extension (the term had been coined there) and reported that 424,500 students had attended 32,146 lectures in 577 centers.[6] Oxford-Cambridge Extension brought these universities to people for whom, until then, universities had been in a world apart; and it gave to the concept of university public service a distinguished background which was to help make the idea acceptable to conservative American faculties.

As in England, the first American impulses toward adult education came from non-university sources. Mechanics' institutes appeared here almost simultaneously with their inception in England and their growth was greatly stimulated by the moral support of such famous men as Benjamin Franklin and the financial support of such philantropists as John Lowell, Jr. Prior to 1840, however, it was the American lyceum that was the real focus of adult education enterprise in this country. Initiated in 1826 by a young Yale graduate, Josiah Holbrook, as a lecture system and public forum for the small towns of Massachusetts, the lyceum movement gathered momentum rapidly. By 1839 some three thousand lycea existed throughout the country, their purpose cultural uplift, instruction in "rational and useful information," and discussion of current issues. In their heyday the lycea were to provide platforms for the leading intellectual figures of the time—Beecher, Phillips, Emerson, Holmes, Taylor, Greeley, Lincoln.[7]

The year 1839 marks another key point in the background of university summer enterprise, for in that year Henry Barnard established the first teachers' institute in Hartford, Connecticut. The idea caught on like wildfire, and by 1847 such institutes were operating in ten states. They usually ran from a day to a week, and were typically organized by state or county superintendents of public instruction for the purpose of upgrading elementary and secondary school teachers by offering them a

[6] James Creese, *The Extension of University Teaching* (New York: American Association of Adult Education, 1941), p. 12.

[7] Roger W. Axford, "The Background of the Adult Education Movement," *Proceedings of the Wisconsin Academy of Sciences, Arts, and Letters, 1961*, p. 346.

variety of "hints" on teaching content and methods.[8] By 1898 more than a quarter of a million teachers were enrolled in almost three thousand institutes covering virtually the entire nation.[9] By that time many of the institutes had evolved into summer normal schools of longer duration and more solid content, some of them housed on college and university campuses.

At the same time, another sort of institute was developing, to serve the interests of the agricultural community. Lycea held in farming communities of Connecticut had early taken on an agricultural flavor, and immediately after the Civil War a Kansas agricultural society began to sponsor what it called a "farmers' institute." The idea caught on around the country, until between 1880 and 1890 farmers' institutes had been established on a more or less permanent basis in twenty-six states, some under the aegis of local clubs, some under state associations, and some under land-grant colleges. A typical institute met for two or three days. Day sessions were devoted to lectures and discussions on practical farm problems, the evenings to "culture" and entertainment. By 1899 institutes were reported in forty-seven states with a total attendance of 500,000 farmers and their wives. A *Harper's* writer testified (as something less than an expert to be sure) that an agricultural revolution was taking place, "greatly assisted if not inaugurated by this systematic, popular instruction."[10]

Institutes and lycea played their part in the development of American university summer work, but a more potent force was Chautauqua. Take one part each Bible class, circus, political convention, and laboratory seminar, mix thoroughly in a large tent, add a touch of library and a dash of college, bring to a boil over the fires of Utopian planning—and you get a rough idea of

[8] Royden Dangerfield, Associate Provost, University of Illinois, has this observation to offer: "Undoubtedly the summer term evolved from the summer county institutes which were established in numerous states for the purpose of upgrading public school teachers. Neither of us is old enough to know where the summer session came from, but my bet is that it came from the pressure of the school superintendent." Personal correspondence.

[9] Data for lycea and farmers' institutes are based on unpublished manuscripts by Vernon L. Carstensen, Professor of History, University of Washington.

[10] Charles Dudley Warner, "Studies of the Great West," *Harper's*, April 1884, p. 74.

Chautauqua. Here was the America of Gladstone, Barnum, Bryan, and Harper distilled into one draught of uplift and spending itself in an orgy of religious and educational evangelism. We are not old enough to have seen Chautauqua in its prime, but we still remember its 1920 version as a hair-curling experience. Television's Continental Classroom and Oral Roberts are but pale and emasculated versions of Chautauqua at its peak.

John Heyl Vincent, a Methodist clergyman who later became a bishop of his church, and Louis Miller, a businessman and church worker from Akron, Ohio, started the Chautauqua movement in 1874 when they purchased a camp-meeting ground at Fair Point on Chautauqua Lake, New York, and began a two-week summer conference for Sunday School teachers. Thanks to sound management, astute promotion, and the aspirations of dedicated men, Chautauqua's annual assembly quickly developed a staggering variety of educational programs: a scientific conference, a temperance conference, a church congress, all covering an array of secular as well as religious subjects. In effect Chautauqua became a folk university, and it was not long before college instructors were called in to give courses on college subjects.

Originally associated with a specific campground in New York, the term Chautauqua later became connected, officially or unofficially, with summer tent assemblies across the country, some at the doorsteps of universities; and some Chautauqua instructors joined the faculties of distinguished institutions.

Incorporated in Chautauqua was a summer teachers' retreat designed, according to its literature, "to benefit secular teachers by combining with the recreative delights of the summer vacation the stimulating and quickening influence of systematic instruction." This idea led an increasing number of colleges and universities to make their facilities available in summer to special groups, primarily to elementary and secondary teachers, although the earliest such efforts were usually conducted by entrepreneurial professors rather than by the institutions themselves.

Finally, in our summary of these early experiments in summer education, we must not overlook the science excursions. Biology and geology professors came early to find that summer offered fine opportunity for field instruction. Harvard geologists took selected students to the Great Lakes area in 1848, and to the Rocky Mountains in 1869. Probably the first permanent summer camp was the Agassiz-Anderson School of Marine Biology founded on the Atlantic Coast in 1873. Imitation followed its success, and somewhat similar ventures were undertaken at Concord, Salem, Plymouth, Martha's Vineyard, and Glens Falls.

In 1876, the rapid growth of new knowledge, the evolving concepts of the purpose of higher education, and the developments in industry and technology that characterized the ecology of the summer university were to find a focus in the founding of Johns Hopkins University. This event marks the point when "university work," with its emphasis on research and productive scholarship, began to be a new ideal for institutions of higher education.[11] The influence of scholars returning from German universities, the lure of new fields of inquiry, and public demand for professional disciplines spurred the ascendancy of the graduate school, with its paraphernalia of year-round laboratories and libraries. Thus, to the new research-oriented professor, the summer period became just another set of months in which to continue his efforts to extend the boundaries of knowledge.

The next important date in summer session history is 1887. The land-grant colleges established under the Morrill Act of 1862 had had no immediate success in formal undergraduate instruction, but they early established agricultural experiment stations for exploring and testing improved farm practices. And in 1887 Congress passed the Hatch Act, providing each state with a federal appropriation for the support of agricultural research. This marked the beginning of Washington's support of a growing range of basic and applied investigations on the campus. And since agricultural research, by its very nature, peaked in summer, the Hatch Act gave significant impetus to the year-round nature of professorial appointments.

At the same time, other funds, both public and private, were becoming increasingly available to education. With the help of

[11] Earl J. McGrath and L. Richard Meeth, "Organizing for Teaching and Learning," in Baskin, *Higher Education*, p. 28.

Carnegie monies, for example, more and more cities and even villages had built libraries in the late 1800's, and the libraries in turn lent their support and sponsorship to educational activities. Addressing the American Library Association in 1887, Professor Herbert B. Adams of Johns Hopkins urged the importation of the English system of university extension to the United States. Public libraries in Buffalo, Chicago, and St. Louis responded. The Philadelphia Society for the Extension of University Teaching, organized in 1890, quickly became the American Society for Extension Lecturing, and stimulated the establishment of twenty-three centers. These centers generally were organizations operating independently of the universities. Typically they were formed by libraries. Lectures on literature, the natural sciences, the social sciences, and a variety of other subjects patterned after English extension were the main forms of educational activity, though some systematic class work was also carried on. Many of the leaders and lecturers were secured from nearby campuses.[12]

In the period between 1888 and 1895 a number of American universities began to offer an English system of extension lectures, with all of its trappings of syllabi, quizzes, and exams. As a matter of fact, systematic public lectures had been given by some colleges as early as 1816. The program enjoyed a momentary popularity. Presidents pushed it and leading professors performed. During 1891, ten thousand people participated in Wisconsin and Minnesota alone. In the same year Indiana University supplemented its summer school for teachers with a series of evening lectures.

At this juncture, in 1892, William Rainey Harper, pirated by John D. Rockefeller from Chautauqua, drew up for their brand new University of Chicago a "unique and comprehensive plan" by which he hoped to "revolutionize university study in this country." He viewed extension not as a sideline or an afterthought but as an integral part of university operations, and he set up, as one of his five coordinate colleges, a Division of University Extension, empowered to offer college courses for college

[12] A. Stephan Stephan, "Backgrounds and Beginnings of University Extension in America," *Harvard Educational Review*, Spring 1948, p. 103.

credit by lecture study, class study, or correspondence study. He also put his institution on a four-quarter calendar, thus bringing summer study inextricably into the fold.

Finally, we must turn our attention to Harvard University, which played a number of important roles in the evolution of university summer enterprise. From its founding, and for nearly two hundred years afterward, the Harvard curriculum had consisted of some thirty-odd courses, all of which had to be successfully completed by each student. In other colleges, too, with some minor variations, the mid-nineteenth century curriculum can be said to have consisted of a limited number of courses in ancient languages and literature, philosophy and religion, and mathematics. In the 1880's, however, Harvard took the lead in the fragmentation and proliferation of courses, and its example was quickly followed by other colleges. The omnibus courses in natural history broke into departments of physics, chemistry, geology, botany, astronomy, and others. Ancient history was superseded by specialization in modern history. And a great host of social sciences entered the academic spectrum. No longer could students leisurely pursue a common curriculum.[13] The alternatives devised to take care of the problem were the elective principle, which Harvard pioneered; the establishment of professional schools; and the adaptation of the summer term to serve as a vehicle for the acceleration and enrichment of regular credit students.

In its early days, the Harvard calendar had included a summer quarter, but not a winter quarter! The reason was clear enough: to allow Harvard students to teach in the common schools, whose calendars in turn reflected the cycle of the agricultural year. Harvard then gradually joined the trend toward two semesters, with a summer hiatus which was used only for the non-credit instruction of teachers. But the memory of the old summer quarter was to linger on, until in 1900 President C. W. Eliot proposed a three-year bachelor's degree sequence for Harvard, utilizing the summer term to produce the acceleration. The sys-

---

[13] McGrath and Meeth, in Baskin, *Higher Education*, p. 29.

tem operated until 1912, one of its products being James B. Conant. Yale, Johns Hopkins, Clark, and other institutions had similar year-round calendars. Gradually the programs collapsed under a variety of pressures, but the status they lent to the summer term was significant.

The effect of all these innovations on the academic world can hardly be overestimated, for they gave the concept of university summer service its first real home, its first real budget, and its first coherent philosophy. Harper and Eliot had broadcast the seed, and it was shortly to find its most fertile soil on the campuses of the emerging state universities where public service was a compelling philosophy.

THE BIG CHANGE

The years from 1901 to 1919 represent what Morison and Commager call the "Progressive Era."[14] It was this period in American history that gave real impetus to university summer enterprise. A brief examination of factors at work in American life at the turn of the century illuminates the background of the modern summer university.

While the nineteenth century had officially ended somewhat earlier, the twentieth began in spirit with the accession to the presidency in September, 1901, of forty-two-year-old Theodore Roosevelt. Politician, cowboy, author, and war hero, Roosevelt was a man of immense vitality and perplexing contrasts. In these respects he was a mirror of his nation, setting forth with buoyant optimism into a future big with change.

The vitality of America was there for all the world to see and to marvel at. The Spanish war had moved America onto the world stage. Immigration was making it the great melting pot and supplying the manpower to keep the wheels of industry moving. Education was becoming a matter of national pride. Public school enrollment had trebled in three decades and showed

[14] For a scholarly yet colorful summary of the period, see Samuel Eliot Morison and Henry Steele Commager, *The Growth of the American Republic* (New York: Oxford University Press, 1930).

no signs of letting up. The automobile and the airplane were becoming household words, concrete symbols of the new American technology on the move.

Yet the contrasts within the society made it all too clear that what Herbert Croly was to call the promise of American life had not yet been reached. For every improvement made, the muckrakers uncovered a new sore spot. Slums, slave wages, political corruption, business and financial trusts, adulteration of foods and drugs, and rape of natural resources all attracted the attention of not only the writers but the nation's political leaders as well. Public service began to compete with other impulses to claim the energies of the ablest Americans. In the search for answers and the talent to supply them the nation turned to its universities for help.

That the universities responded to this plea was primarily due to the efforts of an unusual assortment of educational leaders who shared a vision of a new university in a new America. There had been John Bascom, who well before the turn of the century had predicted that the "university will be permanently great in the degree in which it understands the conditions of the prosperity and peace of the people, and helps to provide them."[15] There was Leland Stanford, who declared that "the great universities of this country must be as firmly and fairly devoted to the needs of American democracy as the modern harvester is to the needs of the American wheatfield." A Princeton president by the name of Woodrow Wilson believed that "it is not learning but the spirit of service that will give a college place in the public annals of the nation." And William Rainey Harper called for bringing "all of the people of the state directly into contact with university men and university thought."

It was Charles R. Van Hise, however, who enunciated in the clearest terms a bold and vigorous new theory for American higher education. The university, he said, should so embody the combined intellectual life of the community that it can and will apply itself on any level to the betterment of the community. It was out of this challenge of a new age and this response on the

---

[15] This and the following quotations are found in Arthur and Lila Weinberg, *The Muckrakers* (New York: Simon and Schuster, 1961), pp. xiii–xxv.

part of educators that the new American university and the summer session arose.[16]

*Public Relations.* With new concepts of public service came that peculiarly modern invention: public relations. Up to the early 1900's, publicity in America was a sometime thing. Then Theodore Roosevelt began to exploit the new mass media to sway public opinion. He saw newspapermen twice a day and staged national conferences on such critical topics as country life and conservation. Business and industry, pilloried by the press agents of the progressive movement, began to feel that if publicity could be used against them, it could be used for them.[17] "Service" came to replace "efficiency" as the watchword of big corporations. Even John D. Rockefeller set out to change his image. It was only natural that public universities would join in the search for devices and functions that would relate impersonal institutions to their constituents. The term "public relations" as such was not to enter the university vocabulary until much later, but this is what William Rainey Harper and Charles R. Van Hise were talking about when they said in the early 1900's that "utilizing the opportunity to carry knowledge to the people will be a practical advantage rather than a disadvantage to the growth of a university along all other lines."[18]

*The "Wisconsin Idea."* "Nothing in the whole half century [1900–1950]," says Columbia historian Allan Nevins, "stands out more strikingly than the expansion of higher education. More and more intellectual leadership came from a new source—the universities. From the West came *the Wisconsin Idea.*"[19] This "Idea" embraced experimental reform based upon detailed research. The extensive use of academic and other experts in government, agriculture, and industry; new university configurations; and an enlightened electorate were all prominent elements. The

[16] For a fuller treatment of these men and their movement, see Clarence A. Schoenfeld, *Academics in Action* (Madison: Dembar Educational Research Services, in press).

[17] Weinbergs, *Muckrakers*, p. xiv.

[18] C. R. Van Hise, "The University Extension Function in the Modern University," *Proceedings of the First National University Extension Conference, 1915*, p. 20.

[19] "Audacious Americans," *Life*, January 2, 1950, p. 80.

campus played an important part, directly through the role of faculty members on various advisory and administrative boards and agencies, and indirectly through emerging extension classes and summer work.

By way of background, Charles R. Van Hise, who became president of the University of Wisconsin in 1903, proposed in his inaugural address that professors be used as technical advisors by the state government. Nine years later some forty-six men were serving both the state and the university. While it is impossible to measure the effect of these university professors upon legislation and state government, it is clear that some of them for a time exercised strong influence. John R. Commons, for example, was the author of an act establishing an Industrial Commission, and served for a period as one of the commissioners. T. S. Adams, who helped write a Wisconsin income tax law, served on the Tax Commission; and a number of other professors held prominent positions.

Equally important was the revival of University extension work. Van Hise told a Washington audience that "a state university should not be above meeting the needs of the people, however elementary the instruction necessary to accomplish this."[20] University extension programs were begun on a small scale in 1907 when the legislature unanimously approved a grant of $20,000 for this work. Consciously patterned as much after privately owned correspondence schools as after the English extension system, the new extension division developed quickly, energetically, and conspicuously. The ideas evolved were not themselves unusual. The remarkable thing was that an organization was conceived and created, and a staff assembled, trained, and made effective. The division consisted initially of four departments: correspondence study, instruction by lectures, debating and public discussion, and general information and welfare. The success of the experiment was reflected in increased legislative support, large enrollments, and wide publicity.

Meanwhile the College of Agriculture had broadened its extension program. Short courses for farmers' wives were added

[20] Quoted in Merle Curti and Vernon Carstensen, *The University of Wisconsin, 1848–1925* (Madison: University of Wisconsin Press, 1949), II, 516.

to those for farmers and farmers' sons, a weekly press service was initiated, and county agricultural representatives or county "agents" were created.

On the Letters and Science campus, faculty members staffed a summer school that attracted increasing numbers of teachers to Madison for refresher work. Other university staff members and alumni assisted a new legislative reference bureau in a unique bill-drafting service. In 1908 E. E. Slosson declared that "under the influence of university men, Wisconsin has become the recognized leader in progressive and practical legislation." Other observers thought they saw in the courses in sanitary sewage, highway construction, and shop mathematics offered by the extension division and the summer school the promise of a new, completely informed, progressive America.

All of these elements—the extensive program of legislative reform, the expert work of the professors, the work of the legislative reference bureau, the vigorous extension programs of the university, and the summer school—were part of the "Wisconsin Idea." Perhaps the influence of the university in the fields of social and political behavior was neither as large nor as lasting as many claimed at the time, but for a decade and a half Wisconsin enjoyed what William B. Hesseltine called "a successful wedding of soil and seminar, a fruitful joining of research and reform."[21]

By 1915 some thirty universities had organized full-blown extension divisions; twenty-five agricultural colleges were actively engaged in extension work; and seven hundred institutions were running summer schools. Wisconsin's pioneering organizational pattern served generally as a point of departure for administrative practices elsewhere, and this, too, helped to account for the influence the "Wisconsin Idea" was to exert on the new year-round American university.

*State Legislation.* An often overlooked contribution to the growth of the early summer term came from various statehouses around the country. In response to criticism of public school

[21] See ibid., pp. 562–677; discussion of this topic was expanded later by Carstensen in "The Origin and Early Development of the Wisconsin Idea," *Wisconsin Magazine of History,* Spring 1956, pp. 181–188.

teaching, legislation was drawn up encouraging and in some cases compelling further university-level work for elementary and secondary school personnel. While approaches varied from state to state, the goals were common. The Indiana experience shows a blending of coaxing and compulsion:

In 1907 the Indiana General Assembly gave impetus to the Summer Session as well as to the Department of Education of the University by enacting laws providing for (1) a classification of teachers, (2) a minimum wage for each classification, and (3) designation by the State Board of Education of the institutions of higher learning to be accredited for this training. Certain salaries were specified for teachers with certain training, and each higher classification carried specific, new privileges for those who qualified. Although 12 weeks of training were stipulated for certification, aspiring elementary teachers with two years of training were to be licensed without further examination. Indiana University was promptly accredited, and the School of Education was established in 1908. Teachers' classifications were then listed in the summer catalogs.[22]

As teachers learned of the new financial benefits, summer study emerged as something much more than the novelty or relaxing diversion that it had previously been. Teachers planned their summers around their state university's summer session. Colleges and universities began to tool up for an increasing summer population. The lucrative partnership between the summer term and the teachers was well on its way.

UNIVERSITY SUMMER TERM CHRONOLOGY

Out of the welter of forces, causes, and influences we have thus far examined has grown university summer enterprise. Says one recent observer: "The unorthodox character of the summer session has its beginnings in Louis Agassiz' field trips and his Anderson School at Buzzard's Bay and in Bishop Vincent's Chautauqua. It is a past worth cultivating . . . ."[23]

[22] B. D. Meyers, quoted in Robert Richey and Bernita Gwaltney, *The Development of Summer Study at Indiana University* (Bloomington: Indiana University Office of Summer Sessions, 1965), p. 15.
[23] Robert Clark, in *Proceedings of the Third Annual Meeting of the National Association of College and University Summer Sessions, 1966*, p. 18.

It is somewhat difficult to say exactly when and where the "true" university summer term was born. Educational records are sketchy, and the line between informal university sanction and official university sponsorship is not a clear one. Historians generally agree that Harvard began the first program of systematic, specialized, short-term summer instruction in 1869,[24] although the courses offered were thought of largely as refresher work for teachers, and it was not until 1891 that they carried credit toward a Harvard degree. By 1879, when the U.S. Commissioner of Education first mentioned summer schools in his annual report, Johns Hopkins was sponsoring a summer zoological laboratory, and the universities of Virginia and North Carolina offered "normal" courses for teachers. By 1893 the Commissioner reported forty-seven summer sessions under university auspices and an additional twenty-two private ventures. Most of these were made up largely of non-credit teachers' institutes and science seminars. Not until 1899 did state universities like Wisconsin begin hesitantly to assimilate the summer term into the "regular" work of the institution.

Then came the era of "the big change." In 1911, when the U.S. Office of Education began to publish summer school statistics in a more organized fashion, the picture becomes clearer. The Commissioner reported that 477 of the more than 500 summer schools held had submitted information. They had enrolled 118,307 students, taught by 8,049 faculty members, in courses for which 180 gave degree credits. The summer period, in other words, had matured as a vehicle for conventional instruction, but it continued to carry with it its inheritance as a focus for public service programs and year-round research.

The formation at Ann Arbor in November, 1917, of the forerunner of the National Association of Summer Session Deans and Directors marked the institutionalization of the summer university. It is significant that membership in the organization was limited by its constitution to "institutions engaged in giving advanced instruction during the summer months." Thus did ex-

[24] Donald F. Warner, Bernice R. Retzlaff, and Harold A. Haswell, *Summer Sessions in Colleges and Universities of the United States, 1960* (Washington: U.S. Office of Education, 1963), pp. 3–5.

ponents of "regular" university work attempt to capture the summer term. But the freewheeling ancestry of the summer university was to die hard; indeed, it was to flourish.

The development of university summer enterprise may become clearer if we take a mythical campus and trace the history of its summer term: Siwash University, founded in 1846, lies fallow in summer until 1871, when Professor Jacob Stone, its professor of languages, is given permission to use university buildings for a private summer institute for teachers. The venture is short-lived, but it is succeeded in 1880 by a summer school for teachers, sponsored by the state superintendent's office. In 1885 two professors of agriculture, together with two graduate students, begin to pursue their researches the year-round. In 1893 the university openly takes over the summer school for teachers, but grants no credit for summer courses. In 1895 the teachers' school is joined by a summer institute for librarians, arranged by an embryo extension department. In 1899 the College of Engineering offers a summer course in surveying and grants credit for it. By 1901 the various summer courses and schools are incorporated into an official University Summer Session, with a small budget and a part-time director to administer it; certain courses carry full credit for qualified students. In 1903 the Summer Session plays host to a non-credit School of Ethics for adults. In 1905 the catalog of the university speaks for the first time in proud terms about the "educational preeminence" of the Summer Session, along with idyllic descriptions of the summer campus. In every respect, writes Director M. Clarke Jones, "the Summer Session has become an integral part of the University." A registration of 661 seems to prove it.[25]

EARLY SUMMER SESSION TRAITS

By the early years of the twentieth century, American institutions of higher education were becoming increasingly striated

---

[25] Distilled from Stecklein, et al., *Summer Session, Minnesota*, pp. 3–32; and Howard S. Miller, *The University of Wisconsin Summer Sessions, 1885–1960* (Madison: University of Wisconsin Office of Summer Sessions, 1960).

as a result of their different traditions, circumstances, and leadership. Hence there was considerable variation in the nature and scope of activities in the five hundred or so summer terms in existence by 1910. In general, however, we can see three main characteristics:

First, the *public service* theme. On the typical campus, summer work started under the guise of an informal summer institute or summer normal for teachers. This bent toward providing specialized education for other than "regular" students continues throughout the development of the summer term as a significant aspect of university summer endeavor.

Second, the *research* theme. On or near the typical campus, summer science camp or experiment station activity pre-dated formal summer instruction. Year-round productive scholarship and graduate training continue throughout the history of the summer term to be of major importance, although they are frequently difficult to document or measure.

Third, the *regular teaching* theme. Somewhat grudgingly, yet steadily, universities added to their summer service and research programs a curriculum for "regular" students. As the summer term sought status, regular work came increasingly to dominate its literature, and today is often mistaken for the entire operation. Those who do so might as well look at a church and say its work is confined to a one-hour service each Sunday morning.

The three themes were frequently at war with one another in the early days of summer development, and continue today to compete for attention and funds. Yet this tension is not bad; in fact, as a hybrid venture the summer term may be said to exhibit heterosis, or "hybrid vigor." Certainly the three faces of the summer-term Eve should lead no one to believe that there is no central thrust.

Certain common aims, indeed, have prevailed among universities in the country as a whole from the beginning of the summer movement. The single basic aim of university summer enterprise has been to make university resources available and useful to as many people as possible throughout the year. A correlative aim has been to encourage and help every individual to develop himself to the extent of his capacity. Implicit in these aims are a basic belief in man's perfectibility and a faith in his capacity to solve his problems peaceably through the application of intelligence.

Yet it would be a mistake to assume that only such lofty generalities inspired the early summer educator. Compelling as these sanguine ideals might have seemed, likewise motivating him were the tangible, practical, workaday requirements of a developing society experimenting with large-scale political democracy while undergoing rapid industrialization.

Whether moved by liberal ideals concerning the nature of man, or by the press of mundane affairs, the prescription of the summer pioneer was one and the same: the application of knowledge. To him the widespread diffusion of knowledge (or the "socialization" of knowledge, as it was expressed at the turn of the century) was an imperative and urgent goal. This sense of urgency and necessity is reflected in the literature of the summer term of the period, as is the confusion between its idealistic and practical motivations. To this day, indeed, some of the original zeal still permeates the movement, though the earlier preoccupation with philosophy and rationale appears to have given way somewhat to operational considerations. So, too, has persisted the dichotomy between the liberal and the pragmatic, both of which are represented amply in modern-day summer campus practices.

GROWTH OF THE SUMMER UNIVERSITY

Nothing in American history has been more striking, as Frederick Jackson Turner has observed, than "the steady pressure of democracy upon its universities to adapt them to the requirements of all the people."[26] As one vehicle of that adjustment, the summer university has been profoundly influenced by the fundamental stresses that have played upon the American people. Hence any account of the development of the summer term since its first flowering is inevitably punctuated by familiar headlines.

*World War I.* By 1916, 734 summer schools were attended by

---

[26] *The Frontier in American History* (New York: Holt, 1922), p. 283.

298,219 regularly enrolled students.[27] Then came the First World War. Almost overnight the summer university in 1917 doffed its civilian garb and abandoned its state or regional orientations to stand muster in a national formation. Campus scientists worked around the calendar to perfect new weapons of war. Red Cross institutes were conducted. Special evening lectures on "Causes of the Great War" made their contribution to anti-German propaganda. ROTC boys drilled assiduously all summer. Administrators went on leave to supervise special military and naval training schools. By 1918 the regular summer curriculum included courses "to fill the needs of the hour." In short, the summer university, designed for peacetime, proved to be a potent, flexible weapon in the arsenal of democracy. Some summer schools folded for the duration, to be sure, but others were begun to the sound of guns. All experienced a drop in enrollment but not in morale.

*The Roaring Twenties.* The American university emerged from World War I, as George E. Vincent said at the time, with "a new sense of confidence and of social obligation." This was particularly true of the summer term. Public interest may have been focused, as Frederick Lewis Allen puts it, "on a series of tremendous trifles,"[28] but the summer university boomed. From 1921 to 1931 formal enrollments nearly doubled to 414,260. The campus during the balance of the year may have been beseiged by bathtub gin and jazz, but the hallmark of the summer campus was the school teacher, back to meet the rising educational requirements of the profession. Some summer classes were broadcast over the new educational radio stations to students off campus.

*Depression.* The Great Depression was a time of trial. Initially student registrations slumped. Colleges, pressed for funds, insisted that summer schools be self-supporting or even turn a profit. Faculty members had to contribute their services or accept miserable salaries and contingency clauses by which appointments were cancelled if classes failed to "fill." Then, even

27 The figures in this section are from Warner, et al., *Summer Sessions,* 1960, pp. 7–9.
28 For a brilliant portrait of the Twenties, see Allen's *Only Yesterday* (New York: Harper, 1931).

as the depression reached its depth, the student tide turned, largely because unemployed school teachers came back to the campus to improve their competitive positions by taking graduate work. Some states even supplied special summer scholarships for the indigent. Enrollments for credit, which had dropped to 303,754 in 1931, rebounded to 370,026 by 1935.

With the advent of another Roosevelt, the summer campus once again came into its own. University professors took off for Washington to take their places in a "brain trust" of presidential advisors, and federal funds came to the campus to stimulate year-round activities: vocational rehabilitation classes under SSA; projects in workers' education, adult education, and citizenship education under WPA; programs for unemployed youths under NYA; new buildings financed under PWA; pilot training under CAA. The emergency demands and supports for educational services led universities to enter wholeheartedly into a partnership among government, campus, and people. The old Wilson-Eliot-Harper-Van Hise thesis had now become federal law. Teacher and investigator, united in a new spirit of public service, gave their summer universities unprecedented power and usefulness.

*Interregnum.* By mid-decade, Americans had decided they really had nothing to fear but fear itself, and settled down to a long period of retooling. Things were getting better because we were planning it that way. Hitler was only a militant version of Charlie Chaplin, and it couldn't happen here anyway. Beer was back, breadlines were gone. The year 1936, says Leo Gurko, was "an interlude in which one could almost hear the country pause for breath."[29]

It was now thirty years since modern university summer enterprise had come into being. What was its status? The universities had a pentagonal approach: (1) regular collegiate courses, enrolling for credit large numbers of students; (2) general courses, pretty much on the college level but not so meticulously measured in units of credit, to satisfy the special needs of adult students; (3) postgraduate, professional, and technical training

[29] *The Angry Decade* (New York: Dodd, Mead, 1947), p. 172.

through institutes, conferences, and short courses; (4) year-round research; and (5) a wide range of informal school, community, and group services. The chancellor of New York University called this penetration of higher education by increasing multitudes "a development without parallel in the social history of the world." In 1937, 869 summer sessions enrolled 429,864 credit students and served a significant number of non-credit youngsters and adults.

The summer university had organization and methodology; it had new-found prestige; it had flexibility in format and philosophy; it had experience. It was an instrument poised to help solve America's domestic problems. But tranquility was not to be. From 1936 on, the country was "like a boat that starts in a quiet part of the river, gets whirled into rougher and rougher current, until its occupants can hear the noise of a great waterfall ahead."[30]

*World War II.* The summer university went to war early, acquiring, in 1940, money, men, and mission. The money came through the U.S. Office of Education—millions for emergency manpower training. The men (and women) came from all walks of life; in just one year, 900,000 people had gone through the summer and winter courses. The mission was a combination of fear, high strategy, imperialism, and missionary zeal. The crash of bombs at Pearl Harbor turned the university into even more of a camp than a campus, and it was to the summer session that presidents and generals frequently looked for know-how in operating special training programs for many types of uniformed personnel, and in promoting all manner of home-front "drives." Administrators themselves marched off to man the mushrooming bureaus in Washington or the machine guns at Anzio and Luzon. Continuing Engineering, Science, Manpower War Training (ESMWT) programs introduced laborers to university institutes. Businessmen turned to summer seminars for help in launching and improving the work of their Committee for Economic Development.

Summer school attendance actually increased during the war,

30 Ibid., p. 70.

after an initial decline from 456,679 credit students in 1939 to 426,849 in 1941. In 1943, it rose to 479,326, and yet again to 515,602 in 1945, in large part because of accelerated military programs on campus. Many institutions adopted the trimester calendar to accommodate such programs.

The shotgun marriage between the summer university and national defense was to have profound implications for the postwar years. Millions of GI's bore out the almost blind faith of the military in the ability of a training program to turn a shoe clerk into a sergeant. Millions of people on the home front demonstrated the ability of "retread" courses to turn coeds into riveters. Scores of government agencies marvelled at the success of propaganda programs in uniting the nation to save scrap, buy bonds, and ration hamburger. Hundreds of schools and colleges were spellbound by their own ability to convert traditional facilities and curricula into emergency activities. Farmers saw their crops—and profits—mount under the impact of university science. Industrialists rejoiced in new markets born of new products developed by campus research. Patients were cheered by new treatments developed in university labs. Every citizen stood aghast at the atomic havoc wrought by university-trained physicists. In substance, a country which had always had a deep-seated belief in the efficacy of education suddenly found new and dramatic evidence to buttress that faith. The flood of GI's to the campus in 1946–47 was merely symptomatic of a general American thirst for knowledge and a deep American conviction that knowledge was power. That thirst and that conviction were to provide the fertile soil for a continued flourishing of the summer university.

*The Postwar Years.* The years immediately following World War II brought growth at a breathless pace, as people, their governments, and their universities entered into a new alliance for progress. Regular summer enrollments soared from 515,602 in 1945 to an incredible 955,429 in 1947—an increase of 85 per cent. A gradual decline to 796,970 in 1953 merely accentuated the subsequent climb to dizzier heights in 1955, when registrations exceeded the million mark. Research and public service activities mounted apace with instruction. It was difficult to disagree with the assessment that the summer term had "come of age" as "a multi-purpose institution serving a varied clientele."[31]

## THE SUMMER UNIVERSITY TODAY

Almost all American universities today attempt to carry on some educational activities in summer. About such activities, as we have said, it is extremely difficult to generalize. For one thing, American colleges and universities vary greatly in their traditions, circumstances, and aspirations. For another, the summer term itself, by its very nature as the university's chief mechanism of response to environmental stresses, both varies from campus to campus and contributes in turn to institutional differences. In other words, a university and its summer enterprise are indigenous, as at home in their surroundings as is a pin oak in southern lowlands. To speak, then, of a university summer term standard, and to seek a uniform pattern of summer activity, are to imagine what never shall be. Yet a book of this type must attempt some synthesis, and this we now hazard.

### OBJECTIVES

What are the major goals of today's university in summer? Toward what star is the summer campus oriented? There are several. Robert W. Richey, Director of Summer Sessions at Indiana University, suggested these "major objectives" in a report to the Association of University Summer Sessions in October of 1964:

1. To provide a program of courses designed to meet the general and special educational needs of summer students.
2. To provide a maximum number of undergraduate students with year-round instructional opportunities.
3. To lend effective continuity to a university's year-round program of graduate education and research.
4. To give new and continuing students a chance to complete degree requirements faster than would otherwise be possible.
5. To offer school personnel and other groups abbreviated technical and professional refresher courses.

31 Warner, et al., *Summer Sessions, 1960*, p. 21.

6. To provide special conferences, clinics, workshops, and institutes for students of all ages who find it particularly convenient to come to the campus in summer.

7. To experiment with new courses and programs to the end that the summer sessions serve as a pilot plant for curricula of heightened stature and service.[32]

8. To increase the possibilities of using outstanding visiting professors in specialized instructional programs.

9. To encourage students to become more proficient in special fields, to broaden educational horizons, to make up subject-matter deficiencies, or to test ability to do college work.

10. To provide an especially rich cultural program for individuals returning to the campus for summer study.

11. To achieve optimum utilization of campus facilities throughout the calendar year.[33]

It is possible that some institutions have other goals, or would state their goals somewhat differently; but Professor Richey's list would probably be ratified, in principle at least, by most American universities and their summer administrators. It is an ambitious list. How well is it being met?

CHARACTERISTICS

The typical American university has for many years operated an extensive program of research on a year-round basis. Indeed, in many universities research assumes a substantially larger proportion of campus enterprise in summer than in any other period of the year, due to the increased availability of faculty time and laboratory facilities.[34]

[32] Witness Dr. Richey's description of his own school's experience: "Through its flexible organization the Summer Session made a distinct contribution to the development of the whole University. The Summer Session offering could include courses which were not, for reasons of tradition, offered by the College of Arts and Sciences or other divisions in which they logically might be offered. This conservatism, strongest in the liberal arts departments, provided stability for the University program but limited embarkation upon new programs. Physical education, school librarianship, school nursing, and audio-visual materials and techniques are fields in which major University development took place in the summer." Richey and Gwaltney, *Summer at Indiana*, p. 24.

[33] From personal correspondence in author's files.

[34] *Year-Around Operation in American Universities* (mimeographed,

The same may be said for educational services.[35] The common denominator of the public service program is a relatively short meeting—variously called an institute, clinic, conference, workshop, or seminar. It carries no academic credit and may range from an introduction to the violin for a junior high youngster to a highly sophisticated colloquium for nuclear physicists. The 1960 U.S. Office of Education survey indicated that 362 institutions sponsored 1,802 institutes for 175,302 registrants that summer.[36] Some summer institutes are sponsored by the summer session itself, others by the university extension division, still others by individual departments. Along with other less formal educational services, these institutes give the summer campus a great sensitivity to contemporary developments, interests, and needs.

The most highly visible portion of the summer university, and that most often reflected in the data, is the summer session itself, consisting of an array of regular university courses pursued by matriculated students. U.S. Office of Education survey data indicate that in the summer of 1960 1,326 colleges and universities registered 960,994 students in their credit sessions.

---

Boulder, Colorado: Association of Summer Session Deans and Directors, 1963), p. 1. The research activity, however, has never been documented on a national scale. Statistics from the University of Wisconsin (Madison) may be representative: In the summer of 1965, approximately $1.85 million per month in faculty salary monies were assigned to "research." This amount compares with an average of $1.7 million per month in faculty salary monies assigned to "research" in the winter of 1964–65, and contrasts with $1.1 million per month in faculty salary monies assigned to "instruction" in the summer of 1965. In the summer months of 1964, $1,848,051 were budgeted for graduate student assistantships, of which only $215,658 were assigned to teaching in the summer session per se, the balance being for research. While it may be that the Wisconsin emphasis on summer research is disproportionate, it is certainly not atypical in the extreme.

[35] Ibid. These University of Wisconsin (Madison) figures again illustrate the point:

| Man-Day Spaces, 1966 | 3 Summer Months | 3 Fall Months |
|---|---|---|
| Matriculated students | 704,311 | 2,341,920 |
| Non-credit students | 551,358 | 22,088 |
| | 1,255,669 | 2,364,008 |

[36] Warner, et al., Summer Sessions, 1960. The following figures are also from this source.

The length of the summer session is a function of the academic-year calendar. In those institutions which use two semesters of approximately seventeen weeks each—and 85 per cent of America's colleges and universities do so—the principal summer term is usually six to ten weeks in length. In those institutions which use three quarters of eleven weeks each, the main summer term is usually two consecutive sessions of five and one-half weeks each. In those few universities operating on the new trimester system, the summer term is fifteen weeks, sometimes split into two sessions of seven and one-half weeks each. Many large universities operate additional overlapping special sessions of from one to fourteen weeks in duration.

Despite recent talk of new calendar plans, most American colleges still offered the standard short summer session in 1960, according to the U.S. Office of Education. The traditional six-week main term remained the most popular, being reported by 580 of the 1,369 institutions (42.3 per cent); next in popularity were the eight-week term (213, or 15.6 per cent) and the five-week term (187, or 13.7 per cent). Universities, as well as liberal arts, teachers, and junior colleges, generally offered one of these terms, while semiprofessional and technical institutes favored the term of ten or more weeks, and schools of religion and theology had sessions of less than five weeks.

The number of terms also followed long-established practice. Nearly half of all summer sessions (680, or 49.7 per cent) were limited to one term, while an additional 445 institutions (32.5 per cent) had two terms. Of the various types of institutions, only universities showed marked tendencies to hold three or more terms.

The amazing variety of summer calendar patterns has been a great advantage to the prospective student, who could have started a term within a day of almost any date he had chosen between May 30 and August 19, 1960. By careful selection of beginning dates, he could have enrolled in a session of almost any desired length from between two and seventeen weeks. Thus, almost anyone who seriously desired to attend a summer session in 1960 could have found a college and term to suit his purposes and his limitations of time.

Though perhaps not on a par with the three main thrusts of the summer university—research, public service, and conventional instruction—cultural and recreational programs have always played an important part in the plans of summer administrators. Indeed, out-of-class activities may be said to have come first, in the sense that early summer schools took as their setting seaside resorts. As a cynical yet appreciative reporter wrote in 1896: "The questions of Hindoo Swamis, theosophists, and sociological celebrities are coming to take the[ir] place, in summer-resort desirability, with fresh eggs, rich cream, and the absence of mosquitoes."[37] As popular interest in almost any sort of summer educational venture increased, however, the *New York Times* warned ominously that if people insisted on going to school in summertime, certain "physiological and psychological laws" would exact their terrible vengeance.[38] Teachers and "hollow-eyed college professors," continued the editorial, should do nothing more strenuous in summer than "singing and praying." Perhaps it was to counter such charges that university summer session directors designed recreational programs to provide relaxation and change, on the assumption, no doubt, that all brain-work and no play would produce even duller teachers.

So lectures, readings, dramatic performances, concerts, sports, tours, picnics, and dances came to mark the summer campus. Those universities fortunate enough to be located in a vacation-type setting were not bashful about saying so; their catalogs were replete with scenic views, temperature tables, and what Madison Avenue today would call "hard-sell" copy. Some of the early recreation programs and cultural activities had the additional objective of protecting the student from wandering off the campus to engage in other forms of entertainment, particularly when the campus was located in a large metropolitan area.

Today the emphasis on the extracurriculum in summer has scarcely abated, although most summer session administrators feel it has academic as well as recreational significance, and plan it as a part of the total educational experience of the student

[37] Quoted in Miller, *Summer Sessions,* p. 9.
[38] Ibid., p. 10.

rather than as a device to attract registrants. Universities in bucolic surroundings emphasize outdoor pastimes, and urban universities capitalize on city concerts, games, tours, restaurants, and theaters. In his summer session literature, however, the director tries not to fall victim to charges that his statements are beneath the dignity of an institution of higher learning. As Joe Keen, former assistant dean of the University of Colorado summer session, puts it, "We're trying to eliminate the vacation idea of summer school."

The emphasis on the extracurriculum notwithstanding, the summer term is scarcely equal to the rest of the year in number and scope of student diversions. Intercollegiate athletics, fraternity hijinks, undergraduate student government activities, holiday interruptions—all are in suspension. Perhaps this accounts for the better academic performance of many individuals in summer.

After eighty years of ups and downs, the American university in summer has emerged as an institution of significant stature and utility. At an all-time peak in enrollments now, the summer campus promises to be of even greater educational service to a wide range of students of all ages in the years ahead. Across the country, academicians and politicians are relying on optimum utilization of campus skills and resources around the calendar in order to teach economically more undergraduates and adults than ever before in history.

Furthermore, there is evidence that the students themselves are increasingly satisfied with the instruction they receive in summer. For example, when Minnesota's Dean Ziebarth had the temerity to ask his students what they thought of summer work in comparison with that of the "regular" year, nine out of ten students expressed definite satisfaction with their summer courses; only 3 per cent were unhappy to the point where they felt they shouldn't have come.[39] Such an encouraging response may well be a direct function of the summer university's vastly expanded instructional program. For where once it offered only the shadow of a curriculum, the summer session today offers an

[39] Stecklein, et al., *Summer Session, Minnesota*, p. 39.

even greater diversity of programs than the student can find during the regular year. On the typical college or university campus there is actually no longer such a thing as a single summer session. At Wisconsin, for instance, there were in the summer of 1965 an eight-week general session, a twelve-week general session, a four-week general session, a ten-week law session, two five-week and two six-week engineering sessions, a short session in agriculture, eight special sessions in letters and science, three short sessions in nursing, and five special sessions in education. All of these offered university credit. Among the non-credit offerings, there was an even more bewildering array of conferences, institutes, and workshops—some 155 in all—including a three-week clinic for high school bandsters, an eight-day meeting of United Auto Worker stewards, and a one-day seminar for insurance men.

Against this backdrop of teaching and public service there is the continuing research program of the campus, which scarcely breaks step from one January to the next. At least as many campus investigations have been brought to fruition during the summer months as in a similar time span between September and June. As a matter of fact, at a university like Wisconsin, which devotes a good share of its scholarly activity to the study of the state's natural resources, summer may actually represent a peak in the probing for new facts.

The summer period, in short, has become an integral part of the total university year, offering university work in almost all departments. At the same time it provides unusual opportunities to professors and their acolytes for independent advanced investigative work in library and laboratory, field and factory. And it typically includes a wide range of non-credit offerings outside the traditional academic pattern, serving directly the cultural, vocational, and professional needs of youths and adults. Thus the summer university has come to reflect directly the modern university's tripartite function of teaching, research, and service, carrying on that function without interruption throughout the year, and extending it in a number of distinctive and effective ways.

What our summer terms offer is in part a specific reflection of the needs of the people who want to attend. In general, summer clientele fall into two classes: the so-called regular student who wants to pursue his academic program around the calendar; and the "special" student of any age who finds it convenient to come to a campus only for an abbreviated summer period. Out of every one hundred people enrolled in a typical Wisconsin summer term, for example, eighteen are Wisconsin graduate degree candidates; twelve are Wisconsin undergraduate degree candidates; one is a Wisconsin professional school student; six are "special" students enrolled for credit for the summer only; and sixty-three are miscellaneous people of all ages who come for short, non-credit institutes and workshops. Further, out of every one hundred credit students, twenty-five are teachers. Of the total summer student body, more than half were enrolled during the previous academic year; half of the men and a quarter of the women are married; the majority of students are over twenty; and they come from every state and U.S. territory and from some forty foreign lands.

To teach such a heterogeneous student body, a typical university will draw upon industry, government, and other campuses for some visiting lecturers. The faculty will also, of course, be made up of stay-at-homes, glad of the chance to pick up the extra cash—and the stimulus—which are the rewards of year-round teaching. This is not to say that all summertime teachers are happy. Asked how they would improve Minnesota's summer session, for instance, Minneapolis professors responded with suggestions that Dean Ziebarth says "defy categorization—ranging from mosquito control and air conditioning to less noise, lighter loads, and better salaries."[40] But the bulk of the Minnesota staff was willing to testify that summer work is at least as satisfying as that of the regular year, particularly in the chance it affords to "try something new." Many an innovation in university teaching content or methods has been born in a summer session workshop, where a professor is under less pressure to conform to time-honored theories and under more pressure to tailor his presentation to fit a workaday world.

[40] Ibid., pp. 40–41.

"While the offering of continuing work to our currently enrolled university students may perhaps be viewed as the core summer role, this is paralleled closely by the opportunity which the summer affords to experiment with flexible curricula designed to meet special educational needs, particularly those of teachers and other professional groups," says Lorentz H. Adolfson, former director of the University of Wisconsin summer sessions. It was under Dr. Adolfson, in fact, that the University of Wisconsin broke away from its traditional eight-week session to introduce two consecutive four-week periods more convenient for teachers. This widespread summer session emphasis on "teaching the teachers" is nothing new. It has been a hallmark of summer session enterprise since the very beginning. Today, however, the emphasis is shifting to year-round education of continuing students, and as a result our American summer sessions are experiencing a phenomenal growth.

PROBLEMS AND PROSPECTS

Nor does there seem to be any cloud about to obscure the summer sun. Prodded by salary schedules that depend on their summer school progress, and by income tax policies that make expenses for professional advancement deductible, more and more teachers are returning to college every summer. More and more universities are introducing special sub-college summer programs for high school students as one way to identify and encourage the country's best young minds at as early a stage as possible. An increasing number of regular undergraduate students stay on at their home campus at least one summer, or visit another. And regular graduate students seldom pause until they get their degrees, not even for the Fourth of July. Meanwhile, new dormitory and classroom facilities are becoming adequate to meet a summer demand about double the present level.

Because it is flourishing, however, the summer university faces two major problems. One is the job of staffing. The summer dean is increasingly hard-pressed to find enough professors to staff many of his departments. In the sciences, for example, lucrative government and industrial research projects siphon off the top talent. Among schools of education, where very frequently the summer curriculum is more extensive than the winter, the national competition for qualified instructors is intense. A second serious challenge is the job of finding a will and a way to preserve the flexibility of the summer session in the face of mounting pressure to convert it into a standard summer semester serving only the increasing numbers of regular students.

Despite these pressures, there can be no question that the American university summer term is strong and is growing stronger. Nor can there be any doubt that it has made and will continue to make a major contribution to American education and American culture. As Bernice Retzlaff of the U.S. Office of Education has said, it utilizes each summer "billions of dollars worth of facilities which would otherwise lie idle, equipping hundreds of thousands of teachers for more effective service to their communities, enabling even more hundreds of thousands of undergraduate students to hasten the completion of their educational programs, and offering graduate students opportunity to pursue advanced degree work in many academic areas."[41]

But these are only a few of its more obvious contributions. The summer term also provides an opportunity for non-academic people who are tied to their jobs and professions during the rest of the year to gain, in the words of Indiana's Robert Richey, "higher technical competence or larger liberal understanding." It thus becomes a point of contact and a useful channel of communication between the university and the professional world.

Further, because of its heterogeneous clientele and less rigid curriculum, the summer term is a time of experimentation. As Minnesota's E. W. Ziebarth says, "departments often seem more willing to experiment with special types of courses during the summer, courses that differ from academic-year offerings in organization of subject matter or in the manner in which it is presented." Or, as Wisconsin's John Fowlkes puts it: "The summer program has tremendous possibilities to serve as a catalytic agent; daring to present, establish, and maintain new arrange-

[41] This and the following quotations are from personal correspondence in author's files.

ments for students and for faculty which upon observation will be adopted for the rest of the year."

Among the more specific advantages of the summer term may be listed the summer programs for intellectually gifted high school students; the foreign and domestic travel courses (now offered for credit by nearly two hundred colleges and universities); the many summer opportunities for field study, notably in the biological sciences; the review or refresher courses for undergraduates; and, last but not least, the increased opportunity for inviting outstanding faculty members from other campuses to serve as visiting lecturers.

And, finally, in the words of Columbia's William Owen: "Summer sessions are marked by a highly motivated student body, an enriched cultural climate, fewer extracurricular distractions, and a wide variety of recreational outlets." The possibilities for learning in an environment "unplagued by football teams, blessed with an unusual proportion of students who are mature and are in earnest in their quest for learning, and unhampered by the innumerable and rigid curricular requirements that make the regular session too often the repetition of routine" are tremendous.[42]

And so the summer term has become an integral part of the year-round operations of the American university, while offering at the same time certain unique advantages not to be found during the "regular year." Yet successful as the university's year-round operation may now be, it is still possible to utilize even more fully the facilities of the campus during the summer months. For this reason today's university administrators must take whatever steps they deem necessary to initiate new programs and expand present ones, with the aim of encouraging students to take advantage of summer offerings.

The university summer term will continue to be marked by three principal attributes: recognition of the summer session as an intimate and essential aspect of the year-round university program of teaching and research; an appreciation of the unique contribution the summer session can make to adult education

[42] Charles J. Turck, Educational Consultant for the State of New York.

and public service; and an understanding of the desirability of achieving optimum utilization of campus facilities throughout the calendar.

Just as Harvard's Eliot helped inspire the creation of the summer university, so Harvard's Thomas Crooks now offers it an accolade: "A summer term with vigorous self-respect," he says,

has a great utility for the university that could not be recreated in a "year-round" operation of the university for its degree candidates only. I am grateful, as are a majority of our faculty, that we have a strong and growing summer term which can be continuously improved by solving specifically-summer problems. If this situation was not present, I would argue for its creation; that is, for a different kind of seasonal operation rather than a major revision of the academic-year calendar which would exclude the favorable aspects of the summer session.[43]

## In Summary

Thus we have seen that the modern American university stems from three separate yet complementary roots: the Crown academy, with its emphasis on prescribed liberal instruction; the German university, with its emphasis on research and advanced study; and the land-grant college, with its emphasis on vocational training and community service. This inheritance stands out in striking outline in the evolution of the university summer period, and dictates the peculiar nature of the summer period today. The American university summer term has shown consistent growth in scope and acceptance until now it is viewed as an integral and essential, if multi-faceted, aspect of year-round university enterprise. We have attempted in this chapter a summary of university activity from June to September: definitions, descriptions, chronology, genealogy, ecology, development, status, trends; to the end that we see the university in summer— through instruction in a wide range of courses, through research and productive scholarship, through varied public services, and through co-curricular programs—carrying on the work of the university around the calendar and adding to that work such

[43] Quoted in *Year-Around Operation*, Appendix D, p. 9.

unique perspectives as continuing education, experimentalism, eclecticism, a particular environment, a fruitful reaction to the new American leisure, and, above all, a balanced way of life that recognizes responsibility for academic traditions and standards as well as responsiveness to public needs.

# 2

# Summer Students

I F ONE WERE SEARCHING for a word to describe the American university summer student body, *diversity* would be the word. Understanding this student body thus becomes a question not of discarding the various past stereotypes but of combining them into the newer configurations that have emerged in recent years.

It is a favorite technique of researchers studying university summer students to present an exact picture of the "average" summer enrollee with a precision that extends to age in tenths of years and accumulated grade-point average in hundredths of decimal points. This specificity is advantageous in helping to identify major trends in student characteristics, attendance, attitude, and ability. Yet at the same time it is deceptive; for it fails to express the often considerable extremes that go together to make up the mean. Thus, while there indeed may be plenty of "average age" students of twenty-four or twenty-five on a summer campus, they should not be surprised to find their classmates ranging in age from fifteen to fifty-five, with backgrounds and interests as broad as the scope of American higher education today.

Those veterans of the summer wars, the returning school teachers, still flock back to campus as the weather turns warm and P.S. 42 locks its doors until September. Yet their classmates are quite likely to be full-time students, either graduates or undergraduates, many of whom never considered anything but school to occupy their "vacation" time. The probation student still makes an appearance, sometimes at the request of the football coach, but the scholarship winner, the Phi Beta Kappan, and the high school prodigy are displacing him. And with them come transfer students, adult special students (often taking credit courses for the first time in decades), and foreign students. In short, diversity rules the summer campus.

The picture will become clearer if we look at a few portraits of typical Minnesota students:

Before starting teaching in an elementary school in a small Minnesota town, Ruth Evans had completed two years at a teachers college. Now she wants to earn a bachelor's degree in the College of Education. The advancement in salary that her school system gives to teachers who hold a degree is an important incentive, but she also looks forward to the change to city life.

Jim Allen is a full-time student in the College of Science, Literature, and the Arts. He attends the Summer Session in order to take some of the courses that would otherwise be part of his senior year program. By completing the work for a bachelor's degree in three years, Jim feels he will make up for "lost time" in military service.

Along with other forestry students, Robert Adams attends field and laboratory courses at the Lake Itasca Biological Station, a required part of his major program.

John Carlson is registered in the Graduate School. During the previous year he taught high school math in a town not far from the Twin Cities, and he plans to return to his job in the fall. Married and in his early 30's, John hopes to earn an MA that will put him on the road to being a principal.[1]

Our present discussion will be confined only to the summer credit student; for it is he that represents "the summer session

[1] Stecklein, et al., *Summer Session, Minnesota*, p. 39.

student" in the literature, and it is the programs available to him that constitute "the summer session curriculum." Later, when we turn our attention to the great numbers of "students" of all ages who come to the summer campus to participate in non-credit conferences, clinics, and institutes, the diversity of the summer student body will be even further accentuated. Whether we study each group separately or combine them, however, the point remains the same: The kaleidoscopic nature of the summer campus presents both a tremendous challenge to and an important opportunity for the American system of higher education.

Who They Are

The University of Minnesota's study of its 1956 summer program —one of the first institutional analyses, and still the most comprehensive—found that over 50 per cent of the degree-credit population were over twenty-five years of age. At the extremes, only 8 per cent were under twenty—the usual age of fall term college freshmen and sophomores—while 13 per cent were over forty—the median age for faculty at many schools.[2] Data at Michigan State placed the median age at twenty-four,[3] while a University of Utah survey found it to be almost twenty-nine.[4] Regardless of numerical variations, it is safe to conclude that the summer session attracts an older and presumably more mature student. The greater preponderance of graduate students is an easy explanation for the phenomenon, but it is not the only one. A University of Wisconsin study examined only the undergraduate population and found that while half of the fall term population was under twenty, barely a quarter of the summer group was.[5] Taking things one step further, a separate

[2] Ibid., p. 45.

[3] Joe L. Saupe, A Survey of Summer School Students, Summer, 1960 (mimeographed, East Lansing: Michigan State University Office of Institutional Research, 1961), p. 7.

[4] Harry Sharp, Students View the 1962 Summer Session at the University of Utah (mimeographed, Madison: Wisconsin Survey Research Laboratory, 1962), p. 1.

[5] L. J. Lins, C. A. Schoenfeld, Robert A. Rees, and Allan P. Abell, Student Reactions to 1961 Summer Sessions: The University of Wisconsin,

Wisconsin study examined only new freshmen, again to find the summer group significantly older.[6] The summer graduate student is likewise older than his fall semester counterpart. Wisconsin found 70 per cent of its summer graduate population to be at least twenty-five years old, a jump of 10 per cent from the spring semester.[7] Clearly, age does not deter students from pursuing their educational goals in summer.

Considering the greater average age of students, it is not surprising that the married student is a familiar figure on the summer scene. Michigan State found half of its total student body married: twice the proportion found in fall.[8] Wisconsin found graduate ratios of married to unmarried approximately the same in summer as in fall. Married undergraduates, however, were proportionately twice as numerous in summer.[9] Even a survey of entering summer freshmen found one in ten married.[10]

In analyzing the summer population by sex, we must remember that summer has traditionally been the time when women dominated the campus. The enrollment of thousands of teachers and teacher candidates for summer-only courses gave most campuses a female majority that in some instances approached two to one.[11] In recent years, as the 1960 U.S. Office of Education summary of the summer session pointed out, men have in most cases recaptured numerical superiority, averaging about 54 per cent for all types of institutions. The percentages often reached sixty in public universities and often dipped below fifty in teachers colleges and liberal arts colleges.[12] The percentage of women

*Madison Campus* (mimeographed, Madison: University of Wisconsin Office of Institutional Studies, 1962), pp. 6–7.

[6] L. J. Lins, Allan P. Abell, and Paul L. Kegel, *Comparison of Summer Session and Fall New Freshmen: The University of Wisconsin, Madison Campus* (mimeographed, Madison: University of Wisconsin Office of Institutional Studies, 1963), pp. 4–5.

[7] Lins, et al., *Student Reactions 1961*, pp. 6–7.

[8] Saupe, *Survey of Summer, 1960*, p. 7.

[9] L. J. Lins, Allan P. Abell, and David R. Stucki, *Student Evaluations of the 1964 Summer Sessions with Special Reference to the Twelve-Week Session* (mimeographed, Madison: University of Wisconsin Office of Institutional Studies, 1964), p. 6.

[10] Lins, et al., *Comparison of New Freshmen*, p. 3.

[11] Warner, et al., *Summer Sessions, 1960*, p. 8.

[12] Ibid., p. 68.

in summer, however, is still far greater than in the regular year. The University of Maryland, for instance, found women making up 43 per cent of its student body in summer as compared with only 34 per cent in the fall and spring:[13] a ratio comparable to other institutional findings.

An obvious reason for the higher feminine attendance has already been mentioned: returning teachers and teacher candidates. A second factor, less frequently considered, is the necessity for many students to work in summer to finance the next year's education. Since a higher percentage of men work during the summer (as shown by a 1961 Wisconsin study),[14] it is fair to assume that this factor would increase the female percentage simply by lowering the male.

Another important difference between fall and summer enrollments was discovered or, more accurately, confirmed by the Minnesota study.[15] The fall group analyzed was heavily weighted toward freshmen and sophomores (almost 50 per cent), followed in order by juniors and seniors (over 25 per cent), graduates (approaching 20 per cent), and specials and unclassified (5 per cent). Came summer, however, and the order exactly reversed itself. The largest of the four groups, with fully 32 per cent of the summer population was the "specials and unclassified," a group difficult to define but impossible to ignore. Close behind came the graduate student (28 per cent), his ranks swelled by returning educators. The upperclassmen followed, comprising 22 per cent, and then the freshmen and sophomores, with 18 per cent. Despite some variations in percentages and rankings, all later studies have confirmed the basic findings of the Minnesota report: that graduate school enrollment shows a great proportionate increase from fall to summer, and often approaches the actual numerical total of the previous fall; that

[13] Clodus R. Smith, *The University of Maryland Summer School, 1963* (mimeographed, College Park: University of Maryland Summer School, 1963), p. 16.

[14] L. J. Lins, *Comparison of Use of Time During 1961 Summer by Undergraduate Students Registered at Madison and Milwaukee During 1961 Fall Semester* (mimeographed, Madison: University of Wisconsin Office of Institutional Studies, 1962), p. 1.

[15] Stecklein, et al., *Summer Session, Minnesota,* pp. 44–45.

the special student introduces a dimension to the summer scene that is almost absent during the remainder of the year; and that, by and large, the freshman and sophomore student has for various reasons, valid or otherwise, not yet chosen to attempt summer study.[16] Let's examine now some of the reasons for, and implications of, these trends in summer enrollment.

## THE GRADUATE STUDENT

The graduate student increase is in part a result of the annual return of elementary and secondary school teachers and administrators for further training. The University of Southern California, for example, found 60 per cent of its 1963 summer graduate students to be on some school system's payroll during the remainder of the year.[17] Michigan State, in 1960, and Maryland, in 1963, reached 65 per cent.[18] And in 1961 Wisconsin, although it classifies many returning teachers as specials rather than graduates, still drew 30 per cent of its graduate student body from the educator ranks.[19] Regardless of the varying percentages, it is safe to say that further education of educators is one of the primary roles of the summer term, and of the school of education in particular. To be sure, it no longer dominates the entire summer program. Gone are the days of a half-century ago which the U.S. Office of Education described as "almost single-mindedly dedicated to meeting the needs of teachers or teacher candidates . . . ."[20] Yet no public-oriented summer term can ignore the educator segment of its population, despite its loss in relative position. As long as American school systems demand and encourage further training on the part of their teachers and

[16] See, for example, Paul E. Hadley and John D. Provart, *A Study of the Summer Session at the University of Southern California* (Los Angeles: University of Southern California Office of the Summer Session, 1964), p. 17; Lins, et al., *Student Evaluations 1964*, p. 5; and *Annual Report of the 1962 University of Wisconsin Summer Sessions* (mimeographed, Madison: University of Wisconsin Office of Summer Sessions, 1962), p. 2.

[17] Hadley and Provart, *Summer at U.S.C.*, p. 51.

[18] Saupe, *Survey of Summer, 1960*, p. 10; and Smith, *Maryland Summer, 1963*, p. 17.

[19] Lins, et al., *Student Reactions 1961*, p. 9.

[20] Warner, et al., *Summer Sessions, 1960*, p. 19.

administrators, the mutually profitable relationship between the American university summer term and the returning educator seems bound to flourish.

In addition, of increasing import to summer session planners and faculty is the ever-growing number of continuing graduate students from the regular year. Wisconsin, for example, found fully 55 per cent of its 1964 spring semester graduate population continuing for the summer term, a figure doubling the next highest re-enlistment rate for that year. It seems no exaggeration to say, therefore, that year-round education has become, or shortly will become, the rule rather than the exception for graduate students. The continuing increase in financial assistance for the graduate student is helping to remove a major barrier to his year-round education. With financial worries eliminated, and with the entire physical and personnel resources of a major university at his disposal (and often more available to him in summer than in the fall and spring), the graduate student cannot help but regard the summer as a valuable part of his educational timetable.

Another growing campus phenomenon with clear summer significance is the postdoctoral fellow, a new breed of animal who is neither strictly a student nor a faculty member. Following the receipt of his Ph.D., this person attaches himself to a department, a research facility, or an individual professor for more advanced work of an informal nature before seeking full-time employment, usually as a teacher. He is present on the campus throughout the year, but there is evidence that his numbers peak during the summer.[21] He is not enrolled at the university, but he plays an important role in the institution's year-round teaching and research program.

THE SPECIAL STUDENT

The category of special student is at best a catchall attempt to classify groups that defy easy classification. Within its confines

[21] There were 339 postdocs on the University of Wisconsin campus at Madison in 1966.

may be found such disparate individuals as the forty-five-year-old housewife returning to college for the first time in twenty-five years for an interesting course in contemporary literature; the summer transfer student from another college picking up a few credits at his hometown university for transfer back to his alma mater in the fall; and the high school junior adding to his language proficiency and getting an early taste of college life by taking a French literature course.

Nothing better illustrates the confusion caused by the specials than the universities' attempts to classify them. At some schools only those returning teachers doing post-baccalaureate refresher work but not actively pursuing a higher degree are lumped with the "specials." At others *all* returning educators are admitted as specials rather than as regular graduate students. One school may treat the recent high school graduate as a full-fledged undergraduate. Another may place him with the specials. Thus comparison between universities is made difficult. Perhaps the one common denominator for these students is that summer provides the most convenient, if not the only, time for pursuing their varied educational goals. Despite problems of taxonomy, however, almost all schools recognize the "special" as a legitimate part of the summer operation.

THE UNDERGRADUATE

Despite the expansion of the graduate and special student populations in summer, we should remember that in terms of total numbers of degree candidates the undergraduate student predominates. U.S. Office of Education figures disclosed that even in the universities almost 60 per cent of the degree candidates were undergraduate students.[22] For teachers colleges and liberal arts colleges the figures ran from 10 to 20 per cent higher. The motivations for undergraduate attendance are varied and will be considered later. As we mentioned earlier, though, it is the juniors and seniors who comprise the decided majority of the summer undergraduate population. Sophomores, and especially

22 Warner, et al., *Summer Sessions, 1960*, p. 67.

freshmen, are not generally receptive to the idea of summer study.[23]

Of those undergraduates who do choose to study in the summer, the overwhelming percentage are drawn from the college or university's own regular-year population. As a rough rule of thumb, in any summer undergraduate lecture of one hundred students eighty will have been enrolled on the same campus the previous semester.[24] The rest will be an assortment of summer transfer students, teachers, and non-college undergraduates.

The vagabond student has been one of the legendary characters of the summer session, though statistics indicate he is the rare exception rather than the rule. At his best, this individual is the summer-only transfer moving to a different campus to study under an outstanding professor or to utilize unique library or laboratory facilities. At his worst, he is the traveling playboy, after wine, women, and song on a campus with adequate recreational facilities nearby. Courses to him are a distraction, but small cost to pay for a summer of fun. Whether genuine or spurious, however, the transfer today rarely makes up more than a small part of the undergraduate total. Even Wisconsin, noted for both academic and social life, draws only 11 per cent of its summer students from other colleges or universities; and of these it has been noted that a considerable number are hometown Madison students attending other schools in fall and spring.[25]

The remainder of the undergraduates, not college students during the rest of the year, are a mixed collection of high school students, business and professional people, housewives, and non-graduate educators. While seldom more than a tiny portion of the total, each helps add further scope to an already broadly based summer student body.

WHY THEY COME

Of all the hoary myths of the summer term student, none is less deserving of credence today than the one that regards him as

[23] Lins, et al., *Student Evaluations 1964*, p. 5.
[24] See Smith, *Maryland Summer*, 1963, p. 17; or Hadley and Provart, *Summer at U.S.C.*, p. 17.
[25] Lins, et al., *Student Reactions 1961*, p. 9.

either an intellectual dilettante or an academic cripple. Born in the early days of summer university education when many professors and governing bodies were, often with good reason, frankly suspicious of the entire summer program, this myth has survived over the decades to color our thinking about the summer student of today. In this section we shall examine the motivation of the summer student: why he comes and, in particular, where the session fits into his overall educational or career plans. In a later section we will examine the quality of his work.

Student motivation is always a difficult factor to pin down, and any studies of it in relation to summer attendance are therefore open to question and revision. Still, simply asking students their reasons for summer attendance gives as accurate a picture of the situation as any other method. And ask their students, universities have.

If any broad generalizations can be made about the admitted reasons for attendance, it would be that they are the very best. Eighty-three per cent of Minnesota's students listed some educational objective as their most important reason for attendance.[26] Furthermore, their responses were quite specific: A third of the group said they were taking courses they would normally have taken in the fall—in other words, accelerating their academic progress to a greater or lesser extent. Twelve per cent revealed they were working toward a degree primarily through summer study. Another 12 per cent were making up courses they missed during the academic year. The remaining students mentioned a variety of educational reasons ranging from the desire to work under a particular visiting professor to the need to take part in a special field trip or travel course. Of the 17 per cent listing a primary reason other than "educational," almost all mentioned some occupational consideration. Again the responses were often quite specific, usually in terms of "I need this degree or course to get a raise or promotion."

More recent studies, while going into greater detail, all tend to support the conclusions of the Minnesota report.[27] Although

---

[26] Stecklein, et al., *Summer Session, Minnesota*, p. 41.
[27] See, for example, Lins, et al., *Student Evaluations 1964*, p. 11; and Smith, *Maryland Summer, 1963*, p. 19.

exact phrasing of questions varied, between 30 and 50 per cent of the total summer population referred to summer attendance as a means of accelerating their programs. About 10 to 15 per cent of the total population mentioned they were working for a degree largely through summer work. As to the contention that remedial students dominate the scene, Michigan State found that only one in eight of its full-time students attended to make up a deficiency or failure.[28]

ACCELERATION AND THE ACCELERANT

The exact nature and degree of student acceleration has long been a problem to summer session planners and administrators. A misinterpretation of data might easily suggest large numbers of undergraduates pursuing programs aimed at graduation in less than four years. But this is not in fact the case. Michigan State discovered few students graduating in less than four years despite an almost 40 per cent response of "graduate in less than usual time" on its 1960 reason-for-attendance questionnaire.[29] Attempting to explain the discrepancy, university officials suggested in their report that numerous individuals change their minds about early graduation as various personal, academic, and financial problems take their toll. They also suggested that many students may think of acceleration in terms different from those of the university administrator. In other words, to many students, four and one-half years may be the normal time to earn a bachelor's degree, thus making anything less than that an "accelerated" graduation.

Two Wisconsin studies put a slightly different light on the situation of the accelerant. The first found that new freshmen entering in the summer and continuing on in fall were much more likely to take a reduced credit load in fall than new freshmen entering in the fall. Thus it would seem that entering freshmen think of summer study in terms of an easier fall semester

28 Saupe, *Survey of Summer, 1960*, p. 17.
29 Ibid., pp. 17–18.

rather than an earlier graduation.[30] A second study confirmed the freshman preference for "lightening the load" and further found that the category of "earning additional credits" was most heavily supported by sophomores. Juniors and seniors listed "make up lost credits" most frequently as their reason for summer attendance.[31]

The accelerated graduate is thus in actuality a relatively rare individual.[32] The summer session can, however, provide a vital service for him. For despite claims to the contrary by proponents of full-scale trimester or four-quarter plans, at most institutions a student can fulfill graduation requirements in six semesters (or nine quarters) and three summer sessions with only a moderate amount of extra work. It is apparently not lack of opportunity to pursue a year-round educational program that limits the number of three-year bachelor's degree candidates. Rather, such factors as mental ability, emotional demands, and financial support loom large.

What position should the university take toward the genuine accelerant? John Little offers an answer:

These students are fully capable and many are desirous of progressing through undergraduate study and perhaps on into graduate work at a much faster pace than has been considered normal. Some universities are now encouraging such acceleration by providing the opportunity for students to take heavier schedules of courses, to do more independent study, and to secure advanced placement and advanced standing credit through comprehensive examinations as well as through formal course work. All of these opportunities are increasingly available in summer and no logical reason exists which precludes the possibility of substantially reducing the traditional time boundaries normally required for the completion of bachelor and advanced degree programs.[33]

[30] Lins, et al., *Comparison of New Freshmen,* pp. 9–10.
[31] Lins, et al., *Student Evaluations 1964,* p. 11.
[32] A possible exception is indicated in this remark by Henry Kronenberg, Director of the Summer Session, University of Arkansas: "Our mid-year graduation list is about the same as in June. I believe that we are beginning to get some speed-up." Personal correspondence in author's files.
[33] John R. Little, in Clarence A. Schoenfeld, ed., *The Shape of Summer*

## MATRICULANTS AND GRADUATES

While for most students summer study marks a continuation of their educational program, for a few it is a beginning or an end. Many schools advise recent high school graduates to begin their college work in the summer. Although present in such appeals is a certain amount of institutional self-interest in boosting summer enrollment in the often underpopulated freshmen courses, this is matched by rather substantial benefits to the student. Usually mentioned are the ability to orient oneself to campus life in the more relaxed summer atmosphere, the opportunity to concentrate on only one or two courses instead of five, and the greater ease of access to instructors on a campus one-half the size of that in fall. Despite the advantages of summer attendance and, in a few cases, the financial assistance offered, new freshmen have for the most part preferred to do other things than attend school. A North Central Conference of Summer Schools survey found only 4,500 new freshmen in a total summer population of 127,000, barely 3 per cent.[34]

According to a Wisconsin study, the beginning summer freshman does reap one most substantial benefit from his decision to begin study in June—higher grades: "Summer session new freshmen earn higher grade-point averages during the summer than they do during the fall or than do the fall new freshmen in the fall semester; the summer session new freshmen continuing in the fall semester, on the average, earn about the same grade-point average in the fall semester as do the fall new freshmen in that semester."[35] We have yet to explain the reason for the better summer performance. Is the grading simply easier? Or do the legitimate academic advantages mentioned by the schools' publicists account for the differential? A later section will consider answers to these questions.

At the other end of the scale the picture is more favorable to the population-conscious summer dean. Increasing numbers of

Sessions to Come (Madison: University of Wisconsin Office of Summer Sessions, 1961), p. 57.

[34] Forest L. Whan, Report to the North Central Conference of Summer Schools, 1964.

[35] Lins, et al., Comparison of New Freshmen, p. 2.

students at both the graduate and undergraduate levels are electing to finish their degree work in summer. This is not hard to understand when one considers the alternatives open to a student falling a few credits short of his degree in June. He could wait for the next fall semester and graduate the following January. On the other hand, he could finish his degree through summer work, effectively graduating with his class and ready to enter the business world or graduate school in September. That students often choose this alternative is shown by the 1960 Office of Education study, which found that over ninety thousand students completed degree requirements during that summer.[36] Another rough indicator of the popularity of summer graduation would be the increase in formal summer commencement ceremonies, a development no doubt pleasing to many faculty and administration personnel but probably less so to the student who would rather do without all the fuss and start his much-delayed vacation. An examination of practices at approximately two hundred colleges and universities revealed the popularity of the formal commencement ceremonies. Half of the schools, including a number of large state universities, finished their summer programs in caps and gowns.[37]

Whether accelerant or non-accelerant, graduate or undergraduate, regular student or special, the summer student seems to know quite specifically why he has come to school. His reasons are varied but almost all show a high degree of purpose and direction. As one observer puts it:

I submit . . . that goals of students attending summer sessions probably are plainer and clearer to them than goals of students in the other academic terms. Certainly, the returned school teacher has clear-cut goals in connection with earning additional credits for certification or for improved salaries and, frequently, educational goals in the forms of degrees. Undergraduate students who continue their education during the summer often do so because of clear-cut goals which they are eager to reach.[38]

36 Warner, et al., *Summer Sessions, 1960*, p. 83.
37 *1966 Summer Session Commencement in a Selected List of Colleges and Universities* (Carbondale: Southern Illinois University, 1966).
38 N. Edd Miller, 1966 NACUSS *Proceedings*, p. 21.

One might ask, in fact, whether it is not the regular-year students who are often indecisive and lacking in motivation. The summer student is rarely just marking time, "waiting for something to turn up." He has definite, if sometimes only short-range, goals in mind, and he has every intention of fulfilling them. This sureness of purpose helps define the summer student body and the summer term as well.

Before abandoning the subject of why students come to summer school, it is worth considering briefly why some students do *not* come. Financial considerations seem to be an especially critical factor, despite increases in institutional and federal loans and scholarships. Dr. L. Joseph Lins in a 1961 study found employment by far the most prevalent summer activity of spring semester students. Over 90 per cent of the men and 75 per cent of the women indicated that some part of their summer had been spent working. Further, a solid majority of those working planned to apply their savings toward future educational expenses. The report concluded that compulsory year-round education could not be undertaken without serious harm to these students: "For a very significant number of University of Wisconsin undergraduates, summer employment savings appear to determine whether or not the students could continue at the University during the regular academic year."[39]

### What They Do

Once again refuting the myths of life and leisure in the "good old summertime," the summer student often keeps a demanding schedule in the weeks he is on campus. The courses he takes are usually as difficult as those offered in the regular year, primarily because they are often the same. In addition, the summer student may hold a part-time or even full-time job to help finance his summer study. Finally, the recreational, social, and cultural opportunities of summer give further breadth to the student's activities, whether he has time for them or not. In short, for many the one-word answer to questions about what the student does in summer is "plenty."

[39] Lins, *Comparison of Time Use*, p. 2.

THE ACADEMIC SIDE

By definition, the student's primary activity should be class attendance and the outside studies connected with it. The classes he takes vary from the basic to the highly specialized. Most, however, are repeated from the fall and spring semesters with only slight, if any, abridgment. Minnesota found fully 80 per cent of its 1956 summer courses drawn from the regular terms.[40] In a more recent survey, the figure was found to reach 90 per cent for many large universities.[41] Examination of the 1966 Wisconsin summer timetable discloses over eighty departments offering courses at all levels and in all schools of the university. Courses in everything from Renaissance sculpture to business statistics to independent research in horticulture to opera workshop are open to the prospective summer scholar. On the national scene, the U.S. Office of Education data give a further idea of the diversity of summer offerings:

Summer sessions have constantly widened the scope of their purposes and offerings and thereby attracted new categories of students to supplement the inservice teachers and teacher candidates who once constituted most, or nearly all, of their clientele. For example, 81 per cent of the institutions [offering summer instruction] presented courses in the social sciences, 80 per cent in English and journalism, 76 per cent in education, and 70 per cent in mathematical subjects.[42]

There are few proofs more convincing than these for the contention that the summer term and the summer student are drawing closer to their regular-year counterparts. The fact of this similarity, quite understandable in terms of our earlier examination of who the summer student is, presents one of the most challenging problems to the summer term administrator. How does one provide a student body, often only a third as large as in fall, with a complete program to match a breadth of interest at least as wide as and often wider than in the fall? That the

40 Stecklein, et al., *Summer Session, Minnesota*, p. 186.
41 E. W. Ziebarth, "The Summer Session: Still an Appendage? Or, a Research View!" Speech to the North Central Conference of Summer Schools, March 18, 1963.
42 Warner, et al., *Summer Sessions, 1960*, p. 14.

summer term is as prosperous as it is today is in considerable measure due to past and present resolutions of this dilemma.

Aside from the normal carry-over courses, however, the summer session has always featured the unique, the experimental, the "different" courses which have lent the aura of "specialness" to summer education. Today, while in the decided minority, these still attract the student and lend added dimension to summer study.

After considering the programs offered in summer schools, the U.S. Office of Education proceeded to examine the students' response to them. Data disclosed that the average summer scholar enrolled for between five and eight credits of summer work in semester-hour schools. At quarter-hour institutions the range was greater, but most students carried over six credits. There was, however, a disturbing discrepancy between credits offered and credits earned, as the report indicated:

Many summer session students do not take full advantage of the credit-load opportunities offered. The part-time student has always been an important proportion of attendance for reasons which are several, well-known and legitimate. At the same time, he represents potential credits lost at a time when the achievement of maximum educational efficiency in terms of staff and plant utilization is becoming a factor of critical national importance.[43]

While this concern of the Office of Education is understandable, it does exaggerate the situation, placing the student at the service of the summer term rather than the reverse. Additionally, it fails to take account of the highly variable nature of individual course requirements. Any student can call to mind numerous examples of three-credit courses demanding five credits of work. To dismiss these individuals as "part-time students" seems to misstate the case. A better summary of student summer credit loads would be to reiterate the point that they fit the students' needs. Both the senior completing his final three credits before graduation and the acceleration-minded sophomore with a "full load" should be legitimate concerns of the summer university.

In the same Office of Education study travel-study programs

[43] Ibid., pp. 73–74.

were revealed to be one field of tremendous potential for summer education. As many as 192 schools offered some 247 foreign and domestic travel courses for credit in the summer of 1960.[44] Though comprehensive figures since then are not available, it would be safe to assume that the number has increased. At least twenty-five academic disciplines were represented, with foreign languages, art, and the earth sciences leading the way. Under the auspices of the University of Tennessee a student could register for Russian language and area studies. The course would be taught in Austria and followed by a field trip to Russia and other countries of Eastern Europe. A Wisconsin-sponsored tour of the holy lands attracted both religious and lay leaders. Kent State upperclassmen were able to spend a summer in an Oxford seminar, thus furthering their knowledge of modern Britain. In one of the most challenging of educational experiments, California co-sponsored an inter-American relations institute in Venezuela at which U.S. and Venezuelan students studied mutual problems. Somewhat closer to home, the University of Minnesota annually invites students to leave for a six-week exploration of biology at the Lake Itasca Forestry and Biology Station in the heart of the Minnesota lake country. Similarly, the University of Wisconsin Engineering School sponsors a civil engineering camp in northern Wisconsin's Chequamegon National Forest. Occupying the facilities of an old CCC camp, the prospective engineers obtain invaluable field experience far from the bustle of normal campus life.

Yet while travel and off-campus courses are certainly one of the more glamorous aspects of summer education, they are by no means the only area in which summer sessions differ from the regular year. The special course imported for one summer only by a visiting professor is familiar to generations of summer students. A more recent development has been the incorporation of intensive language training into the summer program, especially in some of the lesser studied tongues. Often instigated and supported by federal grants, these programs are using the concentrated summer session calendar to advantage, while filling a

44 Ibid., p. 76.

crucial need for specialists in East European, African, and Asian languages and cultures. Interuniversity cooperation in this field is only beginning, but already it suggests fruitful possibilities. A joint program in East Asian and Slavic studies, for example, offers Chinese and Japanese at the University of Colorado and Russian and Polish at Kansas.

### THE WORKING STUDENT

To many students summer work and summer education are by no means mutually exclusive. In fact it would be fair to revise the old stereotype of the summer student racing from the classroom to the beach or sunporch. Today he is racing to his part- or full-time job. Reference has already been made to the Wisconsin study stressing students' needs for summer work in order to finance another year's education. A different Wisconsin study came to the conclusion that a healthy percentage of the summer student body was able to attend a session and at the same time earn extra money either for present expenses or to help cover fall tuition. Forty-five per cent of the undergraduate population and 30 per cent of the graduate had some sort of job during the term, and some undoubtedly returned to full-time work after the conclusion of the session.[45] The hometown student would seem to be at a particular advantage in this respect. The experience of the Kenosha (Wisconsin) Extension Center, an urban, commuter campus, points this out quite clearly. Here over one-third of the summer student body earned more than six hundred dollars each from their summer's employment.[46]

Approaching the problem from a different aspect, studies at the University of Southern California found that one-third of the undergraduates and two-thirds of the graduates expected to finance their summer education through their own work and savings.[47] This expectation was supported by the disclosure that

---

[45] Lins, et al., *Student Reactions 1961*, pp, 12–13.

[46] John M. Valaske, *A Report on the Summer Student at the Kenosha Extension Center of the University of Wisconsin* (mimeographed, Kenosha, Wisconsin, 1962).

[47] Hadley and Provart, *Summer at U.S.C.*, p. 53.

one-third of the total population was employed. Unfortunately no complete survey of the kinds of jobs held has yet been made. If it were, it would undoubtedly further demonstrate the versatility of the American college student.

THE EXTRACURRICULUM

The demands of academic and occupational activities and the influx of "new" students each summer understandably cut down on the organized social and cultural life of a campus. Fraternities and sororities cease formal activities for the duration, often renting rooms to the incoming students. No athletic teams take to field or court. Student government and political action groups either suspend their activities or work on a greatly reduced scale. Homecomings, winter carnivals, or spring weekends find no summer counterpart.

Yet all is not quiet on the summer scene, for summer social and recreational life is measurable, if informal. Athletics, usually of an unorganized sort, are among the favorite pastimes of all students from new freshmen to doctoral candidates. Geographic locations can be utilized to their fullest in summer. Colorado runs a popular mountain recreation program. Wisconsin summertime means swimming and sailing on Lake Mendota, the latter under the auspices of the student-run sailing club. On almost all campuses, dating opportunities are plentiful and inexpensive. Even simply sitting back with a good book on a warm summer afternoon appeals to many students.

On a more organized level, cultural programs are becoming even more a part of the summer scene. The campus movie house and theater group both continue their programs into the summer months. All-campus lectures attract large and knowledgeable audiencies. Musical recitals are plentiful, and give aspiring performers a chance to test their skills at the same time.

Increasingly, summer events are becoming more than just reruns of the regular year. The 1964 Shakespeare Quadricentennial gave several campus theater groups an impetus to expand their summer programs. Stanford University, drawing on the resources of the departments of speech and drama, English, art and architecture, history and music, staged what *Saturday Review* described as the largest and most ambitious American Shakespeare festival. Three major west coast theatrical companies joined in the eight-week program of plays, musical programs, workshops, and special exhibits that made Stanford Summer 1964 something special for the lover of the arts. Vermont and Colorado also sponsored excellent, if less publicized, Shakespearean programs. The former even inspired an institute for secondary school teachers focused on the various aspects of Elizabethan arts and literature. In the summer of 1965, the University of Maine kept a resident company on campus performing works from the Broadway stage, and the University of Maryland continued its popular Theater-on-the-Mall.

In music, Minnesota's Choral Arts Institute, in its fifth year in summer 1965, brought to the campus conductor Kurt Adler and choral arts lecturer Julius Hereford. Columbia organized a summer session band which presented concerts on the steps of Low Library. Also at Columbia a program of graduate student folk dancing proved most enjoyable. Colorado, as the highlight of a full program of musical entertainment, brought Verdi to the Rockies, presenting two performances of *La Traviata*. Indiana's outdoor opera productions have featured *Aïda* and *Turandot*. And, perhaps the perfect example of a "summer-only" event, Indiana also sponsors a Showboat Majestic Theater: plying and playing the Ohio River from Cairo to Cincinnati, the student casts have delighted spectators and called up memories of bygone minstrel show days.

Increasingly, campus administrators are seeing the need for expanded "co-curricular" programs for the summer student body and, more importantly, are translating that need into the financial support needed to bring outstanding artists, speakers, and films to campus. A major factor behind this trend is the student support for such ventures. The Minnesota study found almost 50 per cent of the students had attended at least one film, concert, lecture, or play during their summer on campus.[48] Clearly, the arts have come to stay in summer education.

[48] Stecklein, et al., *Summer Session, Minnesota*, p. 55.

How They Do

In our discussion of reasons for attendance we have seen the high degree of motivation that prompts most students to attend a summer session. To critics of the summer session, however, this is not enough. They want, in Casey Stengel's phrase, to "see how they execute," how they measure up academically. Too many stories of the star athlete regaining eligibility through summer attendance have biased their viewpoint. Even among university personnel many of these complaints are still aired: "There are so many making up failures, so many who are part-time students, and so many for whom summer session is a semi-vacation program that the standard must be lower than it is during the regular year."[49]

For decades the question of summer performance was frequently discussed but rarely analytically studied. Arguments pro and con were based all too often on half-truths, random observations, and intuitions. A few institutions observed and compared students' summer session grades with the same students' fall grades and found the former to be higher.[50] But did this indicate superior summer performance or merely easier grading? Again the jury was divided.

Then a University of Minnesota research team attempted to move beyond mere conjecture.[51] Taking four courses offered in both the regular year and the five-week summer session, the so-designated "pilot study" first determined student capability through study of past grade-point average. Then performance in the particular course, based on numerical scores on similar examinations, was tabulated for both regular-quarter and summer term students and compared with each student's cumulative average. Final analysis of information disclosed in almost every case "no significant difference" between the performance of fall

49 William Prentice, Speech reprinted in "The Summer Session in Higher Education," *Columbia University Seminar Proceedings*, March 10, 1961, p. 21.

50 See, for example, Lins, et al., *Comparison of New Freshmen*, p. 14.

51 Clara Kanun, E. W. Ziebarth, and Norman Abrahams, "Comparisons of Student Achievement in the Summer Term and Regular Quarter," *Journal of Experimental Education*, Fall 1963, pp. 123–129.

and summer students as measured by test scores. In other words, students in summer are just as likely to work up to their previously established capabilities as students in fall.

Not content with this disclosure, the Minnesota project was repeated the following summer. This time instructors were notified beforehand that comparison was to be made between summer and fall learning. Thus, more rigid control allowed for greater similarity in required readings, lectures, and, most important, examinations. Again results were tabulated and again "no significant difference" was found.

More recently the Indiana University summer sessions office sponsored similar research comparing performance in full-semester courses with performance in the two-and-one-half-week summer intersession.[52] The intersession course with its intensive three-hour-a-day, five-day-a-week regimen offered an excellent chance to study the value of a concentrated learning experience. Carrying the Minnesota project one step further, the instructors teaching the same course in semester and intersession were instructed to use the same lectures, readings, and examinations in both sessions. In the final analysis nine courses with a total enrollment of just over a thousand students were accepted as fulfilling all desired criteria. Once again cumulative grade-point averages were determined and matched against performance in the course under analysis. By cumulative average the intersession students scored consistently higher than their semester counterparts, providing further evidence that summer students are often of higher quality than fall or spring term students. By comparison of performance in the course under study the intersession students again surpassed their competitors. Of seven undergraduate courses studied, intersession students performed significantly better in three and as well in the other four. Of four graduate courses, the spring semester students performed better in one and as well in the other three. In plain terms, if achievement on standardized tests may be taken as indicative of the

---

[52] Robert W. Richey, Ralph W. Sinks, and Clifton I. Chase, *A Comparison of the Academic Achievement of Students Enrolled in Nine Courses in the Intersession of 1963 and that of Students Enrolled in the Same Courses in the Spring Semester of 1962–1963* (mimeographed, Bloomington: Indiana University Office of Summer Sessions, 1965).

amount of work expended and the amount of material learned, then a strong case can be made for the summer student being superior to his regular-year counterpart, at least on the undergraduate level. At the very least he is equal to him.

Finally, in a study similar to those at Minnesota and Indiana, Southern California examined commerce and pharmacy students.[53] While the slightly better scores of the summer students could not be interpreted as "statistically significant," the implication was again that summer education had proven itself. As the report concluded: "If this study has significance it would appear to be that those charged with the responsibility for class scheduling need not fear to make greater use of summer programming."

While the Minnesota, Indiana, and Southern California studies cannot, and admittedly do not, offer the final word on the debate over summer performance, they do help to clear away much of the myth surrounding the summer student, by suggesting not only that he is a better student to begin with but that he does comparatively better in the courses he takes. In addition, the studies go a long way toward supporting a fundamental belief of the summer term: that a semester's or quarter's material can be taught as effectively in a more concentrated period.

Supporting the objective data of the reports have been a half-dozen analyses from various summer faculties. Professors at Minnesota, Maryland, and Indiana, for example, all expressed satisfaction with their summer students.[54] Comparisons with regular-year students that indicated any preference at all usually favored the summer population. "Clearer motivation," "greater maturity," and "livelier intellectual interest" were frequently recurring terms of praise. A Heidelberg College report likewise found summer performance superior.[55] Better preparation by instructors, smaller classes, more highly motivated students, and fewer distractions from study were among the reasons noted here.

Superior student performance is a factor influenced by many

[53] Reported in John Bester, "Student Performance in Summer Programs," *American Journal of Pharmaceutical Education*, February 1965, pp. 44–49.

[54] Stecklein, et al., *Summer Session, Minnesota*, pp. 120–122; Smith, *Maryland Summer, 1963*, pp. 46–49; Richey, et al., *Comparison of Academic Achievement*, pp. 32–35.

[55] James H. Moyer, *Report on the 1964 Summer Session at Heidelberg College* (mimeographed, Tiffin, Ohio: Heidelberg College, 1964).

variables, among them the caliber of the summer program itself. Poorly planned programs taught by second-rate teachers not only will fail to attract good students but will blunt the initiative of those who do come. The burden of improvement therefore seems to be on those institutions which have not yet provided a quality summer program. Good students are available to the school that is willing to offer them a first-class summer program.

## IN SUMMARY

In summarizing our discussion of the summer student, we should point out again that measurable numbers of students are involved in summer research without being enrolled in summer courses, and that significant numbers of "students" of all ages come to the summer campus to participate in non-credit conferences, clinics, and institutes. It is, however, the student pursuing conventional collegiate work in summer that we have been primarily concerned with in this chapter. For, as we have said, it is he who represents "the summer session student" in the literature, and it is the programs available to him that constitute "the summer session curriculum."

As we have seen, the summer student has traditionally exhibited characteristics different from those of the "regular-year" student. "He" is more apt to be female, married, and in graduate school; hence he is older, his motivation stronger, and his goals clearer. Whatever the length of the term, he performs academically at least as well as the average student in winter. School teachers and administrators are still conspicuous by their numbers on the summer campus, but in recent years the "regular" continuing student seems to be achieving ascendancy, except on a few campuses especially favored by location or reputation where are found significant numbers of "summer specials"— visiting students who are candidates for a degree elsewhere or who are pursuing informal educational goals. Whatever his classification, the summer student's reasons for attendance are overwhelmingly academic, if we can accept his own words. He may even list "reading" as his favorite summer diversion. Acceleration, however, seems to be more talked about than practiced, at least in terms of statistics on graduations in less than four years.

Despite growing numbers of summer registrants, the fact remains that a majority of American students are not enrolled in summer on a campus, although it would not be fair to say they are therefore not enjoying educational experiences. They are at summer camps, they are traveling abroad, they are seeing America, they are fishing, they are lying in hammocks; mostly, they are working—to earn enough money to return in the fall. That they are not enrolled on campus, however, is usually not because the courses they want or need are not available.

# 3

# The Professor in Summer

Aɴʏ ɪɴꜱᴛɪᴛᴜᴛɪᴏɴ may be said to function like a magnet, attracting the appropriate ambitions of particular men. Within the university there are at least three poles: the individual teacher or scholar, concerned with his own career in the academic world; the department, seeking to improve its position with respect to other departments both on and off the campus; and the institution as a whole, competing with other institutions both academic and nonacademic. Rather than a single academic community, then, there are several academic communities, whose goals are not necessarily mutually supporting.[1]

Although the term was only recently invented, the university has been in truth a multiversity since the early 1900's. The individual career pattern and the departmental enclave constantly threaten to become ends in themselves. The only counter force

[1] See Laurence R. Veysey, *The Emergence of the American University* (Chicago: University of Chicago Press, 1965).

is the creative administrator, sketching as on a gigantic canvas a network of lines, arranged with some order and sense, representing the real and imaginary relations among the units of a sprawling organization. Little wonder that professors and deans alike often "cannot see the wood for the trees: Students are nigh double, likewise the staff; palaces rear on the sites of barns, dollars roll in and up merrily . . . . Events lull us into assurance or indifference of our destiny."[2] (These words, interestingly enough were written in 1907, not in 1967!)

The upshot is that the American university, winter and summer, because it lacks any real cohesion, is hospitable to a wide variety of individuals. At one extreme are those professors or administrators who accept as their own the conventional public image of the American university: undergraduate degrees as the syndicated symbols of social and economic survival; research and extension dedicated to the practical furtherance of the common welfare; football and fun. At the opposite extreme are those who urge a drastic reorientation of the whole American endeavor. And in the middle are those for whom the university environment simply represents a happy medium between the monastery and the marketplace. It is this very "continued flexibility of academic impulse" that has given rise in summer to an enterprise so eclectic as to be called by some the nadir of university operations and by others the epitome of the university at work to lift the life of the commonwealth to higher planes. And it is the diverse interests and abilities of the individuals who comprise the faculty that determine the true nature (if there is one) of the university and its summer term. Let us, therefore, see who they are.

Who is the June professor and what does he do? Before answering such a question it might be well to say what a professor does in January. First, he teaches. Instructional arrangements may range from a lecture hall for a thousand undergraduates to a one-to-one laboratory relationship with a doctoral candidate. Second, he engages in research. His productive scholarship may be classified as "departmental"—that which he does

2 R. M. Wenley, "Transition or What?" *Educational Review*, XXXIII (1907), 433–434.

in addition to his other duties simply because he is a university professor pledged to extend the boundaries of knowledge; as "budgeted" or "organized"—that which he does on released time with institutional funds; or as "contract"—that which he does under an arrangement between himself, his dean, and an "outside" agency. Third, he performs educational services under the cognizance of his university. He may communicate with his colleagues in other climes; he may join informally with community groups; he may participate in structured extension programs; and he may advise agencies from Weyauwega to Washington, from upstate counties to Karachi. Fourth, he contributes to institutional administration—as a member of a departmental committee, on a college board, in a faculty senate, in a campus colloquium, in a professional society. Fifth, he counsels students —informally as a "father confessor" to his "advisees," formally as the sponsor of a student group. Sixth, he may "moonlight"—as a consultant to an industry, as a project leader for a government bureau, as a writer of textbooks, or even as a used-car salesman. And withall, he is typically a family man, blessed and harassed with all the chores of managing a budget, squiring a wife, raising youngsters, repairing a leaky faucet, and occasionally "getting away from it all."

What does he do, then, in summer? The same things he does in winter, with perhaps a change of emphasis. Unlike the summer student, who may often lead a very different life once September returns, the summer faculty member is engaged in a profession which places essentially the same demands on him throughout the year. He is, first and foremost, an employee of an American college or university, paid for teaching and scholarship. To be sure, he may not be doing the same teaching, or the same related research, that he would be in fall. He may not even be at the same institution. But the similarities, in the main, far outweigh the differences; and it follows, therefore, that the story of the summer faculty is in large part the story of faculty in general. In statistical parlance, most comparisons between summer and fall faculties would disclose "no significant differences." In laymen's terms, the professor in summer is going to look pretty much like the professor in fall, winter, or spring.

It is within this framework of basic similarity, then, that we should consider whatever differences do exist between the summer and regular-year faculty. Perhaps the most important of these is that what the professor does in summer is more likely to be what he *wants* to do, or what he does *best*, with the net result that the university in summer experiences a kind of increased staff specialization that enhances all of its major functions: teaching, research, and public service. Taken singly, the differences which produce such an effect are minor and unimportant; but collectively they allow us to define some subtle but important "characteristics" of the summer faculty.

It should be remembered, however, that, while the summer research and extension staffs may actually outnumber the summer teaching staff, it is the latter that is carried in the "summer session budget" per se and hence that has been analyzed in what little literature there is on the summer faculty. This chapter will therefore be concerned primarily with the summer session faculty member as narrowly construed—in his role as a teacher of undergraduate and graduate students—though we recognize that he may perform some research and service chores as well.

## VITAL STATISTICS

Examinations of the summer student body have revealed the "average" student to be older and more mature than his regular-year counterpart. While research on the matter has been limited, it appears that the same may be true of the summer session faculty member: he is (statistically) senior in both rank and experience to his fall semester colleague.

A report of the 1956 University of Minnesota summer session provided one of the first comparisons of faculty rank in summer and in fall. The summer percentages for professors, associate professors, assistant professors, and instructors were almost identical to the fall percentages. That 46 per cent of the summer faculty were either full or associate professors seemed to negate arguments that the summer staff was an inexperienced, poor relation.[3] Four years later a massive U.S. Office of Education

[3] Stecklein, et al., *Summer Session, Minnesota*, p. 106.

study of over 1,300 American university and college summer sessions found the picture even more favorable to the summer session. Nearly 53 per cent of the summer faculty were associate or full professors, a 3 per cent rise over the figures for the preceding fall.[4] Admittedly the figures may be skewed somewhat by the comparative absence of multiple quiz and laboratory sections in summer, which substantially reduces the need for low-ranking instructors.

Not surprisingly, the summer teacher often comes equipped with that "union card" of his profession, the Ph.D. Minnesota found 62 per cent of its summer faculty holding doctorates in 1957, a percentage slightly higher than that for the fall semester.[5] Again the U.S. Office of Education report provided a nationwide picture: an average of 42 per cent of the summer faculty members included in the 1960 survey had their doctorates.[6] While fall data were not available for that year, a 1963 survey of regular-year faculty showed 41.5 per cent to hold doctorates, again suggesting that the summer term is at least equal to the fall in this respect.[7] A slightly more recent Wisconsin study, however, indicates that the seniority of the summer staff may be slipping somewhat.[8]

In regard to teaching experience, if this may be taken as an indication of excellence then summer teachers are certainly of a high caliber. Minnesota found its entire summer faculty to have a median teaching experience of eleven years;[9] and the University of Maryland, while noting some preference for younger faculty, still found almost 90 per cent of its summer faculty to have previously taught a Maryland summer course.[10] The carry-over of faculty from regular year to summer has

[4] Warner, et al., *Summer Sessions, 1960*, p. 53.

[5] Stecklein, et al., *Summer Session, Minnesota*, p. 108.

[6] Warner, et al., *Summer Sessions, 1960*, p. 58.

[7] James Rogers, *Staffing American Colleges and Universities* (Washington: U.S. Office of Education, 1967), p. 19.

[8] *Annual Report of the 1965 University of Wisconsin Summer Sessions* (mimeographed, Madison: University of Wisconsin Office of Summer Sessions, 1965), p. 9.

[9] Stecklein, et al., *Summer Session, Minnesota*, p. 109.

[10] Smith, *Maryland Summer, 1963*, p. 36.

been noted by E. W. Ziebarth of Minnesota. Between 80 and 90 per cent of an institution's summer faculty, he concludes, are drawn from its own regular-year staff.[11] While this does not mean that the summer visiting lecturer is a vanishing figure, a vestige of an earlier peripatetic era, it does further indicate the increasing similarity between the fall and summer terms. Professors assuredly will continue to exchange campuses as long as the mutual benefits that accrue from such arrangements continue. What is gone is the old reliance of many schools on the visiting instructor. The era in which off-campus recruitment of faculty determined the success or failure of a summer program has been happily left behind.

## Why He Teaches

Having examined a few characteristics of the summer faculty member, let us probe deeper into his reasons for choosing to teach in the summer.

### A QUESTION OF MONEY

Three decades ago, the summer session was the chance for the underpaid professor to keep his assets ahead of his debits for the year. Competition for the available positions was intense, with seniority and departmental influence often deciding the outcome. To the winners went a guaranteed pay check for another two or three months and the knowledge that life could continue in pretty much its usual manner. The losers, however, often faced the dismal prospect of either going without work or taking whatever off-campus job was available. Many an employment bureau no doubt mused over what post to give an unemployed philosophy instructor.

Today a far different situation prevails. While academic prosperity is most noticeable at the large universities and well-endowed private institutions, even the small community and teachers colleges have shared in the financial benefits of the

[11] Ziebarth, "Summer: an Appendage?"

postwar period. It would be an overstatement to say that the college teacher has finally achieved his deserved recompense. Certainly few teachers would admit it! But the fact remains that summer teaching is no longer the matter of absolute necessity that it was in the post-depression era. The professor, given financial security in the regular year and other lucrative alternatives in the form of federal and foundation research grants in the summer, can be quite choosy in planning his summer calendar.

There are some qualifications to this picture, as indicated by a recent survey of North Central Conference of Summer Schools faculty conducted by Forest Whan.[12] This study centered on the summer unemployed, the teachers wanting work but unable to find it. Of 5,845 faculty studied, 899 were unable to find teaching jobs in the summer. At their same institutions 632 visiting professors were hired. The situation in these colleges, of which most are small and non-prestigious, indicates that despite the greatly improved nationwide picture faculty prosperity in terms of full employment has yet to be reached.

For the majority able to find work, however, pay scales have improved considerably over the past few decades. The professor, having in the main determined that he can get summer work if he wants it, is now concerned with making that work pay as well as the work he does during the rest of the year. From the data available, he seems to be succeeding. The U.S. Office of Education in 1960 studied his progress:

Directors were asked to estimate whether, assuming equal time and work loads, salaries in their 1960 summer sessions were higher than, equal to, or lower than those of the regular year. . . . Higher salaries were estimated by 25 institutions, equal salaries by 644 and lower salaries by 514. If only the 1,183 responding schools are included, the frequencies in the same order are 2.1 per cent, 54.4 per cent, and 43.5 per cent.[13]

The study also revealed a great variation in standards of summer payment throughout the country. Five were noted as being most prevalent: (1) a fixed percentage of regular-year salary;

12 Whan, Report to the NCC, 1964.
13 Warner, et al., *Summer Sessions, 1960*, pp. 32–33.

(2) the regular salary figured on a weekly or monthly basis and then discounted by a certain percentage and multiplied by the number of weeks in the summer session; (3) a fixed sum per credit hour taught; (4) a fixed sum related neither to regular salary nor to hours taught; and (5) salary as a percentage of tuition revenue. The last, however, a throwback to the earlier finance-it-yourself days, seems to be dying out.[14]

The yearly North Central Conference reports on salary improvement lend support to the U.S. Office of Education figures.[15] If we estimate the mean weekly salary of all respondents, we find that the full professor was making almost $30 a week more in summer 1965 than just two years earlier. The associate professor improved his salary by $17, the assistant professor by $11, and the instructor by $12. In terms of an eight-week session an increase of up to $240 could hardly be called insignificant. Further, the actual professorial average of $260 per week indicates that full parity with fall salaries is well on its way.

A University of Wyoming analysis offers further proof of the approaching equality of salary: "I note," says Dean H. B. McFadden in summary, "that of the 38 institutions surveyed, one reports summer compensation at a higher rate than academic year compensation and 22 judge the two rates to have been equalized. Nine more expect or hope to move toward equal rates within the near future. It occurs to me that the proportions represented here are just the reverse of those which existed not more than 10 years ago."[16]

A final guide to the improving summer salary comes from a survey of 115 major colleges and universities made by Robert Richey and Fred Dressel of Indiana University.[17] Completed in 1963 and then repeated two years later, the survey followed the

---

[14] Ibid., pp. 33–42.

[15] Robert Richey, Graydon Yaple, and William Utley, *North Central Conference of Summer Schools Comparison of Characteristics* (mimeographed, North Central Conference of Summer Schools, 1963, 1964, 1965).

[16] *Summary of Summer Faculty Salary Questionnaire* (mimeographed, Laramie: University of Wyoming Summer School, 1966).

[17] *A Study of Salaries and Fringe Benefits for Resident Faculty in 115 Major Colleges and Universities in the United States* (mimeographed, Bloomington: Indiana University, 1963, revised 1965).

pattern set by the U.S. Office of Education, with one exception: five categories of response were allowed instead of three. Thus summer salaries compared to regular-year salaries could be higher, the same, practically the same, lower, or much lower. Taking just the "higher" and "same" categories of the 1965 report, exactly 50 per cent of the respondents claimed superiority or equality for the summer session. Including the "practically the same" category, the figure reaches almost 75 per cent. Most encouraging was the less than 1 per cent response of "much lower." Compared with 1963, the more recent figures also give grounds for optimism in that the "higher" or "same" categories jumped almost 10 per cent and the "much lower" category was practically eliminated.

Projecting into the future, Richey and Dressel asked their survey group whether changes were expected. Again the results were highly encouraging to the proponent of equal summer salaries. Of the twenty-nine schools responding, thirteen estimated that the differential between fall and summer salaries would be reduced or eliminated altogether. Another thirteen felt it would stay the same. Only three said that the gap would increase.

For the veteran summer instructor the salary improvement must be especially gratifying. While much of the gratification is no doubt monetary, a certain amount of satisfied pride is involved as well. Historically, low pay scales in summer could be attributed to and justified by one of two arguments used by administrators who set summer salary policy: first, the inexorable laws of supply and demand (too many teachers competing for too few positions) called for lower wages for those fortunate enough to receive work; and second, summer teaching simply did not seem to be worth as much as other teaching and therefore deserved less remuneration. In many instances both arguments were used. The task of the summer faculty member was, quite obviously, to alter both situations. His efforts in these directions —helping to recruit more students, encouraging curriculum expansion, and raising standards of summer instruction—have not only improved his own financial position but have been a key factor in the explosion in summer session enrollment over the past decade.

## SOME FRINGE BENEFITS

While salary is, as we have indicated, a major factor in keeping some of the faculty population on campus after June commencement, it is not the only one. Increasingly other considerations are entering into the picture as the professor plots his summer course. Richey and Dressel in their study of salary changes looked also at the so-called "fringe benefits" available to summer teachers. They found that about 65 per cent of all schools studied offered the same retirement benefits, medical insurance, and life insurance to the summer resident faculty that were offered to regular-year faculty. In large public universities the figure approached 75 per cent. A few of the schools not offering benefits indicated that improvement in their situation was expected shortly.[18]

## A MATTER OF PREFERENCE

Going beyond purely financial considerations, what other factors attract a summer faculty? Robert Vogel, director of the Trinity College summer session, offers an answer after some consideration of past history:

Ten years ago there was figuratively each year a line of impoverished instructors outside my door, all of them applicants to teach in the summer session in order to meet the payments on their mortgage. The AAUP might not like to have this said aloud, but the fact is that during this 10-year period faculty salaries across the country have vastly improved. The result has been that this line of instructors has disappeared. It has been replaced by a line of faculty members who want to teach in summer school because they like to teach. They prefer to spend part of their summer teaching rather than in other pursuits open to them—rest, travel, research. To the extent that enjoyment of teaching contributes to quality of teaching we may say it is possible that summer instruction is, on the whole, of a higher level than during the winter.

[18] Ibid.

Beyond this, and probably more important, it has been my experience that there is definitely an increased interest in teaching in summer school because of the particular satisfaction gained from teaching at that time. Faculty members have learned that summer classes are especially rewarding. If it were possible, they would like always to teach under the conditions which they obtain during the summer session. For a second reason, then, there is a special enthusiasm among the summer faculty.[19]

With the future seeming to hold forth prospects of ever-improving faculty salaries, summer teaching will increasingly become the province of those who, as Dr. Vogel suggests, *like* to teach. The resulting situation cannot help but benefit all concerned. The teacher will be doing what he likes, and, as we shall demonstrate later, he will be doing so with fewer distractions. The student will be getting the benefit of competent instructors who have specifically chosen to teach. And those professors whose competence and/or interest lie outside of classroom instruction will be able to concentrate their full energies on research, administration, or whatever else they may wish to undertake, without the burden of having to instruct an unwanted undergraduate course. If Robert Knapp is correct in predicting that "a segment of the college teaching profession will cut themselves off from the main body and become a class dedicated principally to research and only incidentally to instruction,"[20] then the present summer term is already pioneering a significant educational revolution. In any case, the summer term can expect to benefit from both teaching and research of a very high caliber in the years ahead.

SUMMER ACTIVITIES

Now that we have determined who the summer faculty member is and why he is on campus, it seems appropriate to consider

[19] In *Columbia Seminar Proceedings,* pp. 5–6.
[20] In Nevitt Sanford, ed., *College and Character* (New York: Wiley and Sons, 1964), p. 136.

what he does. Once again, the similarities between the summer and the regular year are far greater than the differences.

TEACHING

Almost all faculty paid from the summer session budget per se spend at least part of their time in classroom instruction: over 80 per cent of Minnesota's summer staff indicated they were doing some teaching;[21] and University of Maryland faculty regarded instruction as their most important duty.[22] The related activity of counseling individual students was the next most frequent listing among both groups. Thus, while not every summer employee is actually in the classroom, teaching is far and away the dominant activity. It is still what the summer term is all about. Research and extension activities, as we have said, are largely carried on under other administrative arrangements.

The U.S. Office of Education again provides the most comprehensive data on the usual summer faculty work load in credit hours taught:

The 6-hour load was by far the most common, being employed by 389 colleges and universities (47.6 per cent of responding semester-hour schools) or more than three times as many as the next most frequent, the 9-hour load used at 105 (12.9 per cent). The third- and fourth-ranking loads were 76 institutions with 3 hours and 61 institutions with 8 hours. The 137 colleges and universities employing quarter hours had no affinity for a given teaching load comparable to that of the semester institutions for 6 hours. The most common quarter-hour figure was 15 credit hours, reported by 29 institutions (21.2 per cent), 14 of which stated that they considered the session a fourth quarter. The next in order of frequency were the 10-hour load (24 schools) and the 12-hour load (20, including 14 fourth quarters).[23]

A 1965 North Central Conference report found 7.1 credit hours to be the mean. The extremes ranged from 4 to 18.[24] The 1964

---

21 Stecklein, et al., *Summer Session, Minnesota*, pp. 111–112.
22 Smith, *Maryland Summer, 1963*, p. 37.
23 Warner, et al., *Summer Sessions, 1960*, p. 62.
24 Richey, et al., *NCC Characteristics*, 1965.

report, which computed teaching load in contact hours per week (i.e. student discussion and counseling time as well as actual in-class teaching), reported 12.9 hours per week as the mean, indicating that out-of-class teaching activities almost double the average instructional load.[25]

Is the summer instructor too heavily burdened with his teaching responsibilities? On this point the jury is divided. The U.S. Office of Education suggests that he is:

Despite the lack of complete and comparative data, the suspicion arises that many teachers are more heavily burdened in summer than during the regular academic year, a practice which constitutes a serious danger to effective instruction. A common student complaint of early summer sessions was that they were intellectually robbed by ineffective teaching in summer terms. Thus to overload the faculty at that time would be to compound the felony. In this connection, it must be remembered that, in recent years, the greatly increased amount of graduate work offered at summer sessions has brought the added burden of supervision of theses and dissertations to the faculties of many institutions.[26]

A University of Wisconsin calendar committee concurs with this view:

Even with a 25% stipend for a 9-week session, many faculty will be paid at a lower *rate* for teaching in the summer than during the academic year. In those numerous departments where a normal academic load during a semester included three courses, these courses are taught for a stipend equal to 50% of an academic salary, or 16⅔% per course. In these same departments the normal course load in the summer is two courses; at 25% for a 9-week session this represents 12½% per course. While, even in the proposed 9-week session, there will be slightly fewer class hours in the typical 3-credit course when taught in summer than when taught during a semester (40 compared to 44), this differential is insufficient to remove entirely the discrepancy in percentage of salary just described. In other words, the faculty member in the Summer Session works a little harder at his teaching for a given amount of money than he does during the semester.[27]

25 Richey, et al., *NCC Characteristics*, 1964.
26 Warner, et al., *Summer Sessions*, 1960, p. 62.
27 *Report of the Academic Calendar Committee, Madison Campus, On*

A North Central Conference report, however, takes a different position:

We can be sure that our summer teachers have lighter loads than in fall—in terms of student credit hours taught. And we can be certain that as a result each summer teacher has more time for individual students, or more time for preparation than he would have in the fall.[28]

Which side is right? Is it "summertime and the livin' is easy" or is the true picture one of too many classes with too many students? One resolution might be reached by considering exactly what constitutes a "credit hour." Can we assume, that is, that a teacher must work twice as hard each day to present a course in eight weeks as he does to present it in sixteen weeks? If so, then the daily demands of a six-hour summer teaching load would be double those of the same fall term load, and the teacher would have even *less* time for consultation and preparation than he has in fall (assuming an average six-hour load in summer and a nine-hour load in fall). He would also be receiving less compensation for each hour of his time than even the Wisconsin figures indicate. Obviously, more research is needed to resolve this question; but the evidence does seem to favor the view that the summer teacher is, in nationwide terms, still overloaded and underpaid.

SCHOLARSHIP

Though we have largely limited our discussion here to the summer teaching faculty—those included in the summer session budget per se—the research function of the summer campus cannot be overlooked. Research activity—of the "unbudgeted" sort— among the faculty who are actually teaching seems to be fairly limited. Minnesota, for example, reported a smaller percentage of its faculty engaging in research or original writing in the sum-

---

*Summer Session Matters* (mimeographed, Madison: University of Wisconsin, 1966).

[28] Forest L. Whan, "Report of the Personnel Committee, 1965," Report to the North Central Conference of Summer Schools, 1965.

mer than in the fall and spring terms.[29] Such a decline, however, may well be attributable to a teaching overload; or it may simply be that the summer faculty prefer to teach.

Whatever the reason, the bulk of summer research is carried on by professors on full-time grants outside the summer session budget. For the faculty member pursuing a research project, summer is often the time when he can devote his fullest energies to it. The pressures of teaching and committee work may be substantially reduced. Further, an able staff of graduate assistants may be present to help as needed with the legwork. Finally, for some disciplines, especially in the biological sciences, the summer climate provides the best opportunity for outdoor work. Louis Agassiz's decision of nearly a century ago to found one of the pioneer summer sessions for biological research is still echoed today in summer in-the-field research.

While most summer research is simply a continuation of spring semester work conducted under either institutional or outside auspices, a number of programs unique to summer have arisen. A 1965 Office of Institutional Research report of summer programs for faculty disclosed, for example, an exciting array of grant-sponsored work opportunities: five University of North Carolina faculty members accepted grants under a Cooperative Program in the Humanities; sixteen University of Iowa faculty members were supported by the Old Gold Research Development Fund for projects ranging from a study of baroque flute music to research on the location of large-scale service industries.[30]

A related aspect of the summer research program is the growth of special institutes and conferences reviewing instructional techniques and methods, primarily at the undergraduate level. Often interinstitutional in scope, such programs can give teachers a chance to revitalize often badly outdated programs. Physicists recently gathered at the University of Washington to initiate a long-term project designed to improve undergraduate teaching

[29] Stecklein, et al., *Summer Session, Minnesota*, pp. 111–112.
[30] *For Your Information*, Office of Institutional Research Circular No. 74 (Washington: National Association of State Universities and Land-Grant Colleges, May 19, 1965).

methods in their discipline. Similarly, Colorado encouraged engineers to attend a planning session on the uses of programed learning in different areas of the instructional program. The University of Illinois sponsored forty of its faculty for a summertime review of the methods, materials, and organization of undergraduate courses in various disciplines. And Kentucky awarded ten special fellowship grants to faculty members presenting proposals designed to enhance their effectiveness as teachers.[31] The possibilities for such programs are enormous; but as yet the surface has barely been scratched.

ADMINISTRATIVE AND COMMITTEE WORK

Just as the coming of summer means to the student the cessation of many traditional campus activities—the organized athletic program, fraternities and sororities, and most of the student government apparatus—so, too, does the faculty lay aside much of its "extracurricular activity," its committee work and administrative routine. The reduction in such activity has been noted by Minnesota,[32] and seems to be fairly common throughout the country. In the words of Northwestern's Associate Dean of Faculties, William C. Bradford, "There is a decline in both student and faculty committees and activities in the summer in comparison with the balance of the year. Many of our standing committees come to a practical halt in the summer, although some of them are beginning to continue their activities."[33] Faculty meetings are often discontinued; departmental functions are cut to a minimum after the busy spring work of selecting next year's graduate students and planning next year's courses. In brief, much of the university's paperwork process goes into a happy state of estivation.

The picture should not be drawn out of proportion, however. Administrative responsibilities still exist, and, despite the desire to dump them lock, stock, and barrel into the already overburdened lap of the summer session director, they have to be

[31] Ibid.
[32] Stecklein, et al., *Summer Session, Minnesota*, pp. 111–112.
[33] Personal correspondence in author's files.

met by the appropriate committee representative or department chairman. Further, though such responsibilities are still far less cumbersome in summer than in fall and spring, an increase seems likely in view of the rising summer enrollment.

AFTER CLASS

Properly viewed, the summer professor's life can present an idyllic picture indeed. Leisurely morning walks to air conditioned classrooms. Small classes full of interested, mature students. Afternoons free to take a dip in the lake or "shoot nine" on the campus golf course. Evenings free to meet for coffee with students or simply relax at home. Surprisingly, there may be some truth in the picture. Summer, simply by being summer, offers in most parts of the country unparalleled recreational advantages: swimming, sailing, tennis, golf, fishing—take your pick. Further, campus cultural programs are improving. First-rate plays, films, concerts, and lectures are coming to the campus in increasing number. For the visiting faculty member the chance to explore a new campus and a new city is often all the leisure activity he wants or needs. In fact, it is often why he took the job in the first place.

For one segment of the summer faculty, however, leisure time is a scarce and sometimes nonexistent commodity. For these men and women, "moonlight" has become a verb rather than a noun, with connotations of long hours at their second job, often too little sleep, and almost always too little time to prepare properly the next day's class material. Forced by low pay to supplement their income, these teachers are sharp reminders that college and university salaries are in certain instances still inadequate. Clearly the burden is on the recalcitrant institutions which still maintain low pay scales. In the words of Dr. John Krout of Columbia University: "If we are to secure better teachers . . . we must pay them the salaries to which they are entitled. We are going to have to pay on the same levels that we pay in the regular sessions. We must face the fact that summer sessions are going to be more costly. It is not a way to make the college some extra money."[34]

[34] In *Columbia Seminar Proceedings*, p. 19.

SOME PERSPECTIVES ON PERFORMANCE

Given the fact that the summer professor has elected to teach during the summer, that he evidently enjoys teaching, that he is often more skilled and experienced, and that other academic duties frequently weigh less heavily upon him than during the regular year, one might assume that he would do a better job of teaching. Such indeed seems to be the case.

As part of a comprehensive evaluation of its 1963 summer program, the University of Maryland polled its summer students to determine their attitudes toward the instruction they received. The results must have been gratifying to even the most optimistic faculty member. Fully 27 per cent gave the top rating, "a model of good teaching," to their professors; another 32 per cent thought their instruction to be "better than average." At the other extremes only 10 per cent felt the teaching was "poorer than average" and 5 per cent "an example of very poor teaching." When compared with regular-year teaching, the summer again measured up well. Sixty per cent of respondents felt their summer instruction to be equal to what they received the rest of the year. And of the 40 per cent who rated one session over the other, fully three-fourths preferred the summer term.

Could these favorable responses be attributed in any degree to gratitude on the students' part for reduced work loads, easy examinations, and a general slowing down of pace in the summer term? The findings indicate definitely not. Most students felt summer study to be at least as demanding as any study in the fall or spring, and a good number felt it to be more so.[35]

While the Maryland responses were extremely satisfying, they should not have been completely unexpected. In actuality they almost duplicated the findings of previous studies at Minnesota and Wisconsin.[36] In some instances the variations were as little as one per cent. About the only major discrepancy was in the comparison between summer and regular-year instruction. Wisconsin students, like those at Maryland, graded their summer

[35] Smith, *Maryland Summer, 1963*, pp. 42–45. The breakdown of responses was as follows: summer courses more demanding, 40.7%; about the same, 46.1%; summer less demanding, 13.2%.
[36] Stecklein, et al., *Summer Session, Minnesota*, pp. 52–53; and L. J. Lins, et al., *Student Reactions 1961*, pp. 20–27.

professors higher; but Minnesota students saw both as equally competent.

When the various studies were broken down by student classification, the largest centers of discontent with summer teaching were found among the graduate populations. To be sure, the summer instructors and the entire summer program still scored well; but the graduates were less likely to find "models of good teaching" in their summer courses. An immediate implication of this finding is that, since the more experienced graduate student should be the better judge of teaching quality, summer instruction is not the paragon that a reader of the Maryland, Minnesota, or Wisconsin reports might be led to believe. Further consideration, however, suggests that the difference lies in relative standards of value and should not be resolved by any absolute measure of performance. Thus, such factors as a professor's informality of approach, his availability for after-class discussion, or his interest in individual students—attributes that may be commonplace or irrelevant to a graduate student—can be new and exciting to an undergraduate, fresh from a spring semester of oversized lectures and inaccessible professors. To deny that such qualities are worthy of consideration in an analysis of teaching, especially on the undergraduate level, is to reduce teaching to little more than a mechanical recitation of a certain body of facts and concepts.

ATTITUDES ON PACE

A problem which disturbs many summer faculty is that of the faster summer pace—the necessity to present in six or eight weeks the same material that is presented in fifteen to eighteen weeks during the fall and spring semesters. For those schools in which the summer term has become a fourth quarter or summer trimester equivalent to a "regular" term, this consideration is less relevant; but at the majority of institutions, where the summer represents a condensed version of the regular semester, the debates continue among faculty over course revamping, trimming of instructional deadwood, and the pressures of a five-lectures-a-week regimen.

Is compressed learning a good or an evil? Listen to some random faculty comments gleaned from a study of the University of Indiana intersession. This several-hours-a-day, five-days-a-week, two-and-one-half-week session takes compression about as far as it can go:

It [the intersession] allowed the student to devote full time to one course. . . . The pace was killing for the instructor. . . . Concentration on a single subject provided greater continuity. Less time was needed for review. Time after class for discussions with individual interested students generated much closer contact between student and instructor. . . . One could not do justice to a semester's work in a short term. . . . There was less time for examinations. There were excessive demands on students' attention spans during longer class sessions. A massed-time term was quite difficult for a course of intensive study. . . . The students were more eager to work. Performance on examinations was better. . . . The short term disclosed a lack of any possibility of having a perspective growing from reflection.[37]

However hectic the pace of the Indiana intersession may be, the fact remains, as we have already shown, that students do not suffer. Robert Vogel, a spokesman for the short term, re-emphasizes this point, while at the same time reminding teachers of their own expressed preference for concentrating their attention on single projects:

I am fully aware of all the arguments which faculty members can muster to prove that a particular course, because of its highly abstract nature cannot possibly be given on such a schedule [as the short summer term requires]. It has been my actual experience that few such courses exist. With a certain malicious glee I would point out that faculty members have for years been justifying the need for sabbatical leaves on the ground that a thorough piece of work can be done only when concentrated time can be devoted to it. We are fond of saying that we must get immersed in a subject. If any one of us were asked to do a lengthy piece of writing and if we were given the choice of being relieved of enough of our regular duties that we could devote, let us say, every afternoon from 3 to 5 to it, or were given a shorter period of time during which we could devote all day to it, there would be no question which choice we would accept.

[37] Richey, et al., *Comparison of Academic Achievement*, pp. 34–35.

It is amazing that summer after summer we can demonstrate that students do achieve more when given the opportunity for concentrated attention to a subject, yet during the winter we seem to profit not at all from this experience, continuing to require that they scatter their attention over a variety of subjects.[38]

However reasoned the arguments may be on either side of the question, final resolution must ultimately rest with the individual faculty member. Preference for session length, like preference for class size or lecture method, is, and will remain, an unaccountable matter of personal taste. For the professor who enjoys the faster pace, teaching possibilities in the summer will continue to expand. For the one who cannot operate within the confines of the summer session, research or relaxation offer themselves as quite desirable alternatives. In this choice, as in all things in a university, it is the individual professor, with his particular ambitions and inclinations, who sets the tone and the tendency. For the professor *is* the university, in June as well as in January, and the summer dean had better know it.

## "ADMINISTRATING" THE FACULTY

How, then, does the summer dean intent on creating direction out of diversity approach his faculty? The answer is that to guide is to lead. The American college or university summer administrator can in no sense be an autocrat. True, deans and their staffs have appeared who frankly held that they should direct "their" universities as do executives their industries or even as captains their ships. Certain colleges have been ruled by presidents who were practically dictators; "some inaugurals have suggested coronation ceremonies." But the summer deans in the great academic tradition have steadfastly held that campus leadership should ever be qualified by a full consideration for faculty opinion.[39] This is leadership in the spirit of democratic statesmanship, the only leadership worthy of and adapted to higher education.

[38] In *Columbia Seminar Proceedings*, p. 8.
[39] Ordway Tead, "Higher Education in the Days Ahead," *School and Society*, January 1950, p. 18.

Sound faculty relations are based upon acceptance of professorial prerogatives. The American professor holds with complete conviction the belief that efficiency is not the only measure of campus leadership; that collecting a fancy budget, erecting splendid buildings, and eliminating internal disagreements by imposing faculty regimentation are not in themselves justification for a leadership which, while effective in such ways, fails to represent the hopes and aspirations of the individual professor.

This is not to say that a campus administrator should be simply the tool of the faculty. A faculty needs guidance, of course, and the administrator must lead. But the sound campus administrator does not lead by force, either overt or covert. He leads, first, by detecting the aims and objectives of his faculty and translating them into action. And he leads by interpreting to his faculty his own aims and objectives and winning support in open debate. A crucial quality of campus leadership is, consequently, adeptness at communication—at sensing the climate of professorial thought and at molding that thought. In this light the successful campus administrator is, in the long run, the administrator who is as one with his faculty. As a leader, he is ahead of his faculty, but not so far ahead that he has lost that vital entente which provides for an interchange of power between president and professor.

College administration which abhors the dictatorial format is not, of course, to be justified merely because it follows in the democratic tradition. It is justified on the most pragmatic grounds: it works. It works where authoritarianism fails. Only a campus democracy has the power to release the full resources and energies of a faculty. Anyone who has spent any time in a military machine in which discipline and conformity are exalted far above independence and initiative will recognize what a deadening weight is placed upon individual integrity and performance by a system of "generalship." A campus administrator who rules with a heavy hand is utterly inimical to the very capacities and processes which he is supposed to stimulate and direct.

In the final analysis, the American university summer dean who has not translated his thoughts into faculty thought, and faculty sentiments into his own thoughts and acts, is powerless. He must always give the appearance of being led if he is in fact to lead his highly individualistic colleagues. No campus reform will succeed for which the sentiment of the faculty is not prepared. And no dean will last who does not represent his faculty. It is this vital interplay between "the leader" and "the led" which is the mark of sound faculty relations the year around.

# 4

## Summer Services

Iｆ ᴛʜᴇʀᴇ ɪѕ any red thread running through this book, it is the theme that the summer term cannot be equated solely with conventional collegiate instruction; research is in the picture, and educational services particularly lend their mark. The summer university has helped greatly to introduce and develop the institution's programs of educational service for citizens of the state, the nation, and the world. Characterized by institutes, conferences, clinics, and workshops, as well as less formal types of consultation, the activities cover almost all ages, interests, and academic levels: the whole concept of continuing professional and liberal education is now expanding tremendously. In-service training of teachers is still a major focus of the summer term, but in recent years new thrusts have appeared, ranging from sight-lifting programs for abler high school students to highly sophisticated seminars for adults from bankers to zoologists. In many programs the emphasis is more on policy considerations than on techniques. Many service programs are supported by government and foundation grants, and these may lead either to a reinforcement or a skewing of the institution's preferred posture.

An important category of educational service encompasses those cultural and recreational programs conducted for the benefit of students enrolled in the summer session. Another category that is becoming increasingly significant is perhaps best described as a project that involves applied research—its conduct, interpretation, and application. Whatever the content or form, however, summer educational services are a significant aspect of university enterprise, adding breadth and depth to the institution's programs, and earning for the institution heightened public interest and support.

## A Broad Panorama

Ask a dozen summer term administrators to list their institution's "summer services," ask a hundred summer students to define the university's "services" to them, ask the same question of leading citizens of a state or region, and quite likely no two responses would be the same. The point is not that the university's services in summer are unknown but rather that they defy easy categorization and definition, and they "serve" different people in different ways. For what, after all, constitutes a "service" by a university? Who should be served? What should be the result of the service be?

One approach to answering these questions would be to consider each university operation as one or another form of service. Teaching, research, non-credit extension, administration, co-curricular activities—all serve some portion of the community and thus equally deserve inclusion in the roll call of university services. The entire university, it can be argued, is a service institution, whether its main purpose be to convey an established body of knowledge to its formal student population; to create new knowledge through painstaking writing and research; or to seek a wider audience beyond the strictly academic community, thereby extending the campus boundaries to include the state, the nation, and even the world. This most catholic view is both legitimate and inspiring; yet it is rather too inclusive for our purposes here. Since earlier chapters have dealt with the summer credit student and the summer faculty, discussion of the formal educational services rendered to and by these groups can for the most part be excluded, leaving the remainder of the university's functions in serving its various publics for our topic of consideration here.

An overview of a university summer service program is, as we have said, not an easy thing to achieve. Within the confines of a single campus in as brief a period as three months can be found an enormous variety of clinics, institutes, lectures, conferences, diversions, workshops, seminars (call them what you will) for everyone from teen-agers to "senior citizens," from football coaches to pharmacologists. In the words of Northwestern's William C. Bradford, summer service activities may vary all the way "from a contest in tackle tying to a genuine educational venture on the part of a trade association."[1] Consider just a few examples of representative programs and students:

Three teen-agers, two girls and a boy, lean over a cluttered work desk in the basement of the journalism building. For the past half hour they have been discussing the layout of "their" newspaper. All three are editors of their high school papers and have come to the campus to participate in a university-sponsored high school journalism workshop. Hoping to learn more about the techniques, the responsibilities, and the powers of the press, they have moved into university dormitories and classrooms, listened to and questioned university faculty members, worked on everything from feature writing to photography, and as a climax they have been given space in the campus newspaper to put their new skills into practice. Barely a month before these same students had been supervising a mimeographed sheet reaching barely two hundred fellow classmates. Now they are writing, proofreading, and editing for a full-size press and an audience that may number as much as twenty thousand. If they feel any uncertainty it is more than matched by great doses of energy and enthusiasm. The emphasis is on action. Try the

[1] Personal correspondence in author's files.

unfamiliar, they are urged; don't be afraid to experiment; learn by doing.

It is an evening in late August and once more graduation time has come for a group of summer students. As the ceremonies proceed, one notices that the participants are no collection of eager undergraduates. Rather they are in their thirties and forties, looking every bit the image of the rising young executive that many if not all of them indeed are. These are the soon-to-be alumni of a Graduate School for Banking, an annual two-week summer institute that recruits its "students" from banks and financial institutions across the country. Not that recruiting is any problem. Last summer 1,300 enrolled to begin, continue, or complete this three-summer program that tries to increase the young banker's knowledge of his profession.

A high school German teacher works her way through a translation of Rilke while two dozen of her fellow students follow along intently. The passage is subtle and difficult, a far cry from the "du bist eins" that she is used to offering her pupils. Before now, Rilke had been only a name vaguely remembered from a contemporary literature course a decade ago. Now she and her fellow participants in the NDEA Institute for Teachers of German have a chance to understand his place in German literature. Central to federally-financed institutes such as these is intensive study of not only the language but the culture of a country. If we look ahead only a few months, we can envision these teachers using their new knowledge to bolster high school language programs throughout the state and nation.

The closed end of a horseshoe-shaped stadium begins to fill more rapidly as the eight o'clock performance time approaches. For many in the audience of students, faculty, and townspeople it seems strange to see scenery and floodlights in a setting usually reserved for football players and marching bands. But the season is summer rather than fall and the spectators have gathered to watch a university-sponsored theater troupe play Gilbert and Sullivan under a starry midsummer sky. The performance is one in a series of evening open-air entertainment featuring both student and professional groups and open to the general public.

These sketches are meant to suggest both the diversity and

the vitality of the summer services of a university. While the vignettes can only arbitrarily be called representative of summer services as a whole, they suggest three main trends in the summer service program of the contemporary American university: the expansion of traditional university-sponsored summer workshops and conferences; the development of new federal- or foundation-financed summer institutes; and the carry-over of regular-year services to the summer. These three thrusts may on occasion overlap so as to obscure the lines of difference between them, and on some campuses one approach may dominate the others; but they are all evident to some extent in every summer enterprise. It is to the first of these developments that we now turn our attention.

## THE UNIVERSITY-SPONSORED PROGRAM

The conference, workshop, or institute fostered by the university can be looked upon as one of the signal accomplishments of the summer university. As we have already suggested, precise definition of this kind of program is extremely difficult, due to the infinite variety of forms it may take. In general, however, it exhibits the following characteristics: it is of shorter duration than the summer term itself, often running less than a week, sometimes only a day; it is usually not offered for academic credit; it usually concentrates on a specific topic of interest only to a select audience; and its participants are generally not of college age—most are older, a number younger, some not yet in high school.

### BACKGROUND

The summer institute grew out of the tradition of the university as public servant to the needs of its patron community. More specifically, it had its origin in the unorthodox and irregular courses offered for credit in many of the early summer terms. Such courses were often attacked by critics, and, says the Office of Education, "would not be accepted in regular sessions because of their vocational or recreational overtones; they were scheduled in summer only to attract more students. Where it occurred, therefore, this practice tended to bring disrepute and to emphasize the inferior status of summer programs."[2] Thus universities were faced with the problem of preserving some valuable public service programs while at the same time upholding credit standards, and they compromised by making the institutes and workshops special non-credit offerings. This approach, first initiated in the 1930's, has apparently resolved any difficulties to the satisfaction of all parties concerned. Certainly few educators today complain of the non-credit programs as an unfortunate "reflection on the integrity of the sponsoring institution."[3]

Since 1940, non-credit programs have experienced a tremendous growth. According to the U.S. Office of Education, over the two decades prior to 1960 the number of institutions sponsoring such programs more then tripled, rising from 106 to 362, and the number of individual workshops increased 1,700 per cent (from 106 to 1,802), registering in 1960 175,302 students. Of the total number of summer institutes and workshops held in that year, 56.3 per cent were university-sponsored, enrolling 70.2 per cent of all participants.[4]

The U.S. Office of Education has further noted a shift in subject matter away from the almost complete preoccupation with educational techniques and methods found in the 1940 analysis. While such concerns still dominate nearly 60 per cent of all sessions, the workshops have had to make increased room for national affairs, social problems, and business and professional interests.[5] This broadening of scope is a healthy sign for the workshop program; for it indicates a movement in the direction of the rest of the summer enterprise—away from strictly teacher training toward a wider conception of the role of the university in summer.

The years since 1960 have shown a continued expansion of programs to reach an even greater number of potential partici-

---

[2] Warner, et al., *Summer Sessions, 1960*, p. 77.
[3] Ibid.
[4] Ibid., pp. 77–78.
[5] Ibid., pp. 78–81.

pants, so that now "workshoppers" often outnumber summer degree students. Wisconsin's 1966 special programs, for example, drew twenty thousand participants, about seven thousand more than its regular credit population. Similarly, in 1964 Colorado found its "irregulars" to have a numerical advantage of three thousand.[6]

Even more astounding is the range of offerings. The 1965 session at Wisconsin again provides an illuminating picture of the scope of the summer service program: Among the more than one hundred conferences, workshops, and institutes were an institute for head nurses, industrial management institutes, a Badger Girls' State convention, a midwest junior historian leadership conference, a weaving workshop, a statewide 4-H Club meeting, a national community theater program, seminars on parthenogenesis and metabolism in plants and teaching reading to the retarded, an adult education conference on poverty, summer training in epidemiology, a church music conference, a wind instrument symposium, a National Student Association conference, a midwestern mechanics conference, and a conference on the biology of the peregrine falcon. On other campuses the U.S. Office of Education has reported such oddities as a jazz workshop featuring Duke Ellington and an institute devoted to horseshoeing.[7] Summer 1967 programs include an educators' study of disadvantaged youth and their socio-cultural milieu at Southern California, a seminar in alcoholism and alcohol education at Indiana University, a workshop in women's track and field at Sacramento State, and a conservation workshop in Cornell University's four-thousand-acre Arnot Forest.

PROGRAMS FOR THE PRE-COLLEGE STUDENT

Among the "students" who attend such programs, several groups are of special interest to the planner of the summer workshop. While for many workshoppers and conferees the summer experience is tinged with the nostalgia of returning to a campus

---

[6] *Annual Report of the 1964 Summer Session* (mimeographed, Boulder: University of Colorado, 1964), p. 10.

[7] Warner, et al., *Summer Sessions, 1960*, pp. 78–81.

setting after many years, the high school or junior high school student is being introduced to the campus for perhaps the first time. The university's goal in its high school programs is to develop existing talent and to provide a broadening of interest that may facilitate a student's choice of his college major or career. The student's goals are not so easy to define. Some may go to perfect their specific skills in the arts or sciences. Others may want an informal orientation to the college campus where they soon expect to enroll. Still others may be looking for a different kind of summer vacation for a few weeks. Whatever preconceptions they may come with, however, few students fail to find the programs stimulating and worthwhile.

The variety of activities in this area of summer programing is enormous. An Office of Institutional Research report paints an exciting picture:

The University of Virginia, Clemson University, Washington State University and Oregon State University are among institutions with summer programs designed to give high school students an idea of career opportunities in science by exposing the students to a broad variety of scientific and engineering fields. Purdue University has a similar mathematics seminar for high school juniors, including the study of elementary number theory, linear algebra, and programming digital computers. Purdue makes its powerful IBM computer available for use of the pupils.

Science camps are also popular. The University of Wyoming's junior high school science camp includes faculty instruction in botany and zoology as well as swimming, hiking, and fishing. Pennsylvania State University will host two-week junior conservation camps for more than 200 high school freshmen and sophomore boys.

Among the institutions sponsoring high school music camps and clinics are The University of Wisconsin, the State University of New York at Fredonia and the University of Wyoming. The University of Kansas has a Music and Art Camp, and the University of Alaska has a Creative Arts Summer Camp for art, dance, writing, and drama. Michigan State University combines journalism, theatre, and speech in a Communication Arts Institute.

Among other summer camps being sponsored by state universities are a camp for handicapped children co-sponsored by Washington

State University and an interracial, inter-denominational camp owned by the University Religious Conference of UCLA. UCLA students serve as counselors without pay for 10-day sessions. In a related endeavor, Rutgers University will bring 120 junior high school youngsters, most of whom have exhibited academic or behavior problems, to campus this summer to participate in a daily program designed to increase their chances of both academic and social success in school. The children will continue in the program for three years, during both the summer and the school year.[8]

Despite the obvious variety, certain similarities do distinguish these programs. First, like most other workshop programs, almost all are shorter than normal summer terms. Two weeks to a month would seem the standard running time. Second, most of them, despite claims that they are "unearthing new talent," draw their participants from among students who have already shown a decided interest and ability in a subject. Often the competition for places is intense, with applicants providing the transcripts and letters of recommendation that one associates with formal college admission. Third, most programs rely upon university personnel and facilities to a considerable extent. Workshoppers eat and sleep in university dorms, receive instruction from university faculty and staff, and utilize such diverse university facilities as computers, concert halls, photographic darkrooms, and gymnasia. Finally, most programs provide their own leisure-time activities for their young participants. Athletics, social functions, and tours of local points of interest are organized to add greater dimension to the total learning experience.

PROGRAMS FOR TEACHERS

The historic symbiosis of the summer term and educational personnel continues to be reflected in the workshop and institute program. At Wisconsin in 1965, for example, an annual workshop on family finance sponsored by the National Center for Education in Family Finance attracted fifty participants. This was a

[8] *For Your Information.*

four-credit program made available to selected teams of elementary, secondary, and collegiate educators, featuring financial planning and consumer spending, money and banking, credit, insurance, taxation, and wills. A four-week Educational Policy Studies Institute for educators was built around lectures, conferences, and discussions on the problems of education and social change in the emerging nations, with special emphasis on Nigeria, Turkey, India, and Japan. Secondary journalism teachers and publications advisers were enrolled in a program of two two-week sessions. The first, a workshop, emphasized improved writing and newspaper production skills. A following two-week seminar emphasized newspaper program management and teaching materials and methods. Another special four-week seminar was held for educational administrators. Further workshops of special interest to teachers focused on adult education, business education, home economics, agriculture, elementary school music, English, speech, mathematics, physical education, school psychology, reading, and library science.

Drawing some examples from other campuses, Harvard offers courses for teachers of science and mathematics in the elementary schools as well as a seminar for college admissions officers. Social studies teachers at Rutgers have the opportunity to delve into industrial economics through a management and labor relations course. The University of Arizona schedules programs in public relations and radio and television for teachers and school administrators. And a 1967 program at the State University of New York, Buffalo, will attempt to introduce teachers of history and English to the cultures of Asia; taught by professors from various Asian universities, this series of lectures will introduce American educators to everything from religion to politics to fine arts.

As can be surmised from this brief survey, the variety of teacher programs nationwide is extremely broad. At one extreme are month-long sessions offering provisional university credit and barely distinguishable from regular session courses. At the other extreme are one-day conferences focusing on one or two specific topics.

PROGRAMS FOR BUSINESS AND PROFESSIONAL GROUPS

Doctors, lawyers, merchants, and even the butcher, the baker, and the candlestick-maker draw upon the university's summer facilities for their meetings and workshops. While a certain amount of unabashed conventioneering still occurs in which the university does little more than provide dormitory space, greater attention is being given to educational purposes, with guest lecturers and university staff members providing the instruction. The Graduate School of Banking mentioned earlier is a good example of this newer approach. So is a Theater in Society program offering various studies in the functions, organizational forms, and difficulties of the modern theater to interested directors and managers. Lawyers are benefited by a one-day conference on, say, pre-trial publicity. Real estate appraisers, credit union personnel, hospital pharmacists, labor union leaders—all may gather under campus sponsorship to learn more about their particular fields.

Let's look briefly at some typical programs: The University of Washington Law School has invited practicing attorneys, city managers, and urban planners to join its regular students in a five-week institute in land use and urban planning. Such topics as zoning, the central core and inner city, and annexation, incorporation, and subdivision regulations were offered in two-day segments, thus enabling the interested businessman to enroll only for topics of particular relevance to his work. Another Washington program featured workshops for the social welfare practitioner, supervisor, or administrator. As with many other programs for professionals, academic personnel and highly qualified "outsiders" shared the teaching duties.

At the other end of the country, Harvard invited "working scientists" to a special program in electronics. The course, directed by Dr. Alfred Pandiscio of the Electronics Design Center, was intended to acquaint its students with "the basic principles, capabilities, and limitations of the electronic equipment and techniques they are likely to encounter in their work." Cornell also caters to the practicing scientist or engineer with intensive ten-day courses in digital computing, thermal radiation transfer, and nuclear measurements.

## THE INTERESTED LAYMAN

Summer education is not restricted to those pursuing special work in their chosen vocations. Increasingly universities are attempting to draw alumni and townspeople under their broad educational canvas for special interest sessions like the Princeton Alumni Seminar programs, which have examined American leisure time, consumer affairs, and aesthetics of the city for the benefit of interested adults. The seminar approach at Wisconsin draws groups of about twenty-five participants together for a week-long program. Lectures from faculty members and other qualified and stimulating speakers provide the impetus for discussion. In the words of director Robert Schacht, "Each member of the group enriches the discussions in and out of class with contributions from his own background." Examples from other campuses include enrichment classes in dancing, photography, twilight sketching, classical guitar, and writing for publication at Minnesota, offered in cooperation with the extension division. And Southern California, drawing on the facilities of the Los Angeles County Museum of Art, opens its course in French art to the general public.

However varied the programs may be from institution to institution, there should be unanimous agreement as to the worth of the university summer institute. William Stirton's analysis of a decade ago is even more applicable today:

These workshops, institutes, seminars are important for many reasons. They are born of a demonstrated need, ordinarily one that has currently arisen from the increasingly complex nature of our society. Obviously, therefore, there is no question as to the currency and the immediacy of the application to an over-all educational pattern. By satisfying this kind of need, you serve not only that motivating purpose but, more importantly, you increasingly identify the university, the school, as the place where the American community turns for prompt consideration of current and pressing problems—a focal point of objective analysis where integrity and competency and desire to be of service should be found to be the hallmarks of an educational plant.[9]

## THE NEW FEDERAL AND FOUNDATION THRUST

The educational historian of the twenty-first century charged with tracing the formative factors of the American university will undoubtedly look upon the two post-1945 decades with extreme interest. Catchwords and phrases like "GI Bill," "sputnik," "trimester," "loyalty oath," "Berkeley," and "multiversity" will conjure up memories of the changes and exchanges of this most dynamic era. Of crucial import has been what California's Clark Kerr, the man and the symbol of the "multiversity," has referred to as the university's increasing involvement with the federal government. In a condensation of his 1963 Godkin Lectures at Harvard he traces the course and present nature of this involvement:

Of key importance to American universities is the role of the federal government, particularly through federal support of scientific research. This support, which received its great impetus during and after World War II, has already changed the face of the leading American universities almost as much as did the land-grant program a century earlier. Federal support has today become a major factor in the total performance of many universities, and the sums involved are substantial. Higher education in 1960 received about $1.5 billion from the federal government—a hundredfold increase in twenty years.[10]

During the current year federal tax dollars will provide about one-third of the ten billion dollars required to operate the nation's 2,100 public and private colleges and universities. This federal aid to higher education is hardly new. What is new is the tremendous volume of education-oriented legislation enacted by Congress during 1965. In all, the 89th Congress passed nine-

[9] "The Summer Session in University Relations," Speech to the Association of Summer Session Deans and Directors, October 19, 1956.
[10] "The Frantic Race to Remain Contemporary," in Michael V. Miller and Susan Gilmore, *Revolution at Berkeley* (New York: Dial Press, 1965), p. 17.

teen acts providing support to education—the greater part of it to higher education. By far the most important single piece of legislation affecting colleges and universities was Public Law 89–329, the Higher Education Act, which authorized expenditures of more than $2.25 billion over a three-year period, and called for the designation of an agency to develop a state plan for community services and continuing education.[11]

This increasing involvement of the university with federal and other "outside" agencies has also profoundly affected the summer service program. Royden Dangerfield of the University of Illinois recently outlined the new posture for his colleagues of the North Central Conference on Summer Schools.[12] The main points of his discussion are incorporated in the following survey of federal- and foundation-sponsored programs:

TYPES OF PROGRAMS

Motivated by sputnik and the resulting doubts about education in the sciences, National Science Foundation programs have attempted to boost teaching in the field by adapting institute and workshop methods. Separate programs provide retraining and updating for college, secondary, and elementary level instructors. Averaging about 35 participants, the institutes have covered such fields as fluid mechanics, anthropology, comparative physiology, heterocyclic chemistry, and economics. In most instances college credit is given. In the summer of 1964 73 college, 439 secondary, and 37 elementary level NSF institutes were offered at colleges and universities.

While teacher training is the most publicized aspect of the NSF programs, it is not the only one. Postdoctoral and graduate research are subsidized on many summer campuses, and the NSF Research Participation Program gives high school science teachers a chance to do original research under the guidance of uni-

[11] "A Guide to Federal Aid for Education," *College Management*, December 1965, p. 2.

[12] "Issues, Impacts, and Opportunities for Sponsored Educational Programs," Speech to the North Central Conference of Summer Schools, March 28, 1965. For further evidence of the new posture, see our own Appendix A.

versity professors. Programs for high school students themselves may come under the NSF. In the University of Kansas' highly successful summer science camp, for example, federal funds have covered basic operating expenses and enabled scholarship assistance to be given to those students needing it, while the university has provided staff and facilities.

The 1958 National Defense Education Act and its subsequent amendments have given rise to a wide variety of special programs designed to train personnel in fields of high priority to the national interest. For example, modern foreign language institutes for secondary and elementary teachers help to upgrade language instruction in the more traditional foreign languages. In 1965, sixty-five summer institutes for teachers of Spanish, French, German, Italian, Russian, Chinese, Japanese, and Arabic were held in the United States, and another fourteen were held overseas at Moscow, Tours, Guatemala City, and Bad Boll, Germany. A third facet of the program included four institutes for teachers in the use of English as a second language. In addition, various summer intensive language programs attempt to meet the great need for persons fluent in a number of heretofore little known foreign languages. African and Asian tongues have received predominant emphasis, with such rarities as Tamil, Thai, Urdu, and Yoruba included among the offerings.

A 1964 amendment to the NDEA established several institutes for advanced studies for teachers of English, reading, history, and geography, and for teachers of disadvantaged youth. Additional institutes for persons engaged in, or preparing to engage in, library services or educational media work are also sponsored under this amendment, as are several counseling and guidance institutes which cater to counseling personnel in elementary, secondary, and college positions, and usually run about six weeks.

A related U.S. Office of Education program, though not under the NDEA, authorizes the training of professional personnel to conduct training of teachers in fields related to the education of mentally retarded, hard of hearing, deaf, speech impaired, visually handicapped, emotionally disturbed, crippled, or other health impaired children. As with other federal programs, both institutional grants and traineeship stipends are made available.

While most of the federally financed summer institutes are operated under NSF or NDEA grants, a number of other government agencies sponsor summer training and research programs. We have already mentioned one. Peace Corps training centers, U.S. Army public relations courses, and National Aeronautical and Space Administration research programs are three other examples. In addition, Title I of the new Higher Education Act has already begun to provide further summer institute funds for 1967.

The role of the summer session office in the different federal programs may vary considerably. For some summer-only programs it may exercise supervision with the assistance of the recipient department. At other times it may take a subordinate or cooperative role with another university office such as the extension division.

State agencies, too, have found that the summer university can be a valuable working partner in solving mutual problems. New York State has sponsored refresher courses in mathematics, the sciences, and the Russian language through generous grants from the state legislature. The Washington State Department of Public Assistance has co-sponsored a workshop for social welfare personnel. Indiana University's seminar on alcoholism is paid for in part by a grant from the State Alcoholism Division. The California State Department of Education has helped to fund a Sacramento State College workshop on teaching the Bill of Rights for junior and senior high school social studies teachers. And, on the local level, the Cincinnati Police Division, working with the University of Cincinnati, has sponsored a conference on early adolescent attitudes toward law enforcement; in this program equal numbers of police officers and junior high school social studies teachers have combined to learn how they may help each other in promoting respect for law enforcement.

A final source of outside support for institute programs is the private foundation, association, or industry. In his 1965 report, Royden Dangerfield mentioned the General Electric Foundation, the Sloan Foundation, and Western Electric as important sponsors of university summer programs; and a number of others such as Ford, Rockefeller, and Carnegie also provide significant amounts of funds. The types of programs sponsored by private organizations vary from an Indiana University PTA leadership training workshop to a Southern California tropical studies venture at the University of Costa Rica sponsored by the Organization for Tropical Studies, a non-profit educational corporation for encouraging study and research south of the border. The American Red Cross is a frequent participant in a variety of health and safety programs. At Cincinnati they sponsor a week-long water safety school. At Indiana they join with the State Medical Association, the Cancer Society, and other private health organizations in providing funds for a school and community health workshop.

SOME IMPLICATIONS OF "OUTSIDE" INVOLVEMENT

The success of the NSF and NDEA programs can be called a final vindication of the "workshop" approach which summer schools have increasingly utilized since the turn of the century. To paraphrase William Stirton, Washington has found the summer university a highly appropriate place to turn for prompt consideration and solution of current and pressing problems. Clearly the workshop, institute, and conference programs, both federally and institutionally financed, are here to stay as integral aspects of a university's summer operations.

This increasing involvement of "outside" agencies in university operations does, however, pose some important problems. While the usual fears of "federal control" have largely proved groundless, a more basic issue of federal direction has been raised and may become increasingly significant. As a result of federal assistance programs a university may, consciously or not, place its best summer personnel and resources at the disposal of the government, at the expense of its own institutionally financed endeavors. The now common preference for the sciences over the humanities is only the most obvious example of this subtle federal guidance. Whether the end result of such a commitment will be beneficial will of course vary with the program and the school.

But this is the whole point: each institution will have to take a hard look at its own needs and the needs of its various publics before committing its facilities, time, and personnel. Even a Congressional committee has conceded that federal expenditures for research and development in the nation's universities can diminish the dedication of teachers to that calling, divert professors from teaching to research, benefit a relatively small number of major universities at the expense of the rest of the higher education spectrum, strengthen graduate at the expense of undergraduate education, and help limited areas of the natural and physical sciences at the expense of the social studies and the humanities.[13] One writer goes so far as to say that federal grant programs are affecting institutional priorities so much that some universities stand in serious jeopardy of being wards of Washington.[14] The situation is not unknown in the summer term, where some presidents measure their summer deans in terms of their ability to win NDEA institute funds, and where carpetbagger students shop for bigger and better subventions. But any summer dean who permits the pursuit of federal funds to become an end in itself, rather than a means toward achieving stated educational objectives, is dealing falsely with the integrity of both his institution and his profession.[15]

Despite such *caveats*, however, the potential value of a massive federally financed program to upgrade teaching at all levels can only be called enormous. Moreover, a somewhat less expected benefit of such programs has recently been noted by Donald Bigelow, director of the Office of Education's Division of Educational Personnel Training: As a result of institute programs, he claims,

a dialogue between the college professor and the school teacher has started, one that appears to be a major, if unplanned, development of

[13] Franklin J. Pegues, "Some Notes on a Gift Horse," *Journal of Higher Education*, February 1966, pp. 97–98.
[14] Lawrence E. Dennis, "Will Success Spoil Higher Education?" *Educational Record*, Fall 1965, pp. 457–459.
[15] For a lively discussion of "The Federal Government and Higher Education," see John F. Moose, *Educational Record*, Fall 1966, pp. 429–438. See also "Sponsored Research: Its Role on the Campus; Its Effect on Teachers," *College Management*, December 1966, pp. 18–22.

the last decade and one which holds great promise. Undoubtedly, such communication has helped to question traditional roles and to initiate a full and frank examination of the university vis-à-vis the preparation of teachers in America, long overdue. . . .

While short-term summer programs will doubtless continue to predominate and some academic year programs will be supported, it is hoped that the institute will become a many-sided vehicle providing many kinds of training. Hence, flexibility and variety are being encouraged. Part-time or in-service programs may help to create opportunities for a more intense or immediate experience, and seminars, workshops, colloquia, symposia and conferences are but some of the ways by which the institute concept can be made more meaningful.[16]

Thus, not only do the institutes sharpen old skills and teach new ones, they provide further liaison between elementary, secondary, and college teachers and aid in promoting nationwide standards of excellence in areas too long marked by fragmentation and mediocrity. In sum, the school that sacrifices all else to run a full summer trimester or fourth quarter for its regular-year student body may well find itself defeating its broader educational purposes.

CONTINUING RESPONSIBILITIES

Amidst the excitement of 4-H conventions and the challenge of NDEA institutes for teachers, one is often tempted to assume that the university's regular fall and spring service program folds its tents and silently steals away as the final diploma is presented at June commencement, not to reappear until a cooler climate and a more "normal" student body return in September. Refreshing as this would sound to the overworked directors of the various services, it can hardly be the case. Increasingly the line between summer and regular services is becoming blurred as more and more of the university operation goes "year-round." Thus, as the summer term has become an increasingly diversified operation, it has been able to incorporate a growing number and range of regular-year programs and trappings. Yet, lest we

[16] U.S. Office of Education, Department of Health, Education, and Welfare, Memo, March 17, 1967.

accuse the summer term of shamelessly begging, borrowing, or stealing every program from the regular year, it is well to remember that there are two sides to the coin. The vigorous adoption of workshop and institute programs by the fall and spring curricula highlights the fact that if the summer is becoming more like the regular year the regular year must also be said to increasingly resemble the summer.

### SUMMER EXTENSION

One of the most fruitful of summer services is the university's extension work, which usually includes correspondence courses, lecture services, publication services, library services, and instruction through mass media, as well as a number of miscellaneous "technical" services.[17] While all of these may not fall under the jurisdiction of a formal extension division, all demonstrate the institution's concern for its off-campus publics in the next county or around the world, and in January or July.

The home-study method of university outreach is as important in summer as in fall. Offering guided instruction by mail, correspondence teaching puts university personnel and courses at the disposal of those unable to reach a summer campus. The beneficiaries may be full-time students unable to spare summer job hours to attend formal classes, interested housewives, merchants, professional people, farmers, or even prisoners.

The single lecture or series of lectures by a university professor, although less prevalent than fifty years ago, is still a legitimate arm of extension. Dinner clubs, conventions, and innumerable interest groups still receive information and inspiration as well as a better view of "what's going on at our university" from these summer circuit riders.

Another extension worker that knows no rest is the printing press. Whether a scholarly tome issued by the university press or a four-page throw-away of the agricultural extension service, the

---

[17] The authors have adapted John Morton's *University Extension in the United States* (Birmingham: University of Alabama Press, 1953) for a categorization of the types of university outreach.

summer university continues to supply its varied clientele with whatever their educational needs suggest in the way of printed matter.

For many extension customers the summer university also takes on the role of librarian, fact-finder, and information center. This service is especially important in rural settings where access to any educational facilities may be difficult. The variety of functions the bureau may be called upon to fulfill may range from organizing a community forum on contemporary problems in water conservation to distributing a bibliography on Red China.

No facet of extension work better demonstrates the continuing re-evaluation of a university's capacity for service than its work with radio, television, and film. What early pioneer of university outreach could have imagined an audience of 100,000 listening to a chamber music concert or watching a televised lecture on Russian literature? And who could have foreseen the growth of lending libraries for film strips and motion pictures? Today, as new outlets and networks spring up, a citizen is no further away from the sights and sounds of his university than the dial on his radio or television set. With the glut of re-runs on commercial channels, the summer educational network has a particular advantage in attracting an audience.

Finally, in addition to on-campus seminars and conferences, the summer university may offer its services, either formally or informally to business, professional, community service, and various educational groups. To illustrate the kinds of service possible in this area, President David D. Henry of Illinois cites "public service for economic development of states and regions; direct leadership assistance to the public school systems and public health agencies; and natural resource development."[18] Impossible to measure in terms of class hours taught or booklets mailed, such technical assistance is nonetheless a vital part of the university's responsibility to its community, its state, and its nation.

[18] "The Federal Government and Higher Education," *Journal of Higher Education*, April 1966, p. 190.

SERVICES ON THE CAMPUS

Along with the university's expansion of summer on-campus course offerings has come a realization that student personnel services cannot be ignored for the three summer months. Accordingly, the summer student no longer finds the fringe benefits of university life denied him.

As summer enrollments have grown, old worries about dormant dormitories have vanished. Residence halls roll out their welcome mats for everyone from high school workshoppers to scholarly conferees to continuing students. In addition to the standard room and board provisions, many units continue their social, recreational, and counseling activities throughout the summer.

Beyond the usual academic programs guidance, universities have taken it upon themselves to aid their summer students in resolving the wide variety of problems that may beset them. Housing bureaus suggest non-dormitory living vacancies. Employment offices keep track of part-time job opportunities. Student clinics and health centers minister to the students' physical needs. Placement bureaus aid the recent or soon-to-be graduate. Admissions offices help the beginning student. The list is by no means complete but the point should be clear. The summer student (and the non-enrolled fall student as well) need to have their questions answered, their health, welfare, and safety maintained.

On the lighter side, all work and no play hurts performance as well as public relations. Accordingly gyms, swimming pools, tennis courts, baseball fields, and golf courses are left open for student use in summer. Occasionally, organized leagues encourage formal competition, with trophies for the victors and get-together banquets for all. More often, though, games take place on a spur-of-the-moment basis in keeping with the informal summer posture. For those inclined to less athletic forms of relaxation, boating, fishing, and picnicking areas have been developed and maintained by many universities. Indiana's Beechwood Heights is an outstanding example. Indoor recreation is also popular. Indiana's Student Union provides facilities for billiards, bowling, table tennis, shuffleboard, and record listening, a list that would be duplicated at many schools. The summer university is also beginning to make a considerable effort for the student who wants his educational experience to continue outside of the classroom. Films, concerts, plays, and lectures all help provide a wide variety of leisure-time learning at little or no cost to the student. Colorado's ambitious Creative Arts Program offers over fifty musical, dramatic, and modern dance programs during the summer months. Wisconsin offers a Monday night University Forum speaker program with topics ranging from modern genetics to mass communications. In addition, many universities sponsor their own repertory companies to produce an astounding range of dramatic and musical programs. For a fuller discussion of these, see Chapter 2.

### SUPERVISING SUMMER SERVICES

The administration of summer services confronts the university with several problems which are different in degree if not in kind from conventional institutional matters. Perhaps the most fundamental question, albeit one that is frequently avoided, is: What determines the acceptability of a proposed workshop or conference to the sponsoring institution? Some universities apply quite rigid standards before bestowing a stamp of academic sterling, insisting that a university department assume unilateral control over all aspects of the program. Other institutions require little more than a hotel would in renting out its ballroom. Most universities operate under a fairly eclectic policy which attempts both to protect the academic integrity of the institution and to meet its public relations requirements as well. The University of Colorado's policy statement is probably typical of the stance assumed by most universities engaged in a sizable summer service enterprise:

As an educational institution, the University seeks in its conference program to serve those groups and interests which are related educationally to the University. However, we welcome other *bona fide* organizations who desire to come to Boulder for short professional conventions or conferences. Each request for space is given careful consideration both in terms of our ability to serve efficiently and the appropriateness to University goals of the proposed conference. Our ultimate purpose in making the facilities and resources available for such conferences is to contribute to the overall effectiveness of the University, and to serve the best interests of the people of Colorado.[19]

The question of acceptability naturally raises the question of who in the university hierarchy makes the decision, and then who in fact runs the particular service program. To answer the latter question first, about all we can say on a general level is that somebody will invariably be placed in charge of each institute or other type of program. That "somebody" may be a member of a core of experts maintained by the institution to run conferences, he may be a regular faculty member exploring the wilds of informal education, or he may be a representative of an "outside" group designated *pro tempore* as a quasi-member of the university staff. As to who exercises policy control, the responsibility tends to follow the dollar. Programs funded by the institution will be subjected to whatever normal channels of review the university provides. Programs relying on user fees or outside grants will enjoy relative freedom from scrutiny by anyone other than the individual or department willing to accept responsibility for the enterprise. The one common denominator in the picture is the summer session director. With varying degrees of authority he will evaluate the appropriateness of the program, ration university skills and resources, and maintain some minimum surveillance over the conduct of the program.

As we have implied, universities vary in their methods of financing summer service programs. Some institutions may insist that all non-credit work be self-supporting, either through participant fees or donor grants. Such a policy protects campus coffers, but it also can lead to serving only those groups that have sufficient funds. Other institutions invest quite heavily in non-credit programs. This policy allows for a rich and varied offering, but it can subject the regular credit program budget to

[19] *Annual Report, 1964,* p. 10.

a good deal of pressure. Most institutions have a tacit policy of charging what the traffic will bear, and thus a group of kindergarten teachers may come to the campus for a free conference on how to deal with the retarded youngster, while a group of industrial accountants will pay through the nose for a seminar on new tax regulations. In deciding on the scale of charges the institution is apt to ask, "Who benefits the most from this program, the individual or society?"

Associated with the administration of summer services are a number of technical problems. Is there to be any priority system for assigning university housing? Is there to be any priority system for the allocation of university personnel resources? Are participants to be given full run of university facilities— libraries, union, hospital, recreation areas? To what codes of campus conduct are high school bandsters and metropolitan bankers to be held? To arrive at valid answers to such questions, it is essential that the institution be operating in a climate under which the public service stance is an intimate and indigenous aspect of the total campus enterprise.

## THE PUBLIC SERVICE STANCE[20]

To be worthy of the name *university* work, a summer program of educational services must be *of* and not simply *in* the university. By whatever means it is achieved, there must be a direct and consistent relationship between summer service personnel and all offices, departments, schools, and colleges of the university. Some universities designate continuing education directors for each appropriate unit and leave them anchored in their home departments, surrounded by their residence colleagues. Other universities pool these representatives in a central continuing education complex, but with lines of communication running back to their departmental or other academic unit. The form seems less crucial than the spirit, that spirit being to achieve close articulation of service programs with campus skills and

[20] Adapted from Clarence A. Schoenfeld and Theodore J. Shannon, *University Extension* (New York: Center for Applied Research in Education, 1965), pp. 73–77.

resources, and to build an understanding of the mutual inter-dependence of teaching, research, and university outreach. In the absence of such an ethos, resident organizations are not likely to accept public service ideas and personnel into full fellowship, and service programs cannot utilize available resources fully or effectively.

Whatever the pattern of internal relations, it must be kept flexible, for there is emerging what John W. Hastie calls "a new revolution" in university organization and policies, characterized by increased amounts of time and energy being devoted to particular investigations, by the establishment of new research centers, and by constantly changing relationships among the various fields of knowledge. Faced with the emergence of new areas of study that involve the knowledge and practice of more than one of the traditional disciplines, and with the demand of students and government for research programs in complex subject matter involving expensive and rapidly changing techniques and facilities, the university has responded by creating new departments, by promoting interdepartmental, and sometimes interuniversity, endeavors, by establishing research centers focused on particular areas of concern, and by purchasing new, elaborate equipment.[21] In short, the fences between the various colleges and disciplines keep falling down.

The effect of such changes on summer service programs is, in essence, that they, too, must be flexible if they are truly to serve their publics. They must be prepared constantly to develop and maintain new and direct lines of internal communication, in order that summer educational services may be fully coordinated with the research activities of the campus to the benefit of both. The outreach specialist needs pertinent, timely information. The scientist needs provocative questions. Together they can form a potent team. Indeed, interdisciplinary public service programing could well serve as an important force in furthering and enhancing the "revolution" in campus organization.

Unfortunately, there are several factors mitigating against

[21] John W. Hastie, *Research at Cornell, 1961–1962: Annual Report of the Coordinator of Research* (Ithaca: Cornell University, 1962), p. 6.

service-research teamwork. For one thing, resident scholars are increasingly occupied with theory-oriented research, rather than with the more immediately practical sort of fact-finding research that is grist for the service mill. Administrators and professors alike regard sophisticated investigations as "the open sesame to the world of universal scholarship," as Frank Pinner puts it. College deans and departmental chairmen generally recruit professors whose reputations rest on basic research abilities or intellectual pedigree, without any particular reference to a public service bent. Adept at such contributions as the building of theoretical models, the new arrivals tend to regard with some scorn the applied researches of their older colleagues. Indeed, the higher the qualifications of faculty members, the less they seem to esteem some of the services which have traditionally been performed by the utilitarian university. In the social sciences, particularly, the new professor seems to have a preference for fundamental questions and gross problems, universal in scope, and he shuns what he calls "man-hole counting" or "brush-fire fighting." This separation of faculty interests from immediate public needs has not occurred in spite of the improvement of the faculty but because of it, Pinner points out. And as a result administrators are caught between their responsibilities to their supporting publics and their esteem for the new men they have fought so hard to win.[22]

Another barrier to coordination of the research and public service programs is that the resident scientists who are willing to perform research that "makes a difference now" are cosmopolitan rather than community-oriented. Local and state research has, to some extent, gone out of style. Professors believe they can advance their careers more surely on the world stage.[23] And hence university faculty are more likely to give their knowledge and energy to Washington and Thailand than to Main Street. Many faculty members are finding private "outside" con-

[22] Frank Pinner, "The Crisis of the State Universities: Analysis and Remedies," in Nevitt Sanford, ed., *The American College* (New York: Wiley and Sons, 1962), p. 940.
[23] Delbert C. Miller, "Town and Gown," *College and University Journal,* Summer 1963, p. 24.

sultative activities more lucrative than campus teaching or public service. For some the university seems to be becoming more a base of operations than a retreat. As one university president puts it, "The question is now, not how do you get the professor out of his ivory tower, but how do you keep him at home!" In a sense what has happened may be that international, federal, and foundation funds have effectively "captured" American universities, in competition with meager state and regional appropriations for programs of educational service.

Ideally, teaching, searching, and serving are not at war with one another. Each function complements the others. To slight one is to dilute all three. The need is clear: to make service personnel more effective fact finders and stimulators by exposing them to theory-oriented research, and to make researchers more disposed to assist in summer educational service ventures.

Considering its deep roots in early concepts of the university as the servant of its citizens, we should not be surprised that public service continues to play a key role in the modern summer term. As we have attempted to show, such service has no respect for age, place, occupation, or previous education. Workshops appeal to everyone from novice newsmen to nuclear physicists. Extension work reaches interested persons off the campus in a stunning variety of shapes and forms. And the broad spectrum of special services for regularly enrolled students covers almost every aspect of campus life.

In this overview considerable emphasis has been given the new federally financed programs, primarily those aimed at the upgrading of teachers. While their newness alone would earn them inclusion in this study, these programs are especially significant in terms of their potential for future years. For they have placed the traditional summer concern with raising educational standards in a nationwide context where federal agencies can work with university personnel to produce a better teacher who in turn will produce a better student.

Change is thus the constant of summer service. As we have suggested, there are storm clouds on the horizon and some already overhead. Increased enrollments, new federal programs, and new dimensions in off-campus work are only three of the challenges that will have to be faced in the next decade. Yet if past performance may be taken as an indication of future excellence, there is considerable ground for optimism. Clearly, the summer university has historically responded to the need to serve the many rather than the few, to try the novel rather than stick to the time-tested, to welcome change rather than deny it. That it has succeeded in, even taken pride in, being all things to all people testifies to its strength and augurs well for its future.

# 5

# Summer Organization
# and Administration

Among America's thirteen hundred-odd college and university summer terms, there are probably no two that are identical with respect to organization and administration. At one extreme there is the summer term that has changed but little from the time when its director was a wholly independent operator. At the other extreme is the fourth-quarter or third-semester term in which the summer dean has virtually disappeared as a separate entity. Between the poles, however, the variety of approaches is great.

Complicating things further, very little has been written of summer term organization and administration, and what little has appeared is as apt to be misleading as illuminating. Quite possibly this chapter will add to the confusion, because we are going to introduce some new concepts and dimensions into the discussion; but our objective, at least, is to lend clarification and insight to an area that badly needs systematic study.

At the outset let us agree on one cardinal characteristic of university summer term organization and administration—its utter heterogeneity. Our institutions of higher education are different from each other, and their summer term configurations are more so. From now on in this chapter there will not be a single sentence about which some reader will not say, "That's not how we do it here!" This is because each summer term is the product of a background of varying traditions, development, goals, needs, environment, requirements, rules, latitudes, personalities, principles, policies, processes, and problems. About all we can say for sure about every summer term is that each is indigenous to its particular clime; that is, it has come to fit one institution's concept or one person's idea of how a summer term ought to operate.

In substance, the type of program, the type of institution, the approaches to financing, the philosophy of past presidents, the leadership of the present chief executive, and the bents of the summer session director himself will be the basis for local structure and administrative practices. "Common processes are almost nonexistent. We are always looking around, of course, to see how others are going and what they are doing. Then we take the best of the practices we see, modify the patterns which have grown up at other institutions, and fit them to our own campus idiosyncrasies."[1]

Summer term administration, then, is a very crude "science." Yet, if we keep in mind that all statements concerning organization and administration must eventually be localized and set against a background of local historical perspective, some national analysis and synthesis do seem both possible and desirable. In order to accomplish this, it will be helpful to cut our summer term world down to size. Fortunately this is easy to do. Of the 924 summer sessions responding to budgetary questions in the U.S. Office of Education's 1960 survey, 612, or 66.2 per cent, spent less than $50,000 for instruction, and only 102, or 11.1 per

[1] George B. Smith, "Summer Session Administration," in Schoenfeld, *Shape of Summer*, p. 71.

cent, expended $200,000 or more.[2] The upper brackets were dominated by large universities, and it is to such institutions that the balance of this chapter applies.

We can define our universe in still another way, by agreeing on broad purposes. It is to facilitate the dissemination of university skills and resources throughout the year that the summer term has evolved. Ideally, if a faculty were as motivated by a spirit of summer service as it is by a spirit of scholarly investigation, a special summer unit would perhaps be unnecessary. There is little evidence, however, that summer enterprise in adequate depth and breadth can emerge in the absence of a unit charged with that assignment, so essential are the roles of stimulation, coordination, and management which summer deans perform. Unlike such units as arts and letters, engineering, law, and so on, the summer term is obviously not in itself a basic discipline. It is an administrative agency, not unlike the graduate school. Yet it is not properly described as just a transmission belt or funnel through which flow campus courses and findings to the university publics. It is also a scanning device or radar screen which picks up signals representing public needs, problems, and aspirations; and it is a laboratory in which campus skills and resources are transmuted, channeled, and packaged into educational programs meaningful and useful to a varied clientele.

### BROAD FUNCTIONS AND ASSIGNMENTS

In their organizational patterns even large university summer terms are characterized by a lack of uniformity. This is so because universities themselves differ in organization, because deans have differing approaches to administration, and above all because each university has tended to select out of the total academic spectrum only those summer functions which befit its traditions, facilities, and current priorities. In most university summer operations, however, regardless of specific structure, provision will be made for the accomplishment of the following responsibilities:

[2] Warner, et al., *Summer Sessions, 1960*, p. 32.

1. Executive management—broad planning, supervision, fiscal control, rendering of reports, and particularly, personnel relations.

2. Instruction—the formal classroom and laboratory curriculum.

3. Instructional resources—duplicating, printing, editing, tests, audio-visual materials, library services, programed materials, electronic devices; in other words, the ever-increasing technology of learning.

4. Basic research—fundamental investigations, designed primarily to explore the phenomena of man and nature.

5. Applied research—surveys, field investigations, and so on, concerned with public problems.

6. Educational services—including the gamut of informal as well as the more formal types of institutes, workshops, seminars, etc.

7. Student affairs—admissions, advising, government, housing, extracurricular programing.

8. Administrative support—accounting, registration, recording, stenographic and clerical services, publicity, and so on.

9. Program development, promotion, and evaluation—determining the interests and needs of clientele and the arrangements by which they are willing and able to utilize summer university resources effectively.

10. Liaison—with campus colleges, schools, departments, offices, and faculty members; and with off-campus individuals, groups, organizations, and agencies.

11. Logistics—management of facilities, provision of supplies.

12. Institutional studies—self-analyses, formal or informal, designed to reveal or inspire ways of improving summer operations.

This list will become more meaningful as we consider the various responsibilities functionally and in terms of who does what. For this purpose we may classify the primary functions of the summer university into five areas: formal instruction, research, educational services, student personnel services, and auxiliary services; the supervision of these functions, however, may be somewhat dispersed.

The conventional teaching program of the university in summer is carried on, with three exceptions, in conventional ways. That is, it is the function of individual professors organized into departments which in turn are units of schools and colleges of the university. The three exceptions are these: (1) the summer term often varies in length from a regular term; (2) the summer instructional budget is a discrete increment of the university's annual budget; and (3) the principal administrative officer is typically a summer session director who acts in lieu of the president or chancellor, or at least serves as a special staff officer.

The research program of the university in summer is also carried on in conventional ways, with very few exceptions. It is the function of individual professors, sometimes organized into special teams, and usually under the cognizance of the appropriate dean and the graduate school. Some summer researchers will be on twelve-month appointments, some will be on summer institutional research funds, and others will be on gift, grant, or contract funds. Only in unusual cases will the research program be reflected in the summer session budget, and only rarely will the summer session dean be directly involved in the administration of research. The dichotomy between the administration of research and the administration of instruction, however, will cause some rather excruciating problems for the summer session director, and when he does become involved in sponsoring an occasional research program he enters a mysterious world.

Some of the university's formal and informal educational services in summer will be a part of the institution's year-round extension program. Others will spring up spontaneously in a likely, or unlikely, department and will resist supervision by anybody. Still others will be reflected in the summer session budget per se and hence will come under the direct purview of the summer session director. In some universities the president will hold the summer session dean responsible for coordinating all summer educational services; in others the extension dean will draw the assignment; in still others, the president himself will attempt any necessary coordination. At the very least, one office will usually be charged with developing statistics on the overall program of summer educational services.

Student admissions, testing, orientation, counseling, government, social life, housing, financial aids, cultural programing, and recreational planning—the growing panoply of what have come to be called "student affairs" or "student personnel services," meaning everything done for, to, and with the student outside the classroom—tend to be performed in the usual way by the usual people in summer as in winter. In other words, the director of residence halls works around the calendar, as do the admissions officer, the director of the student union, and so on. Such activities and personnel will not typically be reflected in the summer session budget. There are a few variations, which stem from the peculiar nature of summer offerings and clientele. For one thing, the director of the summer session serves, in effect, as the dean of a college in which are carried "special" students— those students, that is, who are taking regular course work but who are not candidates for degrees at the institution in question. The director admits them, counsels them, supervises them, maintains records, and takes such academic actions as their performance warrants. The summer session director may also become quite directly involved in supplementing the extracurricular program, typically by working closely with the student union staff; and he may also assume considerable responsibility for arranging and supervising the housing of special groups, working closely with the dormitory chief.

The business office, the physical plant department, the public relations officer, the library, the hospital, the audio-visual aids service, registration and records personnel, the institutional studies people, policemen, leaf-rakers, the president—the whole administrative hierarchy of the modern university—also operate in summer just as in the fall and spring. While the summer session director must maintain close relations with all such auxiliary services, they are by no means "under" him; nor are they in his budget, except for certain special aspects such as the summer laboratory schools, which support instruction in the college of education.

Several conclusions can be drawn from this reconnaisance of university summer session organization. First, the most misleading document in the annals of higher education is the so-called summer term budget, in that it reflects principally only one of the university's five summer activities. For example, in the summer of 1965, the University of Wisconsin's total operations cost some $16,000,000 in salary monies, of which less than $2,000,000 were carried in the summer session budget.

Second, summer organization is hardly a model of scientific planning. Like Topsy, it has "jes' growed," in response to varying conditions and without any systematic theory. Yet everywhere it has usually withstood that most pragmatic of tests: it has worked and is working. In fact, the dispersion and flexibility of the summer term power structure may be one of its greatest strengths.

Third, the whole operation comes to a focus not in the office of the director of the summer session but in the offices of the deans of the respective colleges. Theirs is a twelve-month perspective to an extent found nowhere else in the university.

Fourth, the diffusion of summer organization and administration on each campus contributes to the total lack of uniformity among summer terms, and vastly complicates the task of attempting to collect the simplest of national data.

Fifth, invariably the truly unique aspects of university summer term organization are term length, fiscal arrangements, and the director or dean. We will now discuss each of these in turn.

CALENDAR PATTERNS

In the summer of 1965, 86, or 74 per cent, of America's 116 large universities were employing the semester calendar and hence offered a major summer term of from six to ten weeks in length; 23, or 20 per cent, were on a quarter calendar and hence ran an eleven-week summer quarter, perhaps split into two increments; and 7, or 6 per cent, were on a trimester schedule and hence offered a fifteen-week summer term. In addition, two-thirds of these institutions offered one or more special sessions, some of them overlapping the principal session, others running sequentially. Two-thirds of these universities, then, were utilizing their physical plants for between 43 and 48 weeks out of the year in formal types of instructional programs, not counting periods devoted to special educational services. The predominant lengths of principal summer sessions were eight, ten, and twelve weeks.[3]

It is interesting in this light to observe the calendar patterns adopted by new colleges and universities, where established traditions and practices do not present the usual barrier to innovation. During the period 1961 through 1964, 146 colleges and universities were created in the United States, many of which have been frankly experimental in their organization and posture. A number of them have viewed the summer term in special ways. The University of South Florida, Tampa, for example, has adopted a year-round program of trimesters of fifteen weeks each. So has Oakland University, Rochester, Michigan. At Monteith College of Wayne State University, Detroit, the year-round calendar is of the four-quarter variety, featuring a good deal of independent study. Year-long courses characterize New College at Hofstra, Hofstra, Long Island. A number of students have been able to complete their programs there in three years. Whether or not these departures will make a sustained impact on higher education will depend on the degree to which the innovations find acceptance and use by prestigious institutions.[4] Let us see how some of them have found acceptance so far.

THE TRIMESTER

A half-dozen years ago some observers might have been led to say we were reaching a national consensus on the summer calendar; the trimester plan seemed to be emerging as the wave of the future. More recently, "dividing the college year into three parts is beginning to look better on paper than in practice."[5]

The trimester plan first came into use during World War II because of demands of the military for accelerated manpower

---

[3] These data are based on information on year-round calendar patterns and plans in 116 selected universities, compiled by the Association of University Summer Sessions in 1963, 1964, and 1965, and revised in a report of an ad hoc committee to the Association in October, 1966. See Appendix B for full details.

[4] Lewis B. Mayhew, "The New Colleges," in Baskin, *Higher Education*, pp. 1–25.

[5] "Trimester's Tribulations," *Time*, March 11, 1966, p. 66.

training. It virtually disappeared after 1946, until 1960, when a number of institutions seized on the trimester as the answer to the pressures placed on physical plants by mushrooming enrollments. Many other colleges and universities considered moving to a trimester, frequently prodded by laymen who were intrigued by the savings that seemed inherent in the pattern and by the possibilities for accelerated progress toward degrees. Today the trimester may not be dead, but it has lost much of its luster along with its most vociferous advocates.[6]

In 1959–60 the University of Pittsburgh launched its trimester to the accompaniment of much fanfare. By mid-1965, Pittsburgh had run up an operating deficit in excess of fifteen million dollars. A special Ford Foundation committee studying Pittsburgh's problems pointed out that these two facts "hardly seem unrelated."[7] The committee noted that summer enrollments averaged only half of fall totals, yet Pittsburgh was paying 70 per cent of its faculty on a full-year basis. The three-term calendar particularly "failed dismally to appeal to undergraduate students," perhaps because the calendar didn't tie in with the schedules of other schools in the area. While applauding the experimental spirit of the institution, the Ford committee could only conclude that "disappointing student response made the experiment extraordinarily expensive." The Pittsburgh Board of Trustees got the message.

In 1961–62, Florida, in the hopes of handling more students without a big plant expansion, became the first and only state to adopt the trimester statewide. Admittedly the project got off to a bad start in Florida because it was instituted summarily by the legislature with little consultation with the faculties. Moreover, professors were asked to assume a 25 per cent greater teaching load for only an 11 per cent pay increase. Yet the main objections that came to be expressed were educational. "We had to condense 16 weeks of material into about 12 weeks," said Professor

[6] Frederick C. Klein, "Trimester Troubles," *Wall Street Journal*, February 24, 1966, p. 16.
[7] *A Report by a Special Committee of the Ford Foundation to the University of Pittsburgh* (New York: The Ford Foundation, January 1966), pp. 10–12.

David Dawd, "and it simply didn't work. Students attended class less, read less, and emerged with less, yet they got the same credit. They were shortchanged."[8] Said another: "Education is not a 60-yard dash; it should be approached and savored. Students were confused and stunned." Some students agreed: "It was like trying to drink water from a high-pressure fire hose." Summed up Vice President Robert P. Mautz: "We have been extremely unhappy." Governor Haydon Burns ordered the trimester killed at the close of the 1965–66 school year.[9]

The experience at other colleges has been similar. At the State University of New York at Binghamton (formerly known as Harpur College) a year-round calendar, designed to handle about 50 per cent more students, attracted almost no increase because, as President G. Bruce Dearing reported, "students shunned the summer term."[10] In a recent assessment of the Harpur plan, Dearing and H. R. Kells report that none of the major premises upon which the plan was based were borne out in practice. They conclude that "bizarre calendar configurations must be regarded warily . . . because higher education in this country is perhaps still a decade short of the time when space for students will, in fact, be so scarce that resistance to innovations of this kind can be effectively countered."[11]

At the Illinois State Teachers College branch in Chicago, 60 per cent of the professors have been forced to teach year-round. "The trimester has given us maximum use of our physical plant, but it's killing off our faculty," says Dean Jerome M. Sachs. "The whole group needs some time off to rest and restructure courses."[12] Parsons College in Fairfield, Iowa, has been able to maintain summer enrollments of 70 to 80 per cent of fall and winter levels, but only by requiring attendance for all students with below "C" grade averages, and waiving tuition for all students above the "C" level.

By mid-1966 some fifty other institutions were in various stages

8 Klein, "Trimester Troubles."
9 "Trimester's Tribulations."
10 *The New York Times*, November 28, 1965, p. 3.
11 *Journal of Higher Education*, June 1967, pp. 330–333.
12 Klein, "Trimester Troubles."

of evaluating their experiences with the trimester. Many were coming to "a growing awareness that the trimester is no bed of roses," in the words of Russell I. Thackeray, executive director of the National Association of State Universities and Land-Grant Colleges. "Besides the educational aspects, schools are discovering that the economics they achieve through full-time use of facilities aren't offsetting the increased faculty salaries that go with the trimester, and students don't seem ready to give up summer vacations or outside work for full-time school."[13]

The last, best hope of the trimester has probably been, until recently, the University of Michigan. Unlike the situation in Florida, the plan was adopted at Michigan in several stages, with thorough faculty participation. And unlike the Pittsburgh pattern, Michigan's emphasis has been on the flexibility of the new calendar rather than on acceleration. "We are learning from the experiences of others," says Stephen H. Spurr, Dean of the Graduate School. But not everybody at Ann Arbor is happy. Professor Nicholas D. Kazarinoff heads a faculty group calling for a return to the conventional semester. According to the minutes of a January 10, 1966, meeting of Literature, Science, and Arts faculty, he objects to the "teaching speedup" and the pressure that causes more students to drop courses or take "incompletes." Clarence Fanto, editorial writer for *The Michigan Daily*, has criticized "the slim courses offerings" in summer, and the "academic crush" that has brought a "decline in student participation in valuable activities and organizations."[14]

Most Michigan deans regard the trimester as a qualified success, the Ann Arbor *News* reports:

Dean William Haber of the literary college commended the efficiency of the trimester system, noting that from 4,000 to 5,000 more students were being educated during the summer. This, he said, was comparable to suddenly creating a new school the size of Princeton.

Haber attributed the continuation of spring-summer enrollment at only one-third the levels of normal fall and winter term literary college enrollments to the lack of a well-rounded program due to insufficient funds.

[13] Ibid.
[14] Clarence Fanto, "University of Pittsburgh Offers Lesson," *The Michigan Daily*, January 25, 1966, p. 6.

At the education school, where enrollment is up 65 per cent over last summer, Dean William C. Olson agreed with Haber that the inability to offer a complete program constituted the only major problem created by the trimester system. He saw the expansion of enrollment as very satisfactory considering the limited course offerings.

Dean Floyd A. Bond of the business school reported "tremendous pressures which must be relieved" because of continuous operation with no expansion of the administrative staff. But, in general, "the plan has worked," he said. Bond said the business school has concentrated on advanced courses during the spring half of the term in order to allow students to complete degree work, with introductory courses, offered during the summer half of the term for other students. The school has 40 per cent of its regular term enrollment attending the spring-summer term.

Dean Gordon Van Wylen of the engineering college reported that most faculty members preferred not to teach in Ann Arbor during the summer so they could pursue research or outside work. The problem can be compounded by the fact that most other schools are on a different schedule, making the hiring of outside faculty very difficult.

Nevertheless, he said, he has been able to find enough faculty and "deliberate action to get more teachers would be necessary only if there was considerable expansion."

He added that "it was too early to say that the new term was the long-run solution," but that for the 25 per cent of his regular enrollment that is attending the spring-summer term, "it is obviously satisfactory."

The School of Public Health will go on complete year-round programming next year, Dean Myron E. Wegman reported. At the School of Social Work, Dean Fedele Fauri expressed support for the new schedule and reported excellent results with it in his school.[15]

At the time of this article (June, 1966), a College of Literature, Science, and Arts faculty report was expected to recommend some minor revisions in the new Michigan calendar: a delay in starting classes until after Labor Day, with final exams scheduled right after the Christmas vacation, moving up the end of the winter term to mid-May instead of the end of April.[16]

Despite this reasonably promising beginning, however, in the spring of 1967 repeal of Michigan's trimester calendar was asked

15 "Deans Hail Trimester System," Ann Arbor News, June 12, 1966, p. 3.
16 Cleland B. Wyllie, Michigan Director of Media Relations, June 16, 1966, personal correspondence in author's files.

in a resolution recommended to the College of Literature, Science, and Arts faculty by the executive committee of the College.[17] The resolution held that few of the anticipated advantages of the trimester had been realized, that the trimester had resulted in damage to a number of educational values, and that the system seriously interfered with the scholarly work of the faculty outside the classroom. The failure of the trimester here, on the basis not of finances but of educational values, surely marks the beginning of its end as a serious topic for discussion on the American educational agenda.

## THE QUARTER SYSTEM

Generally, the advocates of the trimester plan have argued for its adoption on these grounds: It better enables our colleges and universities to cope with rising enrollments and the "explosion" of knowledge in the postwar period; it provides the student with the opportunity to complete his undergraduate education in three years instead of four, and thus encourages earlier entry into the job market or into graduate or professional school; it offers faculty members additional options in terms of research or vacation time; and it facilitates maximum utilization of the physical plant and instructional resources.

Presumably the same advantages are inherent in a year-round quarter operation. In fact, proponents of this system contend that it is preferable to the trimester in that it fits better with the public school calendar, it is more adaptable to the varying needs of students and faculty, and it allows the student to pursue fewer subjects in a more concentrated manner during a single term.

After a study of the "relative merits of three-semester and four-quarter plans,"[18] the California Coordinating Council for Higher Education endorsed the quarter system as the "best method of achieving year-round operations" at the University of California and the California State Colleges, and proposed that the cal-

[17] *University Record,* University of Michigan, Ann Arbor, April 20, 1967, p. 1.
[18] *A Master Plan for Higher Education in California: 1960–1975* (Sacramento: California State Department of Education, 1960), p. 8.

endar patterns adopted by these institutions be designed so as "to provide ease of transfer from junior colleges and high schools." The CCHE in California opted for the quarter plan because of its "greater flexibility": faculty would have "one more term per year in which . . . to study, travel, or relax"; and "better articulation with other educational institutions" would be possible.[19]

## COMPULSORY ATTENDANCE?

One of the prime arguments for year-round education on either the trimester or quarter model is that it enables institutions to make more efficient and effective use of existing facilities, and to realize, at least in the long run, important savings in capital outlay for buildings and equipment. Optimum plant utilization, however, requires that student enrollments be distributed more or less evenly throughout the several terms; in other words, we must cut the fall "peak" and fill in the summer "valley." Yet an enrollment balance is difficult, if not impossible, to attain in the absence of some degree of compulsion. The question then becomes: Should any compulsion be employed, and if so, how much is acceptable?

The eighty-year experience of many institutions with summer session operations coincides with recent trimester experience in several "lessons learned": First, a significant number of "regular" students need and will attend a summer session strong in course offerings at all levels of collegiate work. Second, an equally significant number of "regular" students will not choose to attend the summer session. Third, the summer period is the only time when a great many youth and adult "special" students can come to the campus for liberal and professional institutes, clinics, and workshops. And fourth, in many departments it is difficult to recruit a teaching staff, so intense is the competition from research and scholarly travel programs. All of these experiences

[19] *A Comparison of the Trimester and Four-quarter Calendars for Year-round Operation of Public Higher Education in California* (Sacramento: California Coordinating Council for Higher Education, February 1966), pp. ii, 16, and 28.

lead to the conclusion that, in the absence of compulsory measures, it is extremely difficult if not impossible to maintain a summer student body and a summer faculty equal in numbers to the spring and fall terms. Yet, as we have said, unless the man-day spaces are made equal in all terms, there is no economy in so-called year-round calendars; in fact, there are hidden expenses.

With respect to compulsory summer term attendance, most educators are unalterably opposed to such a practice on educational, social, and economic grounds. Many students must work for some period during the year in order to earn enough money to continue their education; and the summer offers many employment possibilities. A number of industries, in fact, are built around the employment of seasonal student help: tourism, canning, and construction, for example. Furthermore, the pressures to accelerate, to "succeed," that come to bear on students from grade school days tend to reach a peak in the college years, and dictate a summer hiatus for renewal of mind, body, and spirit in the case of many individuals. Finally, compulsory school attendance during summer is alien to American folkways and disruptive of American family life, and compulsory summer teaching assignments would be repugnant to many faculty members and would lead to a progressive deterioration of staff quality.

There are other considerations, too. For example, were university facilities to be assigned largely to "regular" students in summer, there would be inadequate room and staff for the youths and adults who now come to the campus in summer. Compulsory summer attendance would make it difficult for many students to plan meaningful curricular sequences, unless each term were to offer an identical array of courses. Compulsory class attendance in summer would interfere with those independent researches which are best carried on by students in summer: agricultural studies, for example. Were all university classrooms to be pressed into service around the clock in summer, the university's physical plant would face major air-conditioning requirements. Finally, the terms of a so-called "year-round" calendar do not articulate well with elementary and secondary school schedules, making it very difficult for beginning freshmen and school teachers to avail themselves of summer study.

CALENDAR CRITERIA

Assuming, then, that we neither can nor want to require students to make full use of campus facilities, what criteria should be used in evaluating academic calendar experiences and proposals? Five can be suggested:[20]

1. The quality of our higher educational institutions should be carefully safeguarded; a university calendar is not an end in itself but only a vehicle for implementing or strengthening particular educational values.

2. The student should be allowed sufficient flexibility in entering upon his college program and in pursuing his educational goals.

3. More specifically, the freedom of the student to determine his own time of entry and his own academic pace thereafter should be fully preserved.

4. The student who so desires should be afforded an adequate opportunity to accelerate his academic work through continuous or near-continuous year-long attendance.

5. Existing physical facilities and instructional resources should be utilized to the fullest extent possible consistent with the values above.

A crucial question immediately arises: How should these values be weighted? Obviously, the relative importance attached to each criterion has a direct bearing on the type and degree of calendar change which one may wish to introduce. For instance, substantial alteration of present scheduling patterns may be appropriate given maximum plant utilization as the overriding goal, but may be unnecessary where opportunity for acceleration is the primary objective. In listing these criteria, then, we have arranged them in what we consider to be a proper

[20] See *Academic Calendar Policy*, Working Paper No. 18 (Madison: Wisconsin Coordinating Committee for Higher Education, March 1966), p. 2.

order of importance; major emphasis should be placed on the preservation of institutional quality and of the freedom of the student to proceed at his own academic pace.

Keeping in mind the above criteria, let us look at another approach to the calendar question. Dean Frank Burrin of Purdue University has given a good deal of thought to the matter and has suggested an interesting way to determine the relative merits of a trimester or four-quarter plan.[21] He constructs an imaginary private or municipal university located in a metropolitan area where there is little room for physical expansion. The student body is composed almost entirely of part-time undergraduate students, and graduate students with part-time or twelve-month half-time appointments. During its six-week summer term practically all of its regular term graduate students and 60 to 70 per cent of its regular term undergraduates enroll. During the summer term, less than 10 per cent of the students are from other institutions. The school does not utilize visiting staff from other institutions during its summer term. It employs a higher percentage of its staff on a part-time basis for both winter and summer terms, relying heavily on professional people in business and industry for its teaching staff. Such an institution probably should be operating on a trimester or a four-quarter plan, Dean Burrin says.

On the other hand, Dean Burrin imagines a state college located in a small midwestern city. Its regular term student body is composed primarily of full-time undergraduate students. During its nine-week summer term, however, the graduate school enrollment is increased by 300 per cent (most of these teachers) while its undergraduate enrollment drops to about 40 per cent of the winter level. Virtually all staff members are employed full time on a twelve-month basis, and the institution employs additional summer staff from other schools. During the vacation period between terms, the facilities are used by large groups of adults who come from all over the state for continuing education activities. This institution would be doing a great disservice to

---

[21] "Year-Round Programs—Possibilities for Improvement Without Major Calendar Change," Speech to the North Central Conference of Summer Schools, April 5, 1964, pp. 7–8.

its constituents if it were to make any major calendar changes, Dean Burrin believes.

In summarizing the calendar question we need only say, as we have said before, that no one scheme for year-round operation is likely to sweep the nation, given the great diversity among American institutions of higher education. There is simply no one calendar plan that is best for all institutions. It is a question that must be resolved on the basis of each institution's unique needs and resources.

## FISCAL ARRANGEMENTS

In the great majority of our large universities today, the summer session budget is a part of the institution's annual financial plans. It will typically be treated as a separate section, as opposed to the budget for the "regular year" and the budgets for those units operating year-round, but it will be *in* there and not treated as an incidental appendage, as was once the case. Furthermore, in the great majority of our large universities, the summer session is not asked to "break even." That is, it will receive a share of revenues from public appropriations or endowment funds as well as from student fees. The level of support will seldom be all the director asks for and may, indeed, be less than the level afforded comparable instructional activities in fall and spring; but the time is past in most of our major institutions when the summer term is required to be self-sustaining.

### STUDENT FEES AND FINANCIAL AIDS

In general, summer term student fees represent their just proportion of regular-term fees. In fact, through a curious turn of fate, in some institutions nonresident summer fees are actually scaled lower than winter fees. In those institutions where the summer term is still asked to be either wholly or largely self-supporting, student fees tend to be scaled higher, and may even be exorbitant, in violation of the American tradition that society should subsidize the education of its youth.

Charges for educational services vary enormously. Some institutes are free; others impose punitive fees. In general, the institution attempts to recapture out-of-pocket costs on the enterprise as a whole.

With respect to student loans, scholarships, and fellowships, the summer term still retains its original status as a vermiform appendix. Summer student financial aids are conspicuously below the level of such programs in the regular year, both in the proportionate number of grants and in the proportionate amount appropriated. Complicating the situation further is the fact that there is intense competition for jobs on the summer campus. Many universities compound the problem by employing in summer many students from the regular year who are not enrolled in the summer term. Some federal subventions do not apply in summer; others apply only in summer. The table in Appendix C tells part of the story.

Summer session deans are struggling manfully on most campuses to improve this situation, and there is some evidence that they may be succeeding. Of the eighteen schools responding to the question—"Has summer session student aid increased in the last five years?"—fifteen indicated that it had. Four estimated the increase to be more than 100 per cent; six estimated an increase of between 50 and 100 per cent; and one judged the increase to have been less than 50 per cent. Four schools could not estimate the rate of increase; three indicated that there was no increase.[22]

At Wisconsin, the following changes in current financial aid policy are being considered:

1. Opening up existing summer resident fee-remission scholarships to new and continuing freshmen and sophomores in the eight-week as well as in the twelve-week session, and adopting such standards in the awarding of the grants as will assure full

[22] Ralph Sinks, et al., "A Study of Financial Assistance Granted in 1963–64 to Undergraduate and Graduate Students in Member Colleges and Universities of the Association of Deans and Directors of Summer Sessions," Report to the Association of University Summer Sessions, October 1965.

utilization of the $10,000 annually allocated for such scholarships.

2. Opening up existing summer nonresident fee-remission scholarships to new freshmen who begin in summer as well as to freshmen continuing in summer.

3. Allocating an appropriate number of existing and new "legislative" scholarships to summer students.

4. Reviewing current student loan policies with an eye to awarding loans to appropriate students for the pursuit of summer study.

5. Considering limiting some campus summer jobs to students enrolled in the summer sessions, along with developing "guaranteed" loan-scholarship-job packages.

6. Developing new scholarship and fellowship configurations that will attract foundation and donor support.

7. Considering a policy whereby the statutory nonresident fee-remission scholarships traditionally available in spring and fall may be awarded to new and continuing graduate students enrolled in the summer sessions as Wisconsin degree candidates, provided necessary funds are made available.

One step forward has already been taken: nonresident graduate students holding assistantships or scholarships which will begin in the fall semester are now eligible for summer nonresident fee remissions; this has previously been the case only for graduate students whose appointments were for the preceding semester.

SALARIES AND FRINGE BENEFITS

Since we have already discussed the salary question in Chapter 3, we may summarize here: Faculty salaries in summer in our larger universities are usually equal to regular-year salaries, assuming equal time and work loads, although some institutions still penalize the summer professor. On the other hand, a few universities pay at a higher rate in summer. Salaries for summer instruction generally are computed by taking the nine-month salary of the instructor as a base, and paying an amount determined by the number of additional months he teaches. A number of institutions place a limit on the number of months for which a faculty member can be paid in any twelve-, twenty-four-, or thirty-six-month span.

Retirement, insurance, hospitalization, leave credits, and other fringe benefits now generally accrue to the summer professor in accordance with regular-year patterns.

## THE SUMMER SESSION DIRECTOR

Most large university summer sessions are in the charge of an individual, usually known as the director or dean. On the face of it, this may seem curious. There is, for example, no "first-semester" or "second-quarter" dean. But a little examination will show that universities would quickly invent summer session directors if they didn't already exist. There is, first, the force of history. Because the first summer sessions were patently in but not of the university, early presidents were quick to delegate responsibility. The habit is still with us. There is, too, the practical consideration that presidents and chancellors need vacations, and someone must be left as the senior officer present. Someone must also, as we have pointed out earlier, play the role of dean of the "college" in which are enrolled the significant numbers of "summer-only" special students.

Summer session directors would like to think, however, that there are more valid reasons than these for their existence. Someone must assume the role of creative summer program planner if the session is to grow soundly. Someone must keep the president or chancellor advised of emerging summer problems and their possible solutions. Someone must be willing to ride herd on the three-ring circus the summer term represents. Someone must respond to the peculiar demands of the summer term with respect to student and staff recruitment. In short, somebody has to "think summer" 365 days a year; and that somebody is the summer session director.

The first summer term administrators, as we have shown, were entrepreneurial professors who operated private summer schools on the university grounds. There sometimes were several such entrepreneurs functioning independently on the same campus at the same time. As the university began somewhat reluctantly to enfold these "weed" summer schools, it appointed what one institution called a *conductor*—a designation appropriate, as a later summer director has written, "because he was charged with the responsibility of bringing into harmony the dissonant variations on an educational theme."[23]

By the early 1900's the chiefs of the summer term were uniformly called directors, and they were that. Charged with building flourishing programs yet with making ends meet at the same time, they established the ground rules, dealt imperiously with individual instructors, and marshalled students to classrooms and picnics. As the summer term increasingly took on the mantle of the regular year, the directors began to deal with school and college deans, to rely on the institution's overhead personnel for administrative support, and to win some financial subsidy; whereupon they came to be called deans themselves in many cases.

Today, whatever his title may be, the chief summer session administrator is a coordinator, not an "operator."[24] In military parlance he is a special staff officer, not a commander. He advises, he cajoles, he recommends, he supervises, he may even prod, but he does precious little directing. He is even lucky to know everything that's going on, so various are the large university's summer programs and so automatic their arrangement through on-going channels.

Where do summer session directors come from, and where do they go? Because irregular programs for teachers bulked large in early summer session operations, presidents frequently turned to educators or extensionists for their summer directors. As one writer has put it, "The education-extension route had given these men the experience needed to face such a conglomeration of problems without flinching too noticeably; their colleagues looked on in appalled silence."[25] Many extensionists and educators continue to serve with distinction as summer session directors today. The modern trend, however, is to lodge the function with an academic dean, vice-president, or provost; although it

23 E. W. Ziebarth, in Stecklein, et al., *Summer Session, Minnesota*, p. 22.
24 Smith, in Schoenfeld, *Shape of Summer*, p. 75.
25 Ibid., p. 70.

must be said there are all sorts of exceptions to this rule, depending on local traditions and talent.

Whatever the nature of their associated administrative posts, summer session directors reach them by devious routes. Among the members of the Association of University Summer Sessions, for example, such diverse academic disciplines as the following are represented: education, journalism, geography, bacteriology, international relations of Latin America, speech, business economics, English literature, religion, advertising, constitutional law, philosophy, history of Japan, economics, American drama, the arts, American political parties, and psychology.

Similarly, the graduate thesis topics of these men can only be described as heterogeneous: Public Relations of Conservation, Education of Negro Children in a Non-Segregated School Environment, Embryology of Certain Mammals, Principles of English Literary Translation, Rhetoric of William Ewart Gladstone, Studies in Money Velocity, The Structure of the Old English Poem *Beowulf*, The Influence of Student Mental Ability on the Retention of Test Results by Tenth Grade Students, Christian Conceptions of Sin and Justification in the Light of Depth Psychology, The Michigan Constitution of 1837, Japan and the U.S., 1790–1853, and The Ontological Argument.

The summer session directorship is definitely not a one-way ticket to some academic Siberia. In the history of one university, for example, one summer session director became president of the institution, another became dean of the college of letters and science, a third dean of the school of education, and a fourth chancellor of the branch campus system. When American summer session directors get together for their annual conventions, their ranks always indicate that this or that former lieutenant has gone on to bigger if not better assignments. It must be admitted, however, that some summer session directors die in harness, and others simply fade away.

### STATUS AND STRUCTURE OF THE SUMMER DIRECTORSHIP

No American institution of higher education considers directing a summer session to be a full-time job. In the larger universities, however, it is usually at least a half-time assignment. What does the summer session director do with the rest of his time? He may do some teaching in his "home" department, which can range from philosophy to agronomy; but he is most likely to be an administrator—a dean or associate dean of the university, a college, the extension or evening school, and so on. He usually holds the rank, real or courtesy, of a full professor. He is generally paid less than the average of other deans at his university but more than the average professor there. He tends to be younger than either.

So much for the obvious data. Where in fact does the summer session director sit in the university power structure? It is hard to say. The other "hat" he wears may enhance or detract from his status as summer session administrator. It is the rare summer director who is a regular member of the president's cabinet simply by virtue of his being director of the summer session, but he will invariably participate in any top-level discussions with summer session implications. In general, in most large institutions the summer session directorship tends to be about what the director wants to make it—a significant administrative post with manifold responsibilities and relationships, or something of an afterthought. Dean F. L. Whan of Kansas State has aptly summarized this situation:

If you were told by someone that he is the Chairman of the Department of English, or the Registrar, or the Comptroller, or the Football Coach—you would have a pretty good idea of what he is doing, what his responsibilities are, how much authority he has, and about where on the salary scale he rests—in general, you would know what he means when he gives you his title. Not so in the case of the Dean or Director of Summer School.

If you told one president I happen to know that you are the Director of Summer School, he would immediately imagine you to be rather high on the administrative hierarchy, . . . a relatively high-salaried person, . . . an administrator with authority, and . . . capable of making wise decisions. If you made the same statement to another president I know, he would wonder if your rank is above that of assistant professor, would assume you to be sort of an administrative clerk, would assume you have no authority of your own, and would have no way to determine whether you could make wise decisions.

I wonder if perhaps we—the part-time directors of summer schools —are not the real cause of the confusion. I wonder if most of us are not so wrapped up in our *other* duties that we have no time to worry about the summer term. Our *other* job carries responsibility, authority, and perhaps high salary. Therefore, we forget or ignore what our own administrators think about the summer school portion of our total assignment.[26]

The position of the summer term and its chief will no doubt continue indefinitely to provoke discussion, with each institution settling the issue in its own way. Graydon W. Yaple, Dean of Faculty at Wilmington (Ohio) College, would in effect "abolish the summer session." He does not propose to abolish summer activities, but he does suggest that we "stop giving a special name to that phase of the college program that happens in summer." "I wonder why," he asks, "we have to have a person designated to operate a program in summer who does not operate educational programs in the rest of the year?"[27] Indiana's Robert W. Richey, on the other hand, is all for strengthening the unique nature of the summer session and its principal administrator: Unless we lend more status and authority to the summer dean, he says, we will "find some of the assistant deans throughout the university operating much like newly-commissioned second lieutenants, which makes it difficult to work with them in the planning, organization, and administration of a strong summer program."[28]

Questions of status aside, let us briefly outline the summer power structure as it currently exists. While most of the summer term's functions are subsumed under the continuing activities of other units, the summer session director usually has a small staff to assist him in the preparation and dissemination of informational literature, special student registration and record-keeping, fiscal control, and program planning and supervision. Invariably he will also have an advisory committee. It may be a committee elected by the faculty; more frequently it will be an

[26] "Report of the Personnel Committee," p. 7.
[27] Personal correspondence in author's files.
[28] Ibid.

appointed group composed of those fellow administrators and professors most concerned with, interested in, or adept at summer term matters. Such a committee can be extremely useful in communicating problems and insights to the director, in helping to shape policies, and in communicating summer term perspectives to key units of the university. It must also be said that an ill-chosen or ill-motivated committee can constitute a serious drag.

With few exceptions the summer session director reports directly to the chief administrative officer of the institution, or to his immediate deputy. He will also, of course, have close working relationships with school and college deans, the extension director, and the various strata and substrata of administrative offices, particularly the admissions officer, the registrar, the chief fiscal officer, the dean of student affairs, the dormitory and student union heads, the director of public relations, the superintendent of buildings and grounds, and the secretary of the faculty.

With all these contacts and interests, however, the summer director's range of unilateral decision-making is narrow. Dean Whan of Kansas State has recently made a study of selected midwestern summer schools which is very revealing on this subject. The table in Appendix D indicates clearly that most decisions affecting the summer session are the result of interplay between the summer dean and one or more other people or units.

Another recent study of the emerging "functions and powers of summer session directors" was conducted by Dr. Charles Heidenreich of Sacramento City College. Surveying 274 universities which enroll over 1,500 students in the regular year, he came up with the following results:

The typical director is most directly responsible to the president (37%), vice-president (30%), or academic dean (21%).
He either always (53%) or frequently (21%) has autonomy in budget expenditures.
He is always (65%) or frequently (13%) responsible for publicity and public relations.
He always (73% of respondents) submits an annual report.

The director always (69%) has responsibility for the instructional program; 13%, however, rarely and 9% never control this aspect of the summer program.

37% always, 33% frequently, and 21% occasionally recommend revisions in the course offerings.

53% always, 14% frequently, and 13% occasionally have the power to disapprove departmental course offerings.

84% always edit the summer session bulletin.

52% always, 11% frequently, and 26% never have the power to appoint visiting faculty.

49% always, 13% frequently, and 25% never determine instructional faculty teaching loads.

29% always and 47% never have power to determine faculty salaries.

59% always and 26% never have responsibility for assignment of classrooms and facilities.

31% always, 23% frequently, 15% occasionally, and 21% never take the leadership in suggesting student class loads, fees, and so on.

37% always, 20% frequently, 16% occasionally, and 18% never advise on summer admission policy.

28% always, 19% occasionally, 13% rarely, and 41% never are responsible for student attendance and discipline.

42% always, 10% rarely, and 35% never have responsibility for summer student registration procedures.

The director has responsibility for pre and post sessions, clinics, workshops, and so on always 47%, never 13%.

During academic year the SS director spends 90–100% of time on summer session (4%), 50–60% (14%), 30–40% (32%), 10–20% (42%).

During the summer he spends 90–100% of time on summer session work (42%), 70–80% (19%), 50–60% (16%), 30–40% (11%).

Title held: Dean 21%, Director 60%.[29]

The Heidenreich study merely documents what has been intuitively known: that there is now no really discernible pattern in summer session administration. Is there, however, any pattern which works better than others?

[29] A Study of the Functions and Powers of Summer Session Directors in Selected Institutions of Higher Education in the United States: Summary Report (mimeographed, Sacramento: Sacramento City College, 1965), pp. 2–9.

Raymond C. Gibson, professor of education at Indiana University, suggests two possibilities and rejects two others:[30] Since summer session functions carried on in our major universities cut across every school and department, he believes they should ideally be organized under a vice-president and dean of the summer session who sits directly under the president. It seems to him that the position should, at the very minimum, be equal to that of the director of athletics, whose position in the hierarchy is almost always directly under the president.

If it is necessary to deviate from this choice with respect to the status of the administrator of the summer session, Dr. Gibson would settle for a position as associate dean of the faculty in charge of summer sessions. This would continue to relieve the dean of the faculty of most of his responsibilities for the summer session and would free him for creative planning and innovation indispensable to the on-going program for the regular academic year. It would likewise recognize the year-round assignment of planning and implementing the summer program, with the associate dean of the faculty in charge of such operations.

In the first two schemes of organization, budgetary allocations would be made to the summer session in the same way as they are made to other schools and colleges of the university, perhaps at the same time that annual commitments are made to schools and colleges. Once the summer session budget for each school, college, or division of the university has been agreed upon, the various deans of schools and colleges under the coordination of the dean of the summer session would proceed to implement the planning in terms of curriculum, budgeting, and personnel.

The third type of organization is one in which the dean of summer sessions would be coordinate with deans of the various schools and colleges, and thus he would have to bargain with his peers for programs, personnel, and budgets. Dr. Gibson rejects this approach since in some cases it would mean that the fate of summer session programs might be decided by individuals who do not believe in them.

The fourth type of administrative structure is one in which

[30] "The Organization of Summer Session Programs," Speech to the North Central Conference of Summer Schools, March 29, 1965, pp. 9–12.

the administrator of the summer session holds a title and a position subordinate to those of the deans of the various colleges. This, Gibson believes, is the most difficult and inefficient method by which a summer session can be administered, because all it gives the director is full authority to go begging for support from superiors. The nature of the summer session as a creative and innovative activity in a university, many of the results of which eventually are incorporated into the regular programs of the academic year, indicates that the dean in such a position is apt to dissipate most of his energies in fruitless enterprises.

Whatever administrative pattern achieves dominance, it must be consonant with certain basic summer session characteristics. Dr. Gibson outlines these as follows:

1. The program involves curricula and personnel from every division of the university.

2. Credit and noncredit courses, workshops, and institutes make the summer session uniquely different from the program of the regular academic year.

3. Summer sessions are essentially more innovative than regular academic programs.

4. Budgeting and staffing summer sessions must be coordinated by a central administrative official, but implementation of the program is a function of the substantive divisions of the university.

5. Central office planning, budgeting, staffing, and publicizing the summer program demand a full-time staff working throughout the year.

6. The only other academic program that cuts across the whole university is perhaps the graduate program.

7. Centralization of responsibility and authority for the summer session is more urgent than for the graduate program because of the difference in funding summer sessions.

8. Although an institution may give individual staff members a choice as to whether they work in summer, participation in summer sessions can no longer be at the discretion of substantive divisions of the university.

9. A university is noted for its specialists who very appropriately do not want to be "organization men." They represent a centrifugal force which, uncoordinated, will bring about the disintegration of the university. This has already happened to most large universities.

10. The indispensable function of the administrator is to bring about the synthesis, to put the pieces back together. The summer session is a classic example of such a need. Under adequate leadership, a university is greater than the sum of its parts.[31]

In sum, the volatile, relatively unstructured nature of the summer enterprise makes standard operating procedures somewhat suspect, and places a premium upon successful informal interpersonal relationships. This situation has led one summer session leader to observe "that a study of *ourselves,* individually, would contribute an important factor to the knowledge needed for the solution of the human relations strains which inevitably must be faced in summer session organization and administration."[32] In the final analysis the director's effectiveness will depend on his ability to lead while seeming to be led. And his "place" in the university's power structure, whatever the mechanics of the arrangements, must be broadly as Earl C. Crockett, President of Brigham Young University, has defined it: "As institutions become larger," he says, "the role of the dean, the summer session dean included, becomes more crucial and challenging. The dean must serve as the man in the middle between the president and the faculty. This is the historic role of the dean."[33]

ROLES

Within the context of this larger role, however, the summer director is very busy playing a number of smaller roles. Primarily, as we have seen, he is a coordinator; this, in fact, is why he exists in the first place. The enormous amount of liaison necessary as a result of common use of space, overlapping of staff, and so on—within the academic units, between the academic units and the ancillary services, and within the ancillary services themselves—makes centralization of this role essential. The wise summer dean, however, follows this rule of thumb: the more

[31] Ibid., p. 8.
[32] Smith, in Schoenfeld, *Shape of Summer,* p. 76.
[33] *Proceedings of the First Annual Meeting of the National Association of College and University Summer Sessions, 1964,* p. 10.

administrative detail which can be kept in the usual channels the better.[34]

The summer director's more specific roles touch on almost all aspects of university administration:

*Program Planning.* The summer session director attempts to sense public educational needs, to interpret these needs to academic deans and department heads, then to help translate them into academic programs of high quality, and finally to communicate information about the programs to prospective students. Such program planning is a year-round role that reaches its peak in late fall when the budget is planned for the forthcoming summer term.

*Policy Formulation.* It is the prime responsibility of the director of the summer term to bring to the attention of the university administration the pros and cons of any problem situation that he can foresee or that may occur, and to suggest reasonable solutions in keeping with the broad policies of the institution.[35]

*Fiscal Control.* The summer session director has the task, on the one hand, of holding eager academic departments to course offerings and staffing which are economically feasible; and, on the other hand, of needling backward departments into making the most of their summer opportunities. Sometimes this role will involve formal budget conferences; more likely informal meetings or visits are all that will be required.[36]

*Student Affairs.* As the "dean" of the "special student" college, the summer session director acts on admissions, counsels students, and sees that academic records are kept. In his larger role as director of the summer session as a whole, he concerns himself with matters of housing, extracurricular programing, registration, advising, and educational facilities—working, as we have said, through the year-round personnel assigned to these functions.

The library presents a particular problem. Returns of the 1960 Office of Education questionnaire showed that in 696 institutions summer library hours were identical with those of the regular

[34] Smith, in Schoenfeld, *Shape of Summer,* p. 72.
[35] Ibid., p. 75.
[36] Ibid., p. 73.

session, in 468 they were shorter, and in 67 longer. The respective percentages were 56.5, 38, and 5.4. The incidence of shorter hours was greatest among junior colleges, liberal arts colleges, *and universities*, and least in those types of institutions where year-round education was most common—semiprofessional schools and technical colleges. Longer summer library hours were most often found in teachers colleges.[37]

"Should we have a summer commencement?" This is a perennial question. Only some four hundred institutions terminated their sessions with commencement exercises last year. Superficially, this might seem to suggest that the summer session is inferior to the spring session, when commencements are almost universal. Actually, "the absence probably arises more from motivations of economy, of avoiding discomfort, and of an irrepressible desire to begin postponed vacations than from considerations of status."[38]

*Public Relations.* Preparing and distributing promotional literature, greeting campus visitors, welcoming conference groups, addressing student forums, supplying the press with timely information—the summer director inevitably falls heir to these and related public relations chores.

*"Troubleshooting."* Whatever it may say in the manuals, most of the summer director's time will typically be taken up with a host of human relations problems, running the gamut from the ridiculous to the crucial. In one and the same summer he may: commiserate with a department chairman who can cajole no staff member into teaching; counsel another department chairman who proposes to load his summer staff with expensive visiting lecturers; hold the hand of a homesick junior high musician; salve an ancient English teacher who complains bitterly that the play she has been assigned to read is "salacious"; excuse from the campus a wayward coed who beds down in an off-limits apartment; calm a parent who doesn't want his son rooming with a Negro; exchange words with a graduate school dean who grants research leave to an instructor at the last minute; help the registrar try to get his IBM machine cranking;

[37] Warner, et al., *Summer Sessions, 1960*, p. 82.
[38] Ibid., p. 88.

debate a student union rule that bathing suits are *verboten* in the cafeteria; assure a professor that he need not give a midterm exam if he doesn't want to; fence with a reporter who wants to do a story about sorority life in summer; invent statistics for the president's office on short notice; settle a quarrel between two institute directors over the use of a movie projector; work out a loan for an errant freshman who majored in poker instead of political science; refer a disturbed graduate student to the psychiatric clinic; mediate between a cadre of ROTC cadets and their "Peace in Vietnam" pickets; and tell his wife why he won't be home for supper again tonight!

*Ancillary Activities.* Most universities are run, or appear to be run, by committees. So pervasive are his interests and responsibilities that the summer session director will wind up, in the nature of things, on more than his share. Further, most professional associations are run, or appear to be run, by committees, so that, in representing his institution in the various leagues of summer sessions, the summer dean will wind up on state, regional, and national boards.

Withall, the director must continue to pose as the professor he once was. While he is under no real pressure to publish, he invariably will. While he is under no pressure to teach, he does so when he can. He likewise will enter into some of the educational service programs of his parent department. If he has any time left, he will also attempt to play the role of husband, parent, and human being. He may even play golf.

*Student Model.* The summer session director has a critical role to play in the development of the summer student's personality. He is bound to represent much of what it is that students are supposed to become. As a leader of summer university enterprise he cannot be merely an engineer who keeps the machinery running; he must embody his institution's ideals and goals. He must show in his behavior that he stands for something, that he knows how to make value judgments, and that he has the courage to follow through in action. Deans and directors may overlook their role as models for students, and it may appear at times when things are running smoothly that the students are overlooking it too. But let the summer dean make a mistake, act in violation of some ethical norm, compromise once too often with the forces that oppose the true aims of the university, or display some measure of "phoniness," and the effect on students is immediate and profound. They feel cheated.

It would be a fine thing if all summer session directors could be heroes. If they cannot be, what with all the shopping, housekeeping, and troubleshooting they have to do, they should at least behave so consistently with our basic values that they can be ignored or taken for granted by students on the assumption that all is well. Summer deans, in short, have to be "wise and just and good men without expecting, or getting, any credit for it."[39]

## NATIONAL AND REGIONAL ORGANIZATIONS

In tackling the continuing requirements of his post, the summer session director is fortunately not alone. For inspiration, guidance, commiseration, and assistance in raising standards, he has several national leagues of summer sessions which he can join. Dean John R. Little of the University of Colorado has recently contributed to the literature of summer sessions an excellent statement on these national organizations, which we summarize below:[40]

The Association of University Summer Sessions (formerly the Association of Summer Session Deans and Directors), consisting of fifty member institutions, was formed officially in 1925 for the purpose of "considering matters of common interest relating to the University summer session, particularly with regard to graduate study." The Association is an extremely informal group, relying mainly upon unstructured programs and discussions, although an annual statistical "Summary of Reports" concerning member universities is prepared and distributed at each annual conference. Other less formal studies and reports are often distributed among the members. Although its members have been

39 Sanford, *College and Character*, pp. 296–297.
40 See John R. Little, "Organizations for Summer Administrators: Development, Current Status and Possibilities," Speech to the North Central Conference of Summer Schools, March 29, 1965.

selected from all sections of the country, the Association has never intended nor pretended either to be a national organization or to have any national function. Its strength has been in its close-knit informality, its service to its members, and the members' service to each other.

The North Central Conference of Summer Schools was formed in Chicago in March, 1949, at an informal meeting of forty-five deans and directors of summer schools who were in attendance at the North Central Conference of Secondary Schools and Colleges. A committee then developed a plan for the first formal meeting, which was held in March, 1950. Fifty attended the first meeting and from then on the conference grew steadily to its present membership of 107 institutions.

The Conference has three stated purposes: (1) to assemble at the time of the annual meeting of the North Central Association administrators responsible for summer school programs in interested colleges and universities; (2) to provide opportunity for a review of pertinent phases of summer school operation, especially those of a current nature; and (3) to hear reports of special committees previously assigned to make investigations. Annual conference programs consist of formal and informal presentations of papers and addresses, directed discussions, and an annual business meeting, all with an accent on unstructured informality and with adequate opportunity for questions and discussion.

The Western Association of Deans and Directors of Summer Sessions came about as the result of a joint summer session advertisement placed in the *NEA Journal*. Representatives of eight or ten Rocky Mountain schools began meeting in 1946 to plan the advertisement and stayed on for a couple of days to discuss mutual problems. Although the joint advertisement idea was given up in 1960, the group continued to meet on various campuses throughout the region. Today the group numbers representatives of from forty-five to fifty institutions. In 1963, its name was officially changed from the Rocky Mountain Association to the current designation, and its membership was correspondingly broadened to include representatives from all the Rocky Mountain and Pacific states. The most informal of all associations, it has no officers but depends instead upon the representatives of the host institution to chair and plan the program for its business sessions.

In April of 1964, the National Association of College and University Summer Sessions (NACUSS) was formed as the result of a need for a national body that could speak for summer programs in higher education. The group offers opportunities for the stimulation and professional growth of its members through the exchange of ideas and information. Membership is available to institutions of higher education as well as to individuals, and to representatives of junior colleges as well as of four-year colleges and universities. Membership has grown from 120 members at its first meeting to over 325 at the present time. The organization is both national and regional, with each geographic region (Northwestern, Western, Southern, North Central, Middle States, and New England) having its own leadership through a vice-president. Annual meetings are held, research activities are being planned, and a bulletin, the *NACUSS News*, is published to keep its members in touch with activities of the organization.

Such national and regional organizations perform an irreplaceable role in interinstitutional communications, in in-service training, in sight-lifting, and in giving the summer term a better chance to receive special educational funding. They augur well for the increased interinstitutional cooperation which may be a hallmark of summer organization and administration in the years ahead.

INTERINSTITUTIONAL COOPERATION

In the sense that universities were born as confederacies of colleges, interinstitutional cooperation can hardly be said to be new; however, recent interest and activity have raised it to the level of a new educational dimension. The summer university fostered some of the earliest examples of interinstitutional cooperation and continues to participate in the movement.

The prewar joint program in Scandinavian language studies, alternating each summer between the Universities of Wisconsin and Minnesota, was the forerunner of the current series of summer institutes in Far Eastern languages sponsored by the Committee on Institutional Cooperation (the "Big Ten" plus Chicago). Perhaps the most widely publicized effort of the CIC is its traveling-scholars program, under which graduate students are registered at their home universities and pay fees there but have access to the resources of eleven institutions.[41] The plan was "dry-run" in summer before being extended to the fall and winter terms.

Other forms of interinstitutional alliance are lending new strengths to colleges and universities across the country. In many cases the summer term has been the cradle of the cooperation: witness, for example, the compact formed by Colorado colleges to advertise the halcyon climate of their summer campuses.

Minnesota's Dean E. W. Ziebarth is not sure that interinstitutional cooperation on the part of summer sessions will flower, even in the presence of growing national organizations. In a recent survey of selected universities,[42] Dr. Ziebarth found that, "of the 24 institutions which responded to my questions, 12 gave a generally negative reply, six responded with a qualified negative indicating real interest in cooperation but reflecting little action, and the remainder reported agonizingly slow and barely perceptible motion. There has been much discussion and very little action. We are still coming down the stairs bump, by bump, by bump, and my head aches from being banged in the same old way."

Dean Ziebarth admits, however, that "there are . . . some exceptions to the relatively gloomy picture I have been painting, and it would be possible to develop an impressive-sounding list of illustrations of joint action." He goes on to offer the following examples: Purdue has offered workshops on the Evansville College for Purdue credit; it has also worked with Ball State

[41] Kevin P. Bunnell and Eldon L. Johnson, "Interinstitutional Cooperation," in Baskin, *Higher Education,* pp. 246–271.

[42] "Interinstitutional Cooperation," in Schoenfeld, *Shape of Summer,* pp. 79–93.

and the Dunes Arts Foundation. The University of Missouri maintains cooperative graduate programs with two of the Missouri State Colleges. Northwestern has cooperated with other schools on field trips in geology. Illinois and Michigan are planning cooperative field work in geography in which each school will handle three weeks of work and a third school will handle the last two weeks. Columbia cooperates with Harvard and Cornell in a joint research course in ethnographic studies at several Latin American centers. The University of Minnesota operates a Ph.D. program in classics in cooperation with Iowa and Wisconsin. Minnesota is also beginning work on a Spanish language program with the Universities of Arizona and Guadalajara. Northwestern shares astronomy facilities with the University of Chicago. Colorado and the Colorado School of Mines exchange graduate students and instructors in certain engineering and geological courses. The University of Michigan was host to a five-school program this summer in Near Eastern studies. The University of Minnesota administers the Student Project for Amity among Nations (SPAN) for five other schools; the program involves projects in western European nations, in the Scandinavian countries, in the Orient, and in the Middle East.

In Summary

Whatever the exact configuration of their organization and administration, after decades of seemingly second-class citizenship most summer terms are finally attaining some degree of status within the university hierarchy. Most directors are part-time, but their impact on institutional policies and their ability to command financial support have grown considerably. With varying degrees of authority, they will be concerned with such administrative functions as admissions, registration, student affairs, contract negotiations, curricular planning, fiscal controls, personnel processes, and physical facilities. Most of these matters are being handled in ways increasingly similar to regular-year patterns, although there are still some exceptions.

The growth of regional and national organizations of summer

deans marks the professionalization of summer administration, facilitates the exchange of information, establishes a voice in Washington, tends to raise standards, and augurs well for increased interinstitutional cooperation. And progress in these areas in turn promises stimulation and guidance for the summer director in his varied roles and responsibilities.

# 6

## Summer Problems and Prospects

Conceived under Chautauqua canvas, the American university summer term has gradually assumed the trappings of academic respectability; in this evolution are the seeds of both its growth and its deterioration. The summer term is undoubtedly becoming more like the regular year. But will this "success" spoil the summer session? The answer may lie in the fact that the regular year is becoming more like the summer term, and the two together will stand or fall in terms of their ability to come to grips with and surmount some fundamental stresses playing upon all of American higher education today.

We have now pulled together most of what is known about summer education in American universities. By taking into account the available data and bringing to bear insights based on experience, we have tried to sketch a picture of summer students and their programs, summer professors and their practices, summer public services, and summer term administration. Now it is time to define the summer term's own continuing problems, as well as to present an agenda for the American university in summer in its larger role as an institution whose problems and goals reflect those of higher education in general, and whose traditional affinity for experimentation makes it an ideal workshop for solving those problems and attaining those goals.

## SOME PERENNIAL PROBLEMS

As we have seen, there is hardly anything the summer university has engaged in that somebody hasn't complained about—its motives, its length, its special programs, its advertising methods, its financial practices. Many of the old gripes are irrelevant now, but it is worth reviewing them as a backdrop to current stresses. Most basic, perhaps, the various summer session objectives outlined in Chapter 1 have been said by a few critics to be in fact rationalizations, secondary to the desire to milk the last hour of utilization out of campus facilities, and to augment the limited incomes of professors. There is really no answer to this charge other than to say it applies to any month of the year if it applies at all.

Another continuing complaint, dating from earliest times, has concerned the length of the summer term. Dean Charles S. Slichter wrote in 1927 that six weeks was too short a time in which to produce anything of educational value.[1] His successor felt in 1947 that the wartime fifteen-week summer semester had been too debilitating to both students and staff. Professors and deans continue their search for a magic number of weeks per summer term, but in blissful ignorance of the growing body of evidence that there is little correlation between student academic achievement and length of term, summer or winter.

Pedagogical institutes, off-campus summer science camps, travel courses, and other exotic types of summer enterprise have each drawn criticism as they have been introduced. They continue to be somewhat of an anathema to ultra-conservative faculty; but on the whole such programs are now generally

[1] "Debunking the Masters Degree," *Journal of the Association of American Universities*, XXVII (1927), 107–111.

recognized as acceptable, and even distinguished, aspects of university work.

Another age-old criticism of the summer term has focused on its methods of advertising. In their conventions, summer deans spend a lot of time talking about how best to promote their sessions, because they are all under the gun to "carry out programs of vigorous encouragement of students to take advantage of summer offerings."[2] Wisconsin's 1889 summer prospectus, for example, claimed that "The summer school aims to do earnest, vigorous work, but while seeking especially the patronage of those who spend the summer in this way, [it] affords also rare opportunities for those who seek a delightful summer resort for rest and enjoyment while carrying on one line of study." Suffice it to say this sort of approach has been and continues to be repugnant to all but the most irreverent professors, perhaps because it suggests that admissions standards are suspect.

Early summer terms, as we have shown, were often required to be self-supporting. Instructors, anxious to secure break-even enrollments, eagerly solicited students by unprofessional means, encouraged the imposition of punitive fees, or introduced academically dubious courses under the guise of experimentation. The central evil of insistence on self-sufficiency was responsible for these subsidiary mischiefs, but lax administration also played its part.

As summer terms were integrated into reputable college and university processes, serious efforts were made to overcome their flaws. Today all but a handful of the 1,300 United States summer terms accept on good faith summer credits from sister institutions, and at least a third of these have attained academic equality with the regular year.

It should be emphasized that there always were a considerable number of institutions where the old complaints found no application. Some charges stemmed from generalizing from but a single example. All summer terms have made progress toward alleviating any shortcomings. Says the U.S. Office of Education:

[2] *Special Report* (Madison: Wisconsin State Coordinating Committee for Higher Education, March 1963), p. 1.

Modern summer sessions, as seen in the survey of 1960, have generally eliminated or ameliorated the early defects noted. Their faculties compare favorably with those of the regular session in preparation and experience. Curriculums are standard and inclusive; unusual courses are generally offered as non-degree-credit workshops. Brevity remains—less than 30 per cent of 1960 summer sessions exceeded 8 weeks—but credit and time were carefully correlated. The most serious remaining deficiencies relate to financial policies. These, however, are not universal. Many sessions had overcome their major defects by 1960; some had none to overcome.[3]

If most old complaints have been answered, however, there are some newer needs—and a few older ones—that have not.

IMAGE

For one thing, summer session deans still appear to have an inferiority complex. Whenever they get together they inevitably complain to each other that their summer term is not properly appreciated. Take, for example, this statement from the Report of the Personnel Committee to the 1965 North Central Conference on Summer Schools by its chairman, Dean Forest L. Whan:

My own catalogue reads: "The Summer School is an integral part of the educational program at Kansas State University. Credit earned in K-State summer sessions is transferable to other institutions in the same manner credit earned in other terms is transferred." That our catalogues feel it necessary to so state suggests that our top administrators believe that doubt exists. Nowhere have I been able to find a university catalogue reading: "The fall semester is an integral part of the school program." We hear about student bodies in summer made up of those who fail courses during the regular terms. We hear about disinterested school teachers crowding summer sessions because they are forced to earn credit every so often in order to hold their jobs. We hear that heat and long days of sunlight are for some reason not conducive to the educational process. We hear that neither faculty nor students can do their best if attending school 11 months of the year. (Of course, no one seems to believe that administrators, research personnel, or other 12-month staff are doing poor work because their intellectual activity is not limited to a 9-month year.) All things con-

[3] Warner, et al., *Summer Sessions, 1960,* p. 90.

sidered, there can be little doubt that—regardless of the evidence or lack of evidence—the *image* of summer school is not of the best.[4]

Most of the summer deans at this Chicago convention nodded their agreement. Like most pictures in people's heads, the image of the American university summer term could probably stand some polishing. But the situation does not really seem as bad as summer deans would have each other believe. If all the deans who lack confidence in their wares could somehow undergo some sort of therapy, the summer term image would take on a rosier hue overnight.

TIME

One of the most critical problems of the modern summer term is that the time allotted to the director for his summer administrative duties needs in most instances to be substantially increased. The summer director must fight not only the calendar but the clock. What many presidents may not understand is that the most crucial chores associated with administering the summer term occur not in summer but in the period from November to May when the program and budget are being planned, and staff and physical facilities secured. Indeed, once the summer term opens there isn't much the director can do to influence the course of events other than to sit on student conduct committees. An honest half-time position the year round would seem to be the minimum assignment for a summer dean in an institution that expects to operate an acceptable summer term.

GETTING MONEY

Money is still the final factor which determines educational results. Getting enough money and spending it wisely is the alpha and omega of the summer session director's job. Most directors would say that wise spending is easier than getting. Whether his target is a president, a board of trustees, a foundation, or a legislature, the summer session director is faced annually or bien-

---

[4] Whan, "Report of the Personnel Committee," p. 2.

nially with explaining the needs of his program and documenting those areas that particularly warrant initiation, enlargement, enrichment, or improvement. At the present time the summer session director is riding the crest of public interest in expanded summer operations. That interest, however, is often expressed in terms of juggling the academic calendar in such a way as not to invest more money in education but rather to cut corners. The summer director must convince all parties as best he can that there is no special magic in any particular schedule, and that whenever education in greater quantity is a goal the price tag goes up unless quality is to suffer.

In addition, too many summer sessions are still asked to be self-supporting. As a result, they schedule only sure-bet courses, sign their professors up to sudden-death contracts, pay them below scale, and milk the students. There is simply no excuse for the summer term to enjoy anything but the same level of subsidy as that afforded the balance of the year, and there is no excuse for the summer instructor to be appointed and paid on other than the same basis as the winter instructor. Even faculty fringe benefits should be equal in summer to regular-year standards. Above all, summer fees should be their just proportion of semester or quarter fees. Fortunately this situation, too, is improving, at least according to one report:

Significant differences in status, objectives, composition of student body, length of term, and in salaries and fringe benefits between the academic year and summer have existed in American universities. Universities have been increasingly aware of these differences, and systematic plans have been put into effect during the past decade which have minimized and in many institutions have eliminated nearly all differences except term length and enrollment.[5]

Furthermore, as Maryland's Clodus Smith suggests, self-support need not even be an evil in itself:

The manner in which a university keeps its books has great implications on whether an institution is "self-supporting" in the summer months. We are on a so called "self-support" basis here at the University of Maryland. We are now approaching the 10,000 student

[5] *Year-Around Operation*, p. 17.

mark in the summer session and we feel no great pressures or limitations on what we may offer. We return to the University between $100,000 and $200,000, as based on our bookkeeping procedures.[6]

## GETTING STUDENTS

The plea that colleges and universities give serious consideration to those feasible means of enrollment expansion which may suit their peculiar conditions beats like a drum through the current literature of American higher education. "The greatest untapped potential in American higher education today is the resources of our institutions during the three summer months," has declared Dr. Harold Haswell, former director of higher education programs for the U.S. Office of Education.[7] This charge stems at least in part from an analysis of inadequate data—data, that is, that fail to reflect the research and service aspects of summer enterprise. The personnel and physical resources of many campuses are simply not as idle in summer as a consideration of conventional course enrollments alone would lead one to believe. Yet it would still be foolish to deny that some enrollment expansion is possible. Indeed, nearly a quarter of the institutions surveyed by Dr. Haswell's office in 1960 had plans for immediate expansion of their summer programs. Since this question cannot be divorced from the calendar question, however, let's examine the merits of such plans in this light.

## MAKING PEACE WITH THE CALENDAR

The calendar is probably one of the most critical issues facing the summer university today—in terms of its organization, its finances, its philosophy, its programing, its staffing, and, as we have said, its enrollment (on which many of the other questions in turn depend). We have already examined (in Chapter 5) the various calendar alternatives; and we have suggested some criteria for deciding among them. It is worth reviewing some of these now, with an eye to their broader implications.

---

[6] Personal correspondence in author's files.
[7] "Report from Washington," in Schoenfeld, *Shape of Summer*, p. 36.

Among the devices being held forth by some as a sure road to summer enrollment expansion is the trimester. As we have seen, on paper the trimester looks to be a good way to increase student patronage the year round while economizing on capital investment. Yet in practice it has run up against two very tough questions: What do you do about the teachers and other professional groups who want to come to the summer campus in increasing numbers for short sessions? And how do you get students to attend and professors to teach in summer without using police actions for which neither parents nor presidents have the stomach? The fact is that, until summer curricula, summer credits, and summer scholarships are equal to regular-year standards in every respect, measurable numbers of students will choose to absent themselves from the campus between June and September. P. C. Weaver summarizes this situation as follows:

From the point of view of parents and students, ways must be found by which they may be convinced that summer study brings rewards that are of greater personal, cultural, and economic value than the returns the students are now receiving from their traditional summer experiences. As of the present, I have not met any undergraduate students who are possessed of such a high patriotic or civic sense of obligation that they will attend summer sessions merely for the sake of keeping the institutions operating on a year-round basis . . . . I'm firmly convinced that young people will not come to summer school in numbers unless they are under compulsion to do so.[8]

Furthermore, even if summer study offered benefits equal to those of the regular year—as is often the case with a trimester system—there would still be a good many students who would rather just take a vacation. It is foolhardy to call for "the development of a year-around American way of life in which vacation opportunities, employment, and study opportunities are sought throughout the year."[9] The summer as a vacation period is not going to dry up and blow away simply because a campus committee wills it. It is too deeply imbedded in American folkways, climatic conditions, industrial practices, agricultural pursuits, and

[8] "The Summer Calendar," ibid., p. 49.
[9] *Report of the University Calendar Study Committee* (mimeographed, Ann Arbor: University of Michigan, June 19, 1958), p. 3.

family traditions. Equally ingrained is the attitude that the tempo of life is different in summer, that somehow this is a period when life is easier, a period not conducive to "productivity." And thus many educators believe that "we are never going to make the summer period the equal of others so long as such attitudes prevail";[10] that "The likelihood of maintaining an even enrollment level throughout the year seems remote, for climate, vacation habits, cultural attitudes, the need students have for summer income—all tend to curtail the size of summer college enrollments."[11]

Which brings us now to the question of whether we even *want* to increase summer enrollments to the extent that students are pushed into pursuing summer study. Perhaps speaking as a parent, Lawrence Dennis expresses concern about the severe academic pressures that begin in junior high and mount through the school years until "the pursuit of excellence" may finally take its toll of the mental health of graduate students, to the detriment of society.[12] When a university encourages with too much stringency a regimen of year-round study, it could be contributing to the deterioration of the personalities of adolescents, Mr. Dennis implies. Could it be that "the good old summertime" ought to continue to be just that—a period of occasional withdrawal from the acknowledged tensions of tests, test tubes, and theses?

In sum, it seems a far better alternative to seize on the new American summer leisure to convert occasional idle hours into fruitful hours than to founder in a mass assault on a calendar that is made more of iron than of rubber. To offer to provide many more Americans with meaningful summer educational experiences of varying lengths and breadths is in the best interests of college and community. To attempt to remodel American life or to push students to their breaking point is the rankest effrontery.

And above all we should keep in mind that universities do not

<hr>

10 R. W. Fleming, former Chancellor, University of Wisconsin, Madison, personal correspondence in author's files.
11 *Report to Pittsburgh*, p. 9.
12 "Will Success Spoil Higher Education?" p. 56.

*need* to engage in compulsory summer attendance practices in order to assure a high level of year-round operations. The American university operates year-round now, with programs of teaching, research, and educational services that scarcely break step from one month to the next and that are virtually as strong in summer as in fall, and considerably more varied. Rather than resorting to Gestapo-like tactics in dragooning students and instructors into summer classrooms, then, the American university can continue its outstanding record of voluntary year-round operation through strong summer instructional periods of from two to twelve weeks in length, coupled with continuing research programs, and expanded adult education, extension, and public service activities.[13] It would, in fact, be a great loss if the summer university were to sacrifice such programs for the sake of maintaining a uniform enrollment level of "regular" students. We must therefore add our voice to Robert Clark's, when he says, "Let us extend the academic year into the summer quarter or trimester, and schedule academic year courses for the summer, but alongside, let us continue old programs, distinctive to the summer session, and let us foster new ones."[14]

ADMISSIONS STANDARDS

As if getting students to come to summer school weren't enough of a problem in itself, the summer director is also faced with the problem of admissions standards. Are these, he is continually asked, the same as the standards applied for regular-year students? There is no black and white answer to this question, because student categories are not the same in summer as in fall. In general, however, we can say that, so far as students admitted to candidacy for a degree are concerned, summer admissions standards are identical to those of the fall. In fact, the rules are usually determined by the same committee and administered by the same staff person.

[13] For a different appraisal of "Year-Round Operation," see Robert L. Dickins and Robert H. Ballantine, *Educational Record*, Fall 1966, pp. 467–473.
[14] 1966 NACUSS *Proceedings*, p. 17.

There, however, the similarity ceases. For you typically have in summer, in addition to degree candidates, the "special student" category, which is either unknown or largely unused in the fall. These students, while their long-range goals may be no different from those of the regular students, are summer-only transients, and they are admitted under special arrangements. Let us review the categories of students whom the university will admit as summer specials with a minimum of red tape. These include: (1) The student from another college who is visiting for the summer and who is readmissable to his parent institution the following fall. At some universities most such students will be undergraduates from afar who are attracted by rich course offerings—or lakes and mountains. On other campuses most such specials will be local residents home for the summer. (2) The school teacher or administrator with a bachelor's degree back to pick up professional credits but not for formal graduate work. (3) The adult pursuing ad hoc educational objectives. (4) The superior high school junior accelerating or enriching his education by taking a regular college course.

In addition to these groups, some schools are beginning to make a practice of admitting "borderline" degree applicants as summer specials, and allowing them to stay on in the fall if they prove themselves academically. According to a recent survey of eighty state universities (reported at the April 1966 NCC meeting), forty-five admit borderline applicants for a trial run in summer. Ferris State College in Michigan reports 50 per cent success in "salvaging" young men and women. The State College of Iowa has employed the practice since 1959, with retention rates running from 8 to 75 per cent a summer. Indiana University admitted a test group of thirty-five in the summer of 1965; thirteen (37 per cent) earned high enough GPA's to qualify for fall admission. The performance of none of these groups correlated with normal screening devices. In later semesters their grades tended to decline, but a significant number persisted. Men tended to do better than women.

Until our means of predicting academic success become much more refined, increasing numbers of summer deans will undoubtedly use actual classroom performance as a means of determining the best bets from among the thousands of supplicants at their doors. And the only student who is clearly not admissible, even as a summer special, is the student who has simply "flunked out" someplace.

This eclectic summer special student category has earned for the summer term the disapproval of some educators and the praise of others. The former say summer specials tend to constitute a sort of smog that contaminates the scholarly air of the campus. The latter say summer specials contribute a valuable maturity and cosmopolitanism to the summer student body. As we have already pointed out, however, what little research has been done on the subject suggests that "for all students, summer grade point averages are above those of the fall semester."[15] Both sides claim this proves their point!

GETTING INSTRUCTORS

A summer session's instructional program is no better, and no worse, than the instructors doing the teaching. Getting and placing instructors constitutes one of the central tasks faced by directors, deans, and department chairmen in summer. In many departments the competition for good men is intense—from the research program, from the educational service program, from other institutions, and from the lure of independent study and relaxation.[16] In other departments on the same campus, there may be a surplus of professors, each hopeful of an appointment. Asked recently to list "special problems" they face, midwestern

[15] "Evaluation of the Trial Study Program at West Virginia Wesleyan College," *West Virginia Wesleyan Reports* (mimeographed, Buckhannon: West Virginia Wesleyan College, 1965), p. 7.

[16] "The market for summer faculty has expanded almost in geometric proportions in recent years. This expansion has resulted to a large extent from growing enrollments, coupled with increasing demands of business, industry, and government for highly trained staff. In addition, however, the national and even international orientation of the faculty has encompassed summer employment. Communication within each profession has become such that a faculty member no longer offers his time and loyalties primarily to his own institution." Richey and Gwaltney, *Summer at Indiana*, p. 66.

summer school deans tended to emphasize faculty personnel matters. These comments are typical:

Some departments (such as education and psychology) often have to seek outside help for the summer, and other groups (such as teachers of freshman composition) desire to teach more frequently than positions are available for them.

Institutes and research grants attract many of our better faculty members, as do other institutions, often after our program is in print.

In some departments more people want to work than we can provide for . . . . In other departments it's difficult for us to compete with other institutions.[17]

Complicating the situation is the fact that it is often difficult to get faculty members and their department chairmen to crystallize their plans early and make firm commitments. Research opportunities tend to take priority over instruction, no matter how late they "break"; and outside funds are notorious for arriving at the last minute. Even institute and conference staffing can disrupt the regular curriculum. In some institutions the summer session dean may be able to exact teaching contracts from professors; but in most cases he can only roll with the punch, publish an amended timetable of courses—and keep smiling.

CONTROLLING EDUCATIONAL SERVICES

The mushrooming program of summer conferences and institutes presents three problems—quality control, quantity control, and the much-discussed problem of "federal control" (dealt with in Chapter 4). The university is under increasing pressure from government agencies, from industry, and from lay groups to offer a growing array of summer educational experiences. When these programs draw legitimately on the skills and resources of the campus, and when suitable faculty members are fully involved in curriculum planning and execution, clinics and workshops can be among the most exciting and worthwhile of the

---

[17] Whan, "Report of the Personnel Committee," p. 7.

summer university's ventures. But if the summer session director allows his institution to become little more than a hotel-keeper for this or that convention, he does both campus and clientele a disservice.

The physical resources of the campus are not unlimited. Some rationing of time and space among educational services may become necessary. In particular, the summer session director may have to enter the arena of long-range plant planning—to incorporate adult education criteria in dormitory design, to add suitable rooms to the student union, or to put air conditioning in the continuing education building.

### CONTROLLING AND SUPERVISING RESEARCH

This final problem of the summer university is really a "problem" only for the director; but his decisions and the criteria by which he makes them have important implications for the quality and depth of the summer program as a whole. As with educational services, the research program must be carefully geared to the skills and resources of the particular campus, and should not be emphasized to the extent that it encroaches on the two other major functions of the summer university: in this case, instruction and service.

In those instances where, for one reason or another, the summer session director administers summer research programs, he enters the maze of contract negotiations. There are so few landmarks here that large universities typically assign a special staff officer the sole task of reviewing proposals, checking the fine print in grant documents, and generally assisting in fiscal control.

Since the most important criteria for deciding among the various sorts of proposals should be fully apparent at this point, it seems most useful to approach the research question from the administrative end. There is "big" research and there is "little" research. "Big" research is exemplified by some of the research in physics which involves teams of scientists and the construction of expensive apparatus, such as high energy particle accelerators. "Little" research is carried on by individuals, using sometimes nothing more than books, and costing on the order of $20,000 per project per year at most.[18]

In addition, the summer director has basically two types of research agreements from which to choose in his dealings with the donor—the contract and the grant. The fixed-price contract generally provides for a firm price or an adjustable price for services which are to be provided. It is used most often in projects involving goods and services rather than research and development. To further clarify or confuse, depending on your eye for legal jargon, there are three offshoots of the fixed-price contract: the firm fixed-price contract, the fixed-price contract with escalation, and the cost-reimbursement contract.

In contrast to contracted research, inquiry also may be supported by grants. Such grants may provide, in many cases, a more desirable means of entering into a broad research program. The grant is typically distinguished from the contract on four counts: the research goals tend to be somewhat broader; a lump sum of money is awarded (whereas there are monthly billings under contract); there is low overhead recovery (as much as 75 to 80 per cent lower than under contract); and only a single final report is required (multiple reports are usually required under a contract).

Typically, any research agreement is composed of "common" provisions such as conformance with the Hatch Act, "special" provisions such as restrictions on the publication of data, and "specific" provisions such as describing in detail the task to be accomplished.[19]

MAKING THE MOST OF WHAT WE'VE GOT

The most overriding summer problem, however, is one we have touched on almost everywhere else: How can the summer term be strengthened with a view to inducing greater voluntary utili-

---

[18] Frank T. Dietz, "American Science, Government, and Education," *Phi Kappa Phi Journal*, Winter 1966, p. 9.

[19] Joe H. Munster, Jr., and Justin C. Smith, "A Second Look at Government-Supported Research," *Educational Record*, Spring 1965, pp. 149–157.

zation of campus facilities? On its answers to this question will depend the very future of the summer term; and the answers themselves will depend largely on how summer administrators handle some of the problems we have already posed. Let's review them, therefore, in the light of making the best possible use of campus facilities without coercion:

1. Summer attendance is in part a reflection of curricular offerings. A poverty-stricken list of courses furnishes little incentive for the regular student to stay, or for the visiting student to come. Each university department should contemplate curriculum expansion and enrichment, with an eye particularly to upper-division programs.

2. Summer attendance is in part, too, a reflection of faculty strength. Where the "name" professors are absent in summer, students will be also. Salaries, fringe benefits, and reward systems need to be reviewed with an eye to encouraging summer teaching.

3. Serious efforts must be made to increase financial aid for summer students. Such persons incur a double expense: they must meet the costs of summer attendance while sacrificing income from a seasonal job. Scholarship and loan policies and practices must come to recognize the place of the summer term. Fee reductions may be in order in summer.

4. To increase campus plant utilization and to enable the student to earn maximum credits, some calendar juggling may be desirable. For example, an eight-week session can become a nine- or ten-week session, or a nine- or ten-week session can become two five-week terms.

5. Research activities may lend themselves to more emphasis in summer, particularly those programs requiring extra manpower or benefiting from outdoor investigations.

6. The utility of the summer campus as a site for a wide range of continuing education programs has scarcely been scratched. Youths and adults, housewives and doctors, lathe operators and physicists, bassoon players and engineers—all are ready to convert the new American leisure to purposeful pursuits at the institution which will but construct meaningful learning experiences

on a scale and of a caliber commensurate with public needs and desires.

William Stirton, Vice-President of the University of Michigan, has stated both the problem and its solution more succinctly:

> I know only two institutions that are less efficient in the use of their plant than the schools—I think of the church and I think of the race-tracks; perhaps I should include some consideration of voting booths. Seriously, I am sure that we in the universities can't get by with this casual usage forever . . . . I would suggest that we disassociate our thinking from the conventional traditional summer session which simply filled the interstitial spaces between semesters, and instead think of the tremendous impact and tremendous effect on university relations that can be engendered through a modern summer term concerned with anticipating and meeting modern community and personal needs and giving leadership in the evolution of educational techniques necessary in this increasingly complex society.[20]

A CASE IN POINT

In approaching these various summer term problems, one must be careful to distinguish between those which are merely tactical and those which are strategic. A "problem," according to former Chancellor Robert M. Hutchins of the University of Chicago, is a technical difficulty in the material order; a real *problem* is a confusion about the aim and destiny of the university. *Problems* are seldom exaggerated. "Problems" usually are. As Lord Eustace Percy, rector of the Newcastle Division of Durham University, once said, "Of all modern habits, the worst is to advertise every human activity as a 'problem.' It is bad for morale, as any commander of a military unit knows. The first rule in dealing with human beings is—don't fuss. So with universities."[21]

In the midst of drastic changes in the material requirements of education, it is difficult for university administrators to keep their attention focused on their real problems, so insistent are the "problems" of buildings, equipment, and finance. Yet only to the extent that the real problems of the university can be recognized

---

[20] "The Summer Session in University Relations," pp. 1, 5.
[21] Personal correspondence in author's files.

and solved can the institution and its summer term keep their sense of direction. To make things even worse, however, rarely will summer term problems present themselves neatly packaged and labeled as "tactical" or "strategic." In facing seemingly mundane issues the administrator may actually confront fundamental questions, and in attempting to resolve global conflicts he will inevitably stir up picayune debates. It may be revealing, therefore, to look at a series of actual summer problems recently verbalized by one institution, and to examine that university's response:

*Question No. 1:* Increasingly, schools and colleges are placing professors in the summer sessions budget for consultation with graduate students, thesis advisement, and administration of examinations. Do we need to formulate any general criteria as to what constitutes a minimum "full load"? At present the practices vary considerably from department to department.

*Response to No. 1:* Budgeting faculty time on summer session funds for the purpose of giving individual instruction (as distinguished from formal classroom instruction) to graduate students should be governed by the following considerations:

(a) The university should not take unfair advantage of its faculty. In particular, it should not expect summer staff to direct individually *large* numbers of graduate students in addition to teaching a full course load, nor should it expect faculty not receiving any summer compensation to give more than nominal attention to graduate students during the summer.

(b) On the other hand, the university's resources are not unlimited, and it cannot afford to make *special* budgetary provision for a fraction of faculty time for every graduate student who requests individual instruction.

(c) In judging how far it can afford to budget specific faculty time in summer for individual graduate instruction, the university would do well to remember that it in effect gets a good deal of such instruction "free," since many faculty members in the natural and social sciences who draw summer salary from a federal or gift account are supervising research assistants who by definition are candidates for a graduate degree and are therefore receiving in connection with their research assistantships the very kind of individual instruction which otherwise might have to be provided by faculty paid from the summer sessions budget.

(d) Since the need for, and the resources available to provide, individual graduate instruction in summer vary so widely from college to college and department to department, no fixed formulae are desirable. Specific judgments as to the extent and method of budgeting faculty time for this purpose should be made at the college level by departments in consultation with their dean. The dean should record in his files any specific arrangements made.

*Question No. 2:* Some departments, schools, and colleges reflect the administrative time of chairmen and deans in the summer sessions budget. Others do not. Again, should we seek some minimum uniformity or should we continue to indulge in a variety of practices?

*Response to No. 2:* Great flexibility is necessary and desirable among the various colleges, schools, and departments with respect to reflecting in the summer sessions budget the administrative time of chairmen, directors, and deans; to the end that, throughout the year, all appropriate personnel are adequately compensated for their roles in institutional management, in keeping with prudent fiscal policies.

*Question No. 3:* Some students come to the campus on stipends to participate in a special institute or course which itself is funded by grant monies. Are we correct in saying that such students must pay additional fees if they enroll in or audit a conventional course?

*Response to No. 3:* When certain students come to the campus on stipends to participate in a special institute or course which itself is funded by grant monies, such students must pay additional fees if they enroll in or audit regular courses.

*Question No. 4:* Summer non-credit youth programs are proliferating. In general, we say that the fees for each clinic should attempt to cover out-of-pocket costs. Since the instructional costs vary from clinic to clinic, we wind up with a variety of fees. Is this sound? With some clinics we say that the director of each institute is responsible for his charges twenty-four hours a day. With other clinics, an agent of the summer sessions office and residence halls is responsible for out-of-class activities and "policing." The present disparity in practice is dictated by housing configurations. As more varied housing arrangements become available, which of the two administrative policies should we encourage? Should we turn the whole non-credit operation over to extension? Should we insist on fees for all adult conferences as we do for all youth programs?

*Response to No. 4:* The following policies are suggested with respect to high school clinics:

(a) It is desirable that fees for each clinic should attempt to recover out-of-pocket costs, and it is hence defensible for the fees to vary from clinic to clinic.

(b) The responsibility for curricular and co-curricular matters with respect to each clinic should reside in the sponsoring academic department; and, as far as possible, housing arrangements should be such as to facilitate clinic independence. The summer sessions office, however, in concert with the office of student housing, must promulgate and supervise minimum standards of counseling and deportment.

With respect to adult conferences, it is necessary and desirable that there be great flexibility in sponsorship, administration, funding, fees, and so on; in general, the summer sessions office should encourage and assist conferences and institutes that grow out of or are intimately associated with the regular credit instructional program.

*Question No. 5:* Summer sessions budgeting has been distinguished by a certain lack of foresight. How can the summer sessions office be assisted in developing more accurate projections of staff needs, course needs, enrollments, and fee income (credit and non-credit) at the time biennial budget requests are formulated?

*Response to No. 5:* The respective deans will assist the summer sessions office in developing biennial program projections, fee income estimates, and budget requests.

Such tactical problems and strategic concerns as are typified in this case in point may be more susceptible to solution simply because they are summer term matters. At least the record is quite clear that, in the past and present, the summer university is in the forefront of institutional innovation.

## An Agenda for the Summer University

There is good evidence that more significant experimentation is taking place in higher education today than at any other time in our nation's history;[22] and the university summer term, whose eclectic quality makes it a fruitful setting for innovation, is intimately involved in many of these newer developments. At the same time, however, it faces certain problems, some of which, as we have seen, are peculiar to its own nature and operations, but others of which are reflections of those problems currently faced by higher education in general. John Gardner, formerly president of the Carnegie Corporation, and now Secretary of Health, Education, and Welfare, has recently outlined some of these problems, calling them "the major problems and challenges facing our colleges and universities . . . in this most exciting and trying period in their history."[23] At about the same time Lawrence E. Dennis, former editor of *The Educational Record*, pinpointed several factors contributing to what he termed "the crisis of integrity in college education."[24] Drawing upon the insights of both of these men, and bringing them to a focus within the larger context suggested by Baskin and the various contributors to his book, we may now present an agenda for the summer university in its emerging posture as an integral aspect of year-round higher education.

### Restoring the Status of Teaching

In competition with graduate research and public services, the teaching function, particularly the teaching of undergraduates, is being slighted today, says Dr. Gardner. The summer dean feels

[22] Baskin, *Higher Education*, p. vi.
[23] "Agenda for the Colleges and Universities," *Journal of Higher Education*, October 1965, pp. 359–365.
[24] "Will Success Spoil Higher Education?"

the downgrading of the teaching role in excruciating ways, He is constantly being asked to revise his course timetable because this or that professor has "received a research grant." He is constantly being asked to appoint a young teaching assistant in lieu of the senior professor who is advising in Laramie or Laos. He has to listen to the complaints of students disenchanted by the platform performance of the faculty member who may be a distinguished scholar but is a dud in the classroom.

Restoring the status of teaching is both a simple and an extremely difficult problem. Were undergraduate instruction to assume its rightful place among the criteria used to determine qualifications for professorial appointment, retention, promotion, and pay raises, we would see a rapid reform; but to do so would require monstrous changes in university personnel policies and processes. The summer term could participate in an immediate and effective way by granting to its teaching staff a somewhat higher salary scale than that enjoyed by summer researchers or extensionists; by awarding the successful summer teacher "credits" toward promotion; or by giving a semester or quarter sabbatical for every so many summer terms spent teaching.

## IMPROVEMENT OF TEACHING

The status of the teaching function and the quality of teaching are obviously related problems; a decline in one means a decline in the other. Hence the need for devoting special efforts to the preparation and in-service training of professors has become increasingly important. The most extensive and persistent project for faculty improvement is that sponsored by the North Central Association of Colleges, embracing approximately a hundred liberal arts and teachers colleges in the midwest. Three workshops, each of four weeks' duration, are conducted each summer at the Universities of Michigan and Minnesota, where representatives from the colleges may study current developments in higher education and prepare for stronger leadership in projects back home. During recent summers, the Danforth Foundation has fostered somewhat similar three-week workshops, usually on the campus of Colorado College.

Since 1958 the National Defense Education Act has sponsored many summer institutes to strengthen teaching in science, mathematics, foreign languages, and guidance. While aimed primarily at school teachers, the NDEA institutes have had a salutary effect on college teaching, according to the U.S. Office of Education.

Another approach to this problem, Dennis suggests, is through a drastic overhaul of graduate education, whereby adequate time and attention may be given in graduate programs to the preparation of college teachers. It is one of the great anomalies of American education that a prospective kindergarten teacher must run the gauntlet of suitable professional courses and practice teaching in order to gain state certification, while a college instructor can be appointed without having been exposed to a single moment of systematic study or practical experience in the science and art of teaching. While we might quibble over the number and type of courses necessary to achieve teaching proficiency, it is utterly absurd to claim a modern school of education has nothing at all worthwhile to say to the prospective professor.[25]

The summer term would appear to be an ideal time to introduce into the Ph.D. sequence a decent amount of pedagogical study for those who seek to join our faculties, just as it has become a time for orienting public school teachers to the dimensions of the inquiring mind.

REFORMING THE UNDERGRADUATE CURRICULUM

We cannot of course isolate the problem of teaching quality from the question of what material is to be taught. For this reason Dr. Gardner includes in his agenda a thoroughgoing reform of the undergraduate curriculum, featuring new aims, new teaching aids and methods, more use of independent study, and interdisciplinary approaches—within each field, yet focused on that "breadth so essential for young people." This is no easy task; for the typical professor, appointed because of his grasp of an increasingly narrow field of investigation, is remarkably un-

---

[25] Russell L. Cooper, "Improving College Teaching and Administration," in Baskin, *Higher Education*, p. 197.

qualified to evaluate present undergraduate programs and envisage new dimensions and techniques.[26] Yet enduring curricular reform must come from the faculty if it is to come at all, and if undergraduate programs are to keep in touch with the world in which today's students will be living. The summer term could contribute both the time needed for studying the problem and the place needed for experimentation.[27]

The summer university has already taken some significant steps toward developing a curriculum that can meet the requirements of our complex society. It has responded to society's demands for sophisticated training or retraining of its manpower by presenting specialized sequences for undergraduates and specialized seminars for alumni. At the same time it has responded to a renewed interest in general, or basic, education by affording an opportunity to experiment with integrated liberal studies. It has also reflected in its curriculum the new emphasis on education for world affairs. This trend is typified by the novel area-studies courses offered in summer at Minnesota, Michigan, Wisconsin, and other midwestern universities on a cooperative basis. Mention should also be made of a number of national commissions formed to improve the content and presentation of various courses. Commissions on college physics and on undergraduate mathematics, for example, did much of their work at summer conferences, and are now upgrading or retraining college instructors through summer refresher courses. Finally, the summer university has offered continuing education programs pursued under the auspices of a firm or the government.

The summer term has also proved itself a valuable testing ground for at least four other sorts of curricular innovation: independent study, foreign study, programs for "special" students, and new instructional media. It is worth reviewing these developments briefly, as examples of the possibilities inherent in summer experimentation.

*Independent Study.* The many current attempts to make

[26] Sanford, *College and Character,* p. 10.
[27] For a thorough discussion of "Undergraduate Curriculum Reform," see Christopher Jencks, R. J. Henk, William F. Brazziel, and Donald Bors, *Educational Record,* Summer 1966, pp. 303–346.

greater use of independent study as a means of instruction apparently stem from two forces. For one thing, many senior faculty members are inaccessible from time to time because of research leaves; so the undergraduate must rely more heavily on a variety of surrogates for the immediately present professor. Secondly, new theories of learning and new media of instruction suggest that many students can learn at least as well on their own.[28] One of the earliest forms of independent study was the "independent reading" period of three weeks which followed the six-week period of classroom instruction in a number of summer sessions in the 1930's. Modifications of this pattern are being revived today, to the end that increasingly the summer professor is not so much a dispenser of information as he is a designer and manager of the student's learning.

*Foreign Study.* The student abroad has now become an established part of the American educational landscape. The growth of the movement has been spectacular: in 1950 there were only six programs through which undergraduates could earn credits abroad during the academic year; in 1963–64 there were over 120 programs of many different types. It is not too much to say that the summer session was the cradle of the overseas study movement. Some early summer programs, it must be admitted, were little more than Cook's tours, with the real initiative coming from a travel bureau, "whose blandishments are hardly to be resisted by the professor who is promised a free trip abroad in return for signing up the required number of customers and inducing his college to grant academic credit."[29] Fortunately, however, a number of pioneer overseas programs in summer were very solid projects, at least as demanding as residence instruction, and thoroughly integrated with the domestic curriculum. Out of these programs has grown today's proliferation of foreign study programs, in which the summer university continues to participate and experiment.

*The Special Student.* At least since October 4, 1957, the date of Sputnik, American higher education has experienced a surge

[28] See Bruce Dearing, "The Student on His Own," in Baskin, *Higher Education*, pp. 49–76.
[29] Irwin Abrams, "The Student Abroad," ibid., pp. 79–102.

of concern for the abler student: identifying him earlier, motivating him more surely, and accelerating or intensifying his education. The summer session has proved to be ideally suited to various forms of challenging instruction. As we have suggested before, a summer college program for abler high school students is one way the universities now reach down to give youngsters a taste of college and influence their attitudes while they are still in secondary school. The teaching arrangements that are at the heart of various honors programs for promising undergraduates typically include summer projects in the form of special seminars, independent research, or off-campus work.[30]

Concern for the abler student is matched by a continuing concern for the student with an indifferent record who may be salvageable. Here, too, the summer session plays a role, by giving such students an opportunity to take remedial coursework or simply to boost a sagging grade-point average.

*The New Media.* Televised instruction, programed learning, language laboratories, instructional films, multi-media centers, computers—the spin-off from the technological revolution—are invading the campus. Much of the experimentation has taken place in summer. The summer term has been used particularly for the in-service training of teachers and instructors in the use of the new media. As a science of human learning develops, the newer media systems will be used more extensively and will provide rapid assessment of student learning;[31] the summer university can be expected to continue to play a key role in refining the technology of teaching.

IMPROVING THE INSTITUTION

Improving institutional planning, learning hard lessons about deliberate diversity among institutions and effective cooperation between institutions—these are tasks for the administrator. Here again the summer term can participate by providing time for analysis and place for innovation.

[30] Maxwell H. Goldberg and Norman D. Kurland, "The Abler Student," ibid., pp. 104–126.
[31] C. R. Carpenter and L. P. Greenhill, "Providing the Conditions of Learning," ibid., pp. 128–151.

More and more the job requirements for college administration, as for teaching, are demanding a new kind, or at least a new level, of expertise. In attempting to change college administration from amateurism to professionalism, again the summer university has already had a hand. At the University of Michigan's Center for the Study of Higher Education, some sixty presidents and deans spend a week each June. Harvard has for several years conducted a similar institute. The American Association of Colleges for Teacher Education sponsors each summer a school for executives. So does the Association of American Colleges. Since 1948 Oklahoma State has played host to an annual Summer Conference of Academic Deans.[32] The annual Association of University Summer Sessions meeting itself constitutes an in-service training seminar.

A further problem, however, is that the rise of a cadre of academic administrators, in but not of the faculty community, has created a growing campus chasm, or so Mr. Dennis believes. Research on students is conducted by administrators but not utilized by advisors or instructors. Communications between the administration, the student body, and the staff often are sporadic and jammed by static. Meanwhile some faculty members continue to be caught up in the busywork of committees to the detriment of their scholarly pursuits.

This is part of what Dr. Gardner is talking about when he expresses concern that the campus has lost its sense of *community*. Only a viable community, he believes, can defend its autonomy and shape its future. He traces the decline in campus *esprit* to the mutually related factors of size, student unrest, the rise of professorial "guilds," and the intrusion of government ties. We need, he says, new physical configurations that will mitigate the impact of the campus sprawl, new patterns for the personalization of student life, new dialogues among academic departments; and we need to resist outside demands that diminish the internal coherence of our institutions.

It is beyond the capabilities of the summer term dean to mount a global attack on his university's administrative syndrome, but it does behoove him to set an example of enlightened

---

[32] Cooper, ibid., pp. 196–221.

conduct. The educational world will no longer tolerate institutional autocrats any more than business will retain old-fashioned captains of industry. Modern Americans, and college professors and students particularly, do not respond to dictatorial fiats. The effective campus administrator today must be a man who can serve as a leader, not a task master, by so embodying the spirit of the faculty that he seems indeed to be led; and who can enlist the cooperation of students because he is cooperative with them. He must be partner and colleague, accepting the role of quiet counselor yet always seeking to be a goad, a catalyst, and a servant in helping others achieve their goals and in adapting those special goals to university ends.[33]

### INCREASED PUBLIC SERVICE

While we seek to establish a greater internal coherence in our institutions of higher education, we must not allow ourselves to forget or underrate the university's traditional responsibilities to the publics it serves. After his hitch as president of Princeton, Dennis reminds us, Woodrow Wilson told a group of alumni that "nothing can be private in a university; everything is public." Yet some institutions continue to live in splendid isolation, with no sense of public accountability. More still have ignored the "forgotten fifth" of our population—the culturally deprived who live in disease, poverty, and illiteracy in our urban and rural slums.

We need, for one thing, to bring the city man and his manifold stresses into the same organic relationship with his university as that enjoyed for fifty years between the farmer and his land-grant college. Crime, poverty, racial conflict, slum housing, air and water pollution, inadequate schools and hospitals, strangled highways, vanishing open spaces—these and other symptoms of America's "mis-development" may lend themselves to the same kind of attack as did grade cows, depleted soil, and backward townships. There are no institutions better equipped to serve as a base for urban educational services than colleges

[33] Ibid., p. 197.

and universities imbued with a sense of public service and equipped with vigorous extension divisions and summer terms. And thanks to federal and foundation support, an increasing number of universities have launched a variety of programs of expanding opportunities and compensatory education. Significantly, several of these programs are functions of the summer term, which traditionally has had the most public stance of any of the university's periods.

One of the more important aspects of a university's public service program is its emphasis on what may be called the "right to education." Twenty years ago a President's Commission on Higher Education declared: "If education is to make the attainment of a more perfect democracy one of its major goals, it is imperative that it extend its benefits to all on equal terms."[34] How far we still are from a realization of that dream! While some institutions have assumed leadership roles, others have taken shelter behind high standards of admission, using them cynically to screen out those who have mental capacity but have been poorly prepared for college through no fault of their own.[35]

What can the universities and their summer terms do to encourage our disadvantaged minority groups to make the best use of their educational opportunities? Perhaps they can make a solid contribution by providing a different sort of preparation for the teachers they train: "We need to emphasize the preparation of teachers for the slum school, not the school in the suburb," says one writer. And "we must acknowledge that the real problems of civil rights are not found exclusively in the South."[36] The call to public duty in behalf of the educationally disenfranchised should not sound strange to the ears of the summer term, founded as it was to serve the irregular students of the day.

The right to education is being denied not only to the traditional minority groups. Equally victims are those middle-class students of borderline brains and pocketbooks barred from col-

[34] *Higher Education for American Democracy: Establishing the Goals* (Washington: U.S. Government Printing Office, 1947), p. 38.

[35] John A. Hannah, "Civil Rights and the Public Universities," *Journal of Higher Education*, February 1966, p. 64.

[36] Ibid., pp. 66–67.

leges where rising admission fences and fees are creating economic ghettos favoring the wealthy, talented few. Such institutions hold dearly to a tenacious tradition that quality and size correlate negatively. They aid so-called "needy" students who are permitted to include in their annual budgets hundreds of dollars for travel expenses, fraternity and sorority dues, and plush dormitory rooms, while ignoring those economically and socially underprivileged youths who could commute to the campus. These colleges may continue to enjoy financial success, but their relevancy to society will wither.[37] They may produce an elite class of technicians, but this "elitocracy" will become increasingly less competent to deal with the social situations to which it has never been exposed. A separation of the superior will gain little educationally and will be offset by the creation of a civically incompetent minority.[38]

If they are unable or unwilling to make room for a cross-section of America in the fall, more institutions could leave the doors to learning wider ajar in summer. A growing number are doing so. Under one pattern, the summer term fosters courses and curricula for special students from minority colleges who will return to their parent campuses in the fall. Under another pattern, the summer term is used as a screening device to test the promise of young people who would otherwise be declared inadmissible. This practice has as its rationale a number of studies which indicate, first, that actual campus performance is a much more accurate predictor of college success than are national tests or rank in high school class, and second, that the summer is indeed a favorable time for a freshman to demonstrate his capacity.[39]

INSTITUTIONAL RESEARCH

Perhaps the most pressing item of all for the summer agenda is our own lack of self-knowledge. The paucity of information on

[37] Frampton Davis, "Are the Liberal Arts Colleges Pricing Themselves Out of Existence?" *College and University Journal*, Winter 1966, pp. 25–29.

[38] Earl J. McGrath, "The Liberal Arts Today," *College and University Journal*, Winter 1966, pp. 42–48.

[39] Lins, et al., *Comparison of New Freshmen*.

most aspects of the summer term is evident at every turn. As one writer has said, "Truly what we don't know about the Summer Session is hurting us. What is sorely needed is a major action-oriented research program, coupled with a carefully designed dissemination program which will not only get at the facts but see that they are called appropriately to the attention of educators and the public alike. Such research effort should be planned and directed by those responsible for the Nation's summer instructional programs."[40]

The National Association of College and University Summer Sessions is now actively attempting to encourage the U.S. Office of Education to continue its compilation of summer session statistics on a national basis. If it does not succeed in this attempt, NACUSS may take over the project; it has already made a modest start. In addition, NACUSS hopes to enter into an agreement with the Office of Education, under the Cooperative Research Section, for the establishment of a center to collect all studies and research in summer sessions and place them on microfilm. It further plans to prepare a bibliography of all literature relating to summer programs in higher education.

We must have more information on financial policies and practices, on the composition and objectives of the summer session student body, on the functions and powers of administrators, and on the characteristics of the non-degree-credit workshops, to mention only a few. Case studies of the development and important aspects of summer sessions in individual institutions would give solid bases for valid generalizations.

On a more general level, we do not know what kinds of educational policies or practices have what effects on what kinds of students. We do not know how to distinguish between able students who will perform well and those who will not. We do not know in just what ways the institutional environment affects either students or faculty. We do not even know if that environment differs from summer to winter or, if it differs, whether the differences are good or bad. And finally, we do not know very

[40] Harold Haswell, "Nationwide Summer Sessions Information," 1964 NACUSS *Proceedings*, p. 68.

much about student society—how it operates, and how it might be developed in certain desired directions.

Our task, in short, is to pursue "a continuing examination of means-ends relationships, and of the origins and consequences of ends, so that our means become increasingly effective and our ends ever more intelligently chosen."[41] And the summer term, as a microcosm of the larger campus and as an environment hospitable to experimentation, lends itself admirably to the development of what Nevitt Sanford calls a "science of higher education."[42] If it will undertake this task, in addition to the more mundane task of compiling even the most basic statistics about itself, the summer university will not only be able to enhance its own contribution to higher education but it will be taking a significant step towards the betterment of American higher education as a whole.

## INTERINSTITUTIONAL COOPERATION

We have already presented, in Chapter 5, examples of what the summer university has done in promoting cooperation among different institutions of higher education. This important recent development, as we have said, has introduced an entirely new dimension to the American educational scene, and has given new strength to those colleges that take part. It will be noted, however, that most of the experiments so far have centered in the large colleges and universities. What, then, about the small, independent, liberal arts colleges?

According to Gardner, one of the more urgent problems in American higher education is getting these small colleges "back into the main stream of higher education." Swamped by the sheer number of institutions that are being absorbed by the state systems of higher education, these colleges count for less and less in the numerical scheme of things, and the tough facts of economics are making it more and more difficult for them to survive. While the numbers differ from discussion to discussion, there

---

[41] Sanford, *College and Character*, p. 72.
[42] Ibid., p. 13. See also Henry S. Dyer, "Can Institutional Research Lead to a Science of Institutions?" *Educational Record*, Fall 1966, pp. 452–466.

may be as many as five hundred small colleges on the path to obscurity or oblivion.

Since they are too small to offer the richness of resources that so many of today's students and staff expect, their best chance of salvation, Dr. Gardner believes, is through interinstitutional cooperation, among themselves and in alliance with universities. As a pioneer in interinstitutional compacts, the summer term can take the lead in providing general guidance and practical examples.

## IN SUMMARY

Reviewing our agenda now: We have called upon the summer university to restore the status of teaching, to improve the quality of teaching, to reform the undergraduate curriculum, to improve the very institution itself, to better serve its various publics by involving itself in urban problems and promoting the right of all students to an education, to come to know both itself and its parent institution (not to mention its students and faculty), and finally, to engage in all these and other pursuits in cooperation with other institutions. Furthermore, we have asked it to do this not just for itself but for American education as a whole. It is, to borrow Dr. Gardner's words, "an overwhelming list."

In addition, some of the tasks we have outlined are clearly in conflict with each other, reflecting what Frank Pinner calls the "crisis" of the modern university.[43] The steady and insistent effort to stimulate basic research, which is seen as the open sesame to the world of universal scholarship, conflicts with the public assumption that the main functions of a university are undergraduate training and consultancy for local bodies. The lure of commitments to underdeveloped nations overseas conflicts with the need for services to the neighboring town and countryside; and both conflict with the need to restore a sense of "community" to the campus. The myth that any and all productive scholarship can find its place in the campus mosaic

[43] "The Crisis of the State Universities," in Sanford, *College and Character*, pp. 268–278.

conflicts with the hard fact that some academic endeavors should be encouraged and others discouraged.

Such tensions are always present, however. We cannot ask that universities subject themselves to some kind of gray consensus. Every vital community has internal conflicts and tensions. But we can ask that the contending forces be transformed into healthy forms of interaction and dialogue to the end that our great universities continue to be marked by balance between responsibility for great academic possessions and responsiveness to immediate public needs. Only in this way will success not spoil the summer session. And only in this way will the summer session continue to be an important force in the American higher education system, by continuing both to reflect and to pioneer in the current developments which are taking place in higher education and the nation as a whole.

## Looking Forward

On the basis of trends, one can conclude that the future of the summer student and the summer term looks bright indeed. Enrollments are up throughout the country. High quality students at all levels are choosing to attend. Schools are continuing to improve their course offerings. Campus extracurricular life is flourishing. All in all, prosperity has finally come to the summer session. The prosperity is not without its responsibilities, however, and the summer session of the present will need to face up to some serious challenges in the next decades. The challenges involve far more than merely tooling up to meet increased enrollments, for they imply also some basic considerations about the very nature of the summer program.

The primary fact about summer terms is that they exist and flourish because they fulfill certain explicit student needs. As we have pointed out already, the student enrolls for summer study because he needs a particular course or courses, wants to work toward earlier graduation, or wants to receive the specific financial benefits that his or her employer offers for summer study. The summer student thus knows, by and large, exactly what he wants out of the summer education for which he has sacrificed time and money. If he can't get it he will either go elsewhere or not attend at all. In short, while for large segments of the American population college attendance for nine months has become a social as well as an economic necessity, attendance for twelve months has not. Nor does it seem likely to become so in the near future. The summer term must continue, therefore, to sell itself by offering its prospective students what they are looking for.

The experiences of schools which have offered a trimester program bear out this conclusion. Established as a result of a supposedly overwhelming need for faster production of college-trained men and women in the immediate "post-sputnik" years, the trimester program promised an undergraduate degree in three years for those willing to attend three fifteen-week trimesters a year. For several years the trimester seemed to many educators *the* answer to the problems facing higher education, and serious questions were raised as to how most efficiently to deal with, and eventually dispose of, the old, now apparently outmoded summer session. Then disillusion set in. Despite the efforts spent improving the summer trimester and the reams of material put out to publicize the improvements, the students simply did not want to attend, and by early 1966 it was generally conceded that American folkways still argued against compulsory year-round education.[44]

In this light, let us review now some of the tasks before us. Clearly the future of the summer university will depend on its ability to maintain its essentially eclectic posture—that "vigorous and historic tendency" toward "relatively uninhibited experimentation in new ideas and techniques."[45] In particular, it must retain the "all things to all persons" approach that has increasingly come to characterize it. While the full-time continuing student will become more and more prominent, he cannot be allowed to dominate the summer campus to the exclusion of other groups. Those older summer veterans, the specials and the educators, must also be provided for. Even though the summer term need no longer point to teacher retraining as its raison d'être, it cannot ignore the increasing demands of the nation's schools for better trained personnel. So, too, the diverse elements of the special student population should continue to be welcomed to the summer campus.

In a time of increasing selectivity on the part of college admissions officials, programs of trial admission of "borderline cases" to the not yet overcrowded summer term provide a good screening device as well as a source of summer enrollees. Of even greater potentiality are programs for the admission of outstanding high school students to regular summer undergraduate work. Treated just as another student, they are able to use the credits earned when they reach actual university standing. The few schools that have attempted such programs have found the results highly satisfactory. Continued expansion of travel-study programs for both the regular student and the interested layman is also needed, and greater efforts should be made to expand other sorts of off-campus research and study programs. Graduates and undergraduates should be encouraged to pursue topics of special interest in the summer months, receiving academic credit for such diverse work as studying geology in the Canadian Rockies or researching an American history thesis at the Library of Congress.

While certain old values must be maintained, new considerations must also be taken into account. More financial assistance will have to become available, especially in the areas of year-round scholarships and expanded job opportunities. Present conditions generally range from barely acceptable to deplorable. Greater care must be taken in offering a complete program for the prospective three-year bachelor's candidate. Graduate schools likewise must accept the fact that they are running a full-blown year-round operation. Co-curricular offerings should be increased. Here university funds must help provide for student recreational, social, and cultural pleasures in summer just as they do for the rest of the year. Such student service programs as student health, student counseling, and student housing must also be expanded. In short, the summer student deserves the full benefits of university attendance.

A final challenge arises out of the joint need to make the

summer more like the regular year, while at the same time maintaining its unique attributes. The challenge is one that has been voiced clearly and loudly by both students and faculty in recent years. It is the real challenge of the "revolt of the students": the real motivating force behind the "Berkeleys" throughout the country. Stated from an institutional point of view: How can the university retain its concern for the individual in the face of burgeoning enrollments and computerized administration? Stated from the student's point of view: How do I avoid the deadening impersonality of being merely a face in the multiversity crowd? And how do I square traditional ideas of a "well-rounded education" and "learning at the feet of great men" with the modern realities of assistant-run courses, little contact with research-oriented professors, and strong encouragements "to pick a major early and stay with it"? While all this is not exclusively a summer term problem, it cannot help but become of greater significance to summer education in the years ahead.

The situation comes into even sharper focus when we consider that many of the summer term values both past and present fulfill the demands of educational activists in both the student and professorial ranks. Greater student-teacher contact is desired. The summer has always provided this, not only by enrolling smaller student populations, but also because the faculty has been primarily a teaching faculty. Today, with faculty financial position vastly improved over previous decades, the summer teacher is teaching by choice, not by necessity. Further, he is less burdened with time-consuming committee work. The student quite naturally becomes the beneficiary. So, too, he benefits by the diverse, more motivated student body around him. The chance to meet and study with persons outside his usual narrow social group is another of the lasting values of summer. Finally, beyond the completely tangible is an intangible summer spirit, a feeling of belonging, of importance, of purpose. This feeling has been expressed in many ways, but the following summer student's anonymous comment would seem to speak for most:

There is an indescribable friendliness and togetherness about summer school that makes my heart warm to . . . my home. Not a "home away from home" but "my home." Somehow, everyone drops the pretense —the acting, the sophistication—in summer. Girls wear shorts to classes, even men students yield to the temptation to be cool. Profs joke about their rank among their fellows (as measured by the time their classes meet and which side of the building they are located). We all have something in common which seems to bind us together. Seniors, grad students, summer freshmen, and profs all become friends. Everyone is "in this together."[46]

If the summer session can retain this spirit it not only will aid its own programs and prospects but will provide an invaluable lesson for all higher education.

Throughout this book we have tried to make it abundantly clear that the American university summer term, after eighty years of development in comparative obscurity, has now emerged into unexpected limelight as the focus of those problems and challenges agitating our institutions of higher education. We have seen, first, how the summer session is the scene of continuing conflicts that lend vitality to academic enterprise: the perennial dialogue between faculty and administration, with a new breed of executive emerging to perform a role of quiet leadership, whether he occupy a professor's chair or a president's suite; the pervasive conflict between responsibility for academic standards and traditions and responsiveness to public needs and wants, the balancing of which is the genius of the modern university; and the related debate between conformity to time-honored curricular modes and structural patterns, and flexibility in outlook and execution. Whatever the solution to these and other problems, we know that it must be indigenous; that is, summer term calendars, clientele, curricula, and administrative structures must be in keeping with the background and aspirations of the particular institution or region they are designed to support.

As our various institutions move to shape the summer university of the future, we can expect to see at least seven major trends:

---

[46] In Howard Knutson, *Report on the 11-Week Summer Session* (mimeographed, Cedar Falls: State College of Iowa, 1964).

1. The summer as a period of experimentation, particularly in the areas of interdisciplinary programs and special offerings for groups with particular needs.

2. Modernization of educational facilities and techniques, such as the harnessing of electronic developments to classroom purposes.

3. Constant evaluation, with increased investment in those programs that serve well and a discarding of others.

4. The summer administrator emerging as an internal coordinator and external interpreter of the methods and aims of higher education.

5. A mutual blending of the characteristics of the regular year with those of the summer term to the end that the year-round pattern of university enterprise is more homogeneous from season to season.

6. Increased interinstitutional cooperation.

7. Increased attention to the solution of domestic and international problems.

In sum, the problems of the summer term are largely the problems of higher education in general. By its very nature a peculiar breed of academic animal, the summer session is in an advantageous position to find and experiment with new ways and means of solving some of the dilemmas of the university. The summer session's role in revising curricula, its use of independent study and foreign travel, its ready acceptance of "special" students, and the improvement of its teaching and administration—all are signs that the summer term has accepted this challenge, to the end that it has become a significant device which each American university can increasingly employ to attain its goals. For many of us, this presages a summer enterprise "as broad as human endeavor and as high as human aspirations."

Reference Matter

# Appendix A

FEDERAL AND FOUNDATION SUPPORT OF UNIVERSITY OF
WISCONSIN INSTRUCTIONAL PROGRAM, MADISON CAMPUS
SUMMER 1966

| | SUMMER SESSIONS PROGRAMS | | |
|---|---|---|---|
| Program | Granting Agency | Department | Amount |
| Early Childhood Education | SDPW | Home Econ | $ 2,227 |
| School Administrator's Inst for Ed Res | USOE | Ed Admin | 55,000 |
| Summer Inst in Mathematics for Secondary Teachers | NSF | Math | 39,230 |
| Adv Science Seminar in Interstellar Gas Dynamics | NSF | Astr | 24,785 |
| NDEA Inst in School Library | NDEA | Libr | 48,870 |
| Ed Media Specialists Inst | NDEA | Curr & Inst | 60,289 |
| Army Adv Pub Rel Course | US Army | Journ | 15,304 |
| Family Finance Seminar | Nat Com | Curr & Inst, Bus | 16,192 |
| Teacher Internship Program | | | |
| Secondary | Ford | Wis Imp Prog | 28,000 |
| Elementary | Ford | Wis Imp Prog | 22,000 |
| International Studies | Ford | L & S | 36,880 |
| Banking Schools | Bankers Assoc | Bus | 3,900 |
| Credit Union School | CUNA | Bus | 5,730 |
| Public Service Commissioners | NARUC | Bus | 4,000 |
| Nursing | WSBN | Nurs | 2,655 |
| Psychiatric Nursing | NIMH | Nurs | 1,800 |
| TOTAL | | | $366,912 |

(*Continued on following page*)

YEAR-ROUND PROGRAMS
THE SUMMER SESSION PARTICIPATING

| Program | Granting Agency | Department | Amount |
|---|---|---|---|
| Undergrad Res Participation | NSF | Psych | $ 29,400 |
| Undergrad Res Participation | NSF | Econ | 12,600 |
| Undergrad Res Participation | NSF | Math | 14,000 |
| Undergrad Res Participation | NSF | Civ Engr | 12,600 |
| Res Participation for High School Teachers | NSF | Zoology | 45,800 |
| Year Inst in Math & Science for Secondary Teachers | NSF | Curr & Inst | 143,700 |
| TOTAL | | | $258,100 |

SUMMER PROGRAMS
THE SUMMER SESSION COOPERATING

| Program | Granting Agency | Department | Amount |
|---|---|---|---|
| Clinical Aspects of Nursing | HEW | Ext Nurs | $ 2,570 |
| Summer Inst in Computing Machines and Their Applications for College Teachers | NSF | Ext Engr | 41,530 |
| Occupational Health Nursing Practices | NSF | Ext Nurs | 4,050 |
| Conf on Statistical Experimental Design for College Teachers | NSF | Ext Nurs | 30,400 |
| In-Service Inst in Physics for Secondary Teachers | NSF | Ext Physics | 7,130 |
| In-Service Inst in Geometry for Secondary Teachers | NSF | Ext Math | 17,020 |
| TOTAL | | | $102,700 |

# Appendix B

CALENDAR PATTERNS IN 116 SELECTED UNIVERSITIES

| UNIVERSITY | YEAR-ROUND ACADEMIC ORGANIZATIONAL PLAN[a] | | WEEKS OF OPERATION PER YEAR[b] |
|---|---|---|---|
| | Academic Year[c] | Academic Summer | |
| Alabama | S: 2 18-wk | 2 5½-wk terms with an increasing number of 11-wk courses | 47 |
| Alaska | S: 2 16-wk | 1 6-wk term with 3- & 1-wk courses in some fields; complete summer semester at military installations & at Anchorage Community College | 38+ |
| American (D.C.) | S: 2 16-wk | 2 5-wk terms; 1 8-wk night term | 42 |
| Arizona | S: 2 17-wk | 2 5-wk terms | 44 |

*Source:* Report of an ad hoc committee of the Association of University Summer Sessions, October 1966.

[a] Excluding orientation, advising, registration, and commencement.
[b] Excluding pre- and post-sessions and other special short terms.
[c] In this column, S = semester, T = trimester, and Q = quarter.

| University | Year-round Academic Organizational Plan | | Weeks of Operation Per Year |
|---|---|---|---|
| | Academic Year | Academic Summer | |
| Arizona State | S: 2 17-wk | 2 5-wk terms; 1- or 2-wk pre-session; 2- or 3-wk post-session | 44+ |
| Arkansas | S: 2 17-wk | 2 6-wk terms | 46 |
| Baylor | S: 2 18-wk | 2 6-wk terms | 48 |
| Boston | S: 2 16-wk | 2 6-wk terms | 44 |
| Bowling Green | S: 2 16-wk | 2 5-wk terms | 42 |
| Bradley | S: 2 17-wk | 2 5-wk terms | 44 |
| Brigham Young | S: 2 17-wk | 2 5-wk terms | 44 |
| California (Berkeley) | S: 2 17-wk | 2 6-wk terms | 46 |
| California (Los Angeles) | S: 2 16-wk | 2 6-wk terms | 44 |
| Chicago | Q: 3 11-wk | Full 11-wk qtr; 9-wk Educ session | 44 |
| Cincinnati | Q: 3 10- & 11-wk | Full 10-wk qtr term with 3 3 1/3-wk terms & 2-wk inter-session | 45 |
| Colorado | S: 2 17-wk | 10-wk main term; 2 5-wk terms | 44 |
| Colorado State | Q: 2 12- & 1 11-wk | 1 10-wk qtr with 2 5-wk sessions | 45 |
| Columbia | S: 2 17-wk | 3 6-wk sessions, 1 concurrently & overlapping, all both undergrad & grad | 46+ |
| Connecticut | S: 2 16½-wk | Concurrent undergrad sessions (6- & 8-wk); grad sessions (6-wk session, 3-wk post-session, 2-wk workshops) | 39+ |

| UNIVERSITY | YEAR-ROUND ACADEMIC ORGANIZATIONAL PLAN | | WEEKS OF OPERATION PER YEAR |
|---|---|---|---|
| | Academic Year | Academic Summer | |
| Cornell | S: 2 17-wk | 1 6½-wk term, plus 1- to 14-wk "Special Programs" | 40½ |
| Delaware | S: 2 16-wk | 2 6-wk terms | 44 |
| Denver | Q: 3 11-wk | 1 9-wk term; equiv to a 4th qtr | 42 |
| De Paul | S: 2 16-wk (day) Q: 3 12-wk (eve) | 1 6- & 1 4-wk term (day); 1 8-wk term (eve) | 42 |
| Duke | S: 2 17-wk | 2 5½-wk terms | 45 |
| Fairleigh Dickinson | S: 2 16-wk | 2 6-wk terms | 44 |
| Florida | T: 2 15-wk | 3rd trimester split into 7½-wk terms | 45 |
| Florida State | T: 2 15-wk | 3rd trimester split into 7½-wk terms | 45 |
| Florida, South | T: 2 15-wk | 3rd trimester split into 7½-wk terms | 45 |
| Florida A & M | T: 2 15-wk | 3rd trimester split into 7½-wk terms | 45 |
| Fordham | S: 2 16-wk | 1 6-wk term; 1 8-wk night term | 38+ |
| George Washington | S: 2 16-wk | 2 5-wk terms; Educ has 1 6-wk session, 3 3-wk terms; Law has 2 6-wk terms, 1 13-wk term | 42+ |
| Georgia | Q: 3 11-wk | 1 9-wk term | 42 |

| University | Year-round Academic Organizational Plan | | Weeks of Operation Per Year |
|---|---|---|---|
| | Academic Year | Academic Summer | |
| Harvard | S: 2 17-wk | 1 8-wk A & S term; 1 7-wk term for Educ | 42 |
| Hawaii | S: 2 18-wk | 2 6-wk terms | 48 |
| Houston | S: 2 16½-wk | 1 12-wk, 2 6-wk terms | 45 |
| Idaho | S: 2 18-wk | 1 8-wk term | 44 |
| Illinois | S: 2 17-wk | 1 8-wk term | 42 |
| Indiana | S: 2 17-wk | 1 8½-wk term; 2½-wk pre- & post-session | 47½ |
| Iowa | S: 2 17-wk | 1 8-wk term; added 4-wk independent study unit & 12-wk term primarily for undergrads | 46 |
| Iowa State | Q: 3 11-wk | 11-wk qtr divided into 2 5½-wk terms | 44 |
| Johns Hopkins | S: 2 15-wk | 1 12-wk term | 42 |
| Kansas | S: 2 17-wk | 1 8-wk term | 42 |
| Kansas State | S: 2 17½-wk | 1 8-wk term | 43 |
| Kent State | Q: 11½, 10½, & 10½ wks | 1 10-wk qtr; 2 5-wk terms | 42½ |
| Kentucky | S: 2 16-wk | 1 8-wk term | 40 |
| Lehigh | 2 17-wk terms | 2 5½-wk terms | 45 |
| Louisiana State | S: 2 17-wk | 1 9-wk term | 43 |
| Loyola (Chicago) | S: 2 17-wk | 1 6-wk term; 1 4-wk term; 7½-wk night term | 44 |
| Maine | S: 2 16-wk | 1 12-wk session of 3 overlapping 6-wk terms & 4 3-wk terms | 44 |

| University | Year-round Academic Organizational Plan | | Weeks of Operation Per Year |
|---|---|---|---|
| | Academic Year | Academic Summer | |
| Maryland | S: 2 16-wk | Overlapping 8- & 6-wk terms | 40 |
| Marquette | S: 2 17-wk | Basic 6-wk term; 8-wk term | 42 |
| Massachusetts | S: 2 16-wk | 2 6-wk sessions | 44 |
| Mass. Inst. of Technology | S: 2 17-wk | 1 10-wk term | 44 |
| Miami (Florida) | S: 2 16-wk | 2 5½-wk terms | 45 |
| Miami (Ohio) | T: 2 15-wk; & 1 7½-wk term | 1 7½-wk term | 45 |
| Michigan | T: 2 15-wk | 1 15-wk term, as well as 2 7½-wk half-terms with the 2nd much like a traditional summer session | 45 |
| Michigan State | Q: 3 11-wk | 1 11-wk qtr with 1 5½-wk half-qtr term | 44 |
| Minnesota | Q: 3 11-wk | 2 5-wk terms | 43 |
| Mississippi | S: 2 16-wk | 2 5½-wk terms; some 11-wk courses; a few 3-wk courses | 43+ |
| Missouri | S: 2 18-wk | 1 8-wk term | 44 |
| Montana | Q: 3 11-wk | 1 9-wk qtr with 2 4½-wk terms | 42 |
| Nebraska | S: 2 17-wk | 1 8-wk session with inter-spersed sessions of 6, 4, & 3 wks; 4-wk post-session | 46 |
| Nevada | S: 2 17-wk | 1 12-wk term; 2 6-wk sessions | 46 |
| New Hampshire | S: 2 17-wk | 1 8-wk, 2 4-wk, 1 6-wk term | 42+ |

| University | Year-round Academic Organizational Plan | | Weeks of Operation Per Year |
|---|---|---|---|
| | Academic Year | Academic Summer | |
| New Mexico | S: 2 17-wk | 1 8-wk term | 42 |
| New York University | S: 2 16-wk | 1 12-wk, 1 6-wk, 2 3-wk terms | 44 |
| New York, State Univ. at Buffalo | S: 2 16-wk | 2 6-wk terms; midsummer 6-wk term; 3-wk post-session | 44 |
| N. Carolina | S: 2 17-wk | 2 6-wk terms (1 qtr) | 46 |
| N. Dakota | S: 2 17-wk | 1 8-wk term | 42 |
| Northeastern | 3 10-wk terms | 2 5-wk half-terms | 40 |
| Northwestern | Q: 3 11-wk | 1 10½-wk qtr; 8-wk, 6-wk, 3-wk terms | 43½+ |
| Notre Dame | S: 2 17-wk | 1 6-wk term | 40 |
| Ohio | S: 2 18-wk | 2 5½-wk terms | 47 |
| Ohio State | Q: 3 11-wk | 1 10-wk qtr with 2 5-wk terms | 43 |
| Oklahoma | S: 2 16-wk | 1 9-wk term | 41 |
| Oklahoma State | S: 2 16-wk | 1 9-wk term | 41 |
| Omaha | S: 2 17-wk | 2 5-wk terms, with 1 8-wk eve term | 44 |
| Oregon | Q: 3, of 12, 11, & 11 wks | 1 11-wk term | 45 |
| Oregon State | Q: 3 11-wk | 1 11-wk session, 1 concurrent 8-wk session | 44 |
| Pennsylvania | S: 15-wk fall, 16-wk spr | 2 6-wk terms | 43 |
| Penn State | 3 10-wk terms | 1 10-wk term | 40 |
| Pittsburgh | 2 15-wk terms, 1 9-wk half-term | 6-wk session offered concurrently with last 6-wks of 3rd term | 45 |

| University | Year-round Academic Organizational Plan | | Weeks of Operation Per Year |
|---|---|---|---|
| | Academic Year | Academic Summer | |
| Puerto Rico | S: 2 16-wk | 1 6-wk term | 38 |
| Purdue | S: 2 16-wk | 1 8-wk session; 3 3-wk terms | 40+ |
| Rhode Island | S: 2 17-wk | 2 5½-wk terms | 45 |
| Rutgers | S: 2 17-wk | 1 3-wk, 1 8-wk, 1 concurrent 6-wk term | 45 |
| St. Johns | S: 2 16-wk | 2 5-wk terms; 1 midsummer concurrent 6-wk term | 42 |
| St. Louis | S: 2 17-wk | Concurrent 8-wk, 6-wk terms followed by 5-wk term | 47 |
| S. Carolina | S: 2 17-wk | 2 6-wk terms | 46 |
| Southern California | S: 2 17-wk | 1 12-wk, 1 11-wk, 1 7-wk, 1 4-wk term | 46+ |
| S. Dakota | S: 2 17-wk | 1 8-wk term | 42 |
| Southern Illinois | Q: 3 11-wk | 1 11-wk qtr for lower div; 8-wk term for upper div and grad | 44 |
| Southern Methodist | S: 2 16½-wk | 2 6-wk terms | 45 |
| Stanford | Q: 3 11-wk | 1 8-wk term; a few 10-wk courses | 41+ |
| Syracuse | S: 2 17-wk | 1 6-wk, 1 4½-wk term | 44½ |
| Temple | S: 2 16-wk | 2 6-wk, 1 3-wk term | 44 |
| Tennessee | Q: 3 11-wk | 1 11-wk qtr | 44 |
| Texas | S: 2 17-wk | 2 6-wk terms, except in Engr, Pharm, Law, Architecture | 46 |

| University | Year-round Academic Organizational Plan | | Weeks of Operation Per Year |
|---|---|---|---|
| | Academic Year | Academic Summer | |
| Texas Christian | S: 2 18-wk | 2 6-wk terms; some eve 9-wk courses; some 3-wk courses in Educ | 48 |
| Tulane | S: 2, of 17 & 16 wks | 2 6-wk terms; considering 12-wk courses | 45 |
| Utah | Q: 3 11-wk | 1 2-wk workshop term; 1 8-wk session | 43 |
| Utah State | Q: 3 11-wk | 2 5-wk terms; emphasis on full 10-wk qtr | 43 |
| Vanderbilt | S: 2 17-wk | 1 11½-wk abbreviated sem; 2 5½-wk terms | 45½ |
| Vermont | S: 2 15-wk | 1 8-wk, 1 overlapping 6-wk, 2 4- and 3-wk sessions | 38+ |
| Virginia | S: 2 17-wk | 1 10-wk, 1 8-wk, 1 6-wk term; 3-wk intersession for Educ | 44+ |
| Washington (Seattle) | Q: 3 11-wk | 9-wk qtr; many courses avail in 2 4½-wk terms | 42 |
| Washington State | S: 2 17-wk | 1 8-wk term | 42 |
| Washington (St. Louis) | S: 2 17-wk | 2 5½-wk terms; 1 overlapping 8-wk term | 45 |
| Wayne State (Detroit) | Q: 3 11-wk | 1 11-wk qtr with an additional 5½-wk midsummer term | 44 |

| University | Year-round Academic Organizational Plan | | Weeks of Operation Per Year |
|---|---|---|---|
| | Academic Year | Academic Summer | |
| Western Michigan | S: 2 17-wk | 1 8-wk term; overlapping 6- & 2-wk terms | 42 |
| Western Reserve | S: 2 17-wk | 1 6-wk, 1 5-wk term | 45 |
| W. Virginia | S: 2 18-wk | 1 10-wk term | 46 |
| Wichita State | S: 2 18-wk | 1 8-wk term | 44 |
| Wisconsin | S: 2 17-wk | Basic 8-wk term; 3-, 4-, 5-, 10-wk terms in special areas | 48 |
| Wyoming | S: 2 17-wk | 2 5-wk terms | 44 |
| Yale | S: 2 16-wk | 10-wk term for Med & Forestry; 8-wk Music term. (Although it has been traditional that no summer work may be counted toward a Yale degree, some exceptions are appearing.) | 32+ |

# Appendix C

COMPARISON OF SUMMER AND FALL STUDENT FINANCIAL
AIDS IN 16 LARGE UNIVERSITIES

| University | Summer Enrollment as a Percentage of Fall Enrollment | Total Number of Summer Students Aided as a Percentage of Fall Students Aided |
|---|---|---|
| New York University | 96.1 | 10.2 |
| University of North Carolina | 66.2 | 22.7 |
| Indiana University | 63.6 | 32.6 |
| University of Colorado, Boulder | 62.4 | 14.6 |
| University of New York, Buffalo | 57.3 | 13.6 |
| Harvard | 49.0 | 7.3 |
| University of Washington | 48.9 | 16.0 |
| University of Iowa | 44.2 | 7.3 |
| University of Virginia | 43.6 | 13.5 |
| University of Wisconsin | 43.6 | 51.4 |
| University of Southern California | 39.6 | 9.0 |
| University of New Mexico | 39.4 | 2.5 |
| University of Illinois | 35.4 | 41.1 |
| Montana State University | 35.3 | 43.5 |
| University of Arizona | 34.9 | 10.1 |
| Columbia University | 30.3 | 16.0 |

Source: Ralph Sinks, et al., "A Study of Financial Assistance Granted in
1963–64 to Undergraduate and Graduate Students in Member Colleges and
Universities of the Association of Deans and Directors of Summer Sessions,"
Report to the Association of University Summer Sessions, October 1965.

# Appendix D

WHAT AUTHORITY DOES THE SUMMER SCHOOL DIRECTOR
HAVE IN MAKING DECISIONS AT 29 LARGER SCHOOLS?

| DECISIONS TO BE MADE AFFECTING SUMMER SCHOOL | NUMBER REPORTING AUTHORITY FOR DECISION RESTS IN: | | | |
|---|---|---|---|---|
| | Director (Dean) | Director and Others | Others Only | No Inf. |
| *General* | | | | |
| Setting beginning and closing dates | 3 | 19 | 7 | — |
| Determining length of 4th of July holiday | 4 | 15 | 9 | 1 |
| Determining Summer School budget requests | 12 | 17 | — | — |
| Determining Summer School catalogue format | 18 | 11 | — | — |
| Determining publicity used or publicity policy | 15 | 14 | — | — |
| Decision on air conditioning a new building | — | 7 | 22 | — |
| Decision on air conditioning an old building | — | 8 | 21 | — |
| Determining summer parking policies and fees | — | 8 | 21 | — |
| *Decisions About Classes* | | | | |
| Determining the courses to be offered | 2 | 25 | 2 | — |

*Source:* Forest L. Whan, "Report of the Personnel Committee 1965," Report to the North Central Conference of Summer Schools, 1965 (mimeographed), Table 18. Reprinted by permission of the author.

| DECISIONS TO BE MADE AFFECTING SUMMER SCHOOL | NUMBER REPORTING AUTHORITY FOR DECISION RESTS IN: | | | |
|---|---|---|---|---|
| | Director (Dean) | Director and Others | Others Only | No Inf. |
| Setting the minimum class size permitted | 5 | 18 | 6 | — |
| Setting the maximum enrollment for a class | 3 | 19 | 7 | — |
| Dismissing classes to hold convocations, etc. | 10 | 11 | 8 | — |
| Vetoing departmental course offerings | 12 | 13 | 4 | — |
| Overruling a department not wishing to teach | 4 | 20 | 3 | 2 |
| Number of sections of a course to schedule | 4 | 16 | 9 | — |
| Determining time of day a course is offered | 4 | 13 | 12 | — |
| Determining which classroom will be used | 3 | 12 | 14 | — |
| Cancelling a class because of low enrollment | 13 | 15 | 1 | — |
| Course cancellation because of staffing difficulties | 7 | 18 | 4 | — |
| Scheduling NSF or other institutes | 2 | 17 | 9 | 1 |
| *Decisions about the Summer Staff* | | | | |
| Selection of the staff members to be hired | 1 | 19 | 9 | — |
| Determining loads to be handled by those hired | 3 | 17 | 9 | — |
| Setting loads for 11 or 12 months teachers | 3 | 12 | 13 | 1 |
| Approving sabbatical for 12 months teachers | 1 | 7 | 15 | 6 |
| Leave without pay for 12 months teachers | 1 | 5 | 17 | 6 |
| Hiring substitutes for 12 months teachers on leave | 2 | 17 | 7 | 3 |
| Changing 12 months to 9 months status of teachers | — | 5 | 20 | 4 |

| DECISIONS TO BE MADE AFFECTING SUMMER SCHOOL | NUMBER REPORTING AUTHORITY FOR DECISION RESTS IN: | | | |
|---|---|---|---|---|
| | Director (Dean) | Director and Others | Others Only | No Inf. |
| Permitting 12 months teachers vacation during summer | — | 7 | 19 | 3 |
| Changing amount of teaching of 12 months teachers | 1 | 12 | 11 | 5 |
| Setting limits on per cent hired in given rank | 1 | 12 | 8 | 8 |
| Rotation of employment in large departments | 1 | 12 | 14 | 2 |
| Releasing a teacher from an agreed-upon contract | 5 | 20 | 4 | — |
| *Decisions about Salaries Paid in Summer* | | | | |
| Establishing a summer salary scale or formula | 2 | 21 | 5 | 1 |
| Setting portion of salary paid if load is light | 7 | 14 | 2 | 6 |
| Establishing amounts paid to visiting teachers | 7 | 20 | 2 | — |
| *Decisions about Students and about Housing* | | | | |
| Establishing enrollment procedures | — | 19 | 9 | 1 |
| Establishing summer school fees | 2 | 14 | 13 | — |
| Determining summer admission requirements | — | 18 | 11 | — |
| Establishing the orientation program | — | 16 | 9 | 4 |
| Determining disciplinary action | — | 6 | 22 | 1 |
| Permitting exceptionally heavy student load | 5 | 13 | 11 | — |
| Setting charges for on-campus housing | — | 4 | 24 | 1 |
| Establishing on-campus housing policies and hours | — | 2 | 25 | 2 |
| Determining hours that on-campus food is served | — | 7 | 22 | — |

| DECISIONS TO BE MADE AFFECTING SUMMER SCHOOL | NUMBER REPORTING AUTHORITY FOR DECISION RESTS IN: | | | |
|---|---|---|---|---|
| | Director (Dean) | Director and Others | Others Only | No Inf. |
| *Decisions about Recreation and Cultural Programs* | | | | |
| Arranging convocations and other all-campus speakers | 3 | 22 | 3 | 1 |
| Arranging for music or artist series | 3 | 21 | 4 | 1 |
| Planning "after-hours" recreational programs | 1 | 21 | 6 | 1 |

# Selected Bibliography

*Annual Report of the 1964 Summer Session.* Mimeographed. Boulder: University of Colorado, 1964.

*Annual Report of the 1965 University of Wisconsin Summer Sessions.* Mimeographed. Madison: University of Wisconsin Office of Summer Sessions, 1965.

*Background Materials on University of Wisconsin Summer Session.* Mimeographed. Madison: University of Wisconsin Office of Summer Sessions, 1958.

Baskin, Samuel, ed. *Higher Education: Some Newer Developments.* New York: McGraw-Hill, 1965.

Bester, John F. "Student Performance in Summer Programs." *American Journal of Pharmaceutical Education,* February 1965.

Burrin, Frank. "Year-Round Programs—Possibilities for Improvement Without Major Calendar Change." Speech to the North Central Conference of Summer Schools, April 5, 1964.

*Columbia University Seminar Proceedings, March 10, 1961.* "The Summer Session in Higher Education."

Dangerfield, Royden. "Issues, Impacts, and Opportunities for Sponsored Educational Programs." Speech to the North Central Conference of Summer Schools, March 28, 1965.

Dennis, Lawrence E. "Will Success Spoil Higher Education?" *Educational Record,* Fall 1965.

"Evaluation of the Trial Study Program at West Virginia Wesleyan College." *West Virginia Wesleyan College Reports.* Mimeographed. Buckhannon: West Virginia Wesleyan College, July 30, 1965.

*For Your Information.* Office of Institutional Research Circular No. 74. Washington: National Association of State Universities and Land-Grant Colleges, May 19, 1965.

Gardner, John W. "Agenda for the Colleges and Universities." *Journal of Higher Education,* October 1965.

Gibson, Raymond C. "The Organization of Summer Session Programs." Speech to the North Central Conference of Summer Schools, March 29, 1965.

Goodnight, S. H. *The Story of the Origins and Growth of the Summer School and the Summer Session 1885–1940.* Mimeographed. Madison: University of Wisconsin Office of Summer Sessions, 1940.

Hadley, Paul E., and Provart, John D. *A Study of the Summer Session at the University of Southern California.* Los Angeles: University of Southern California Office of the Summer Session, 1964.

Heidenreich, Charles A. *A Study of the Functions and Powers of Summer Session Directors in Selected Institutions of Higher Education in the United States: Summary Report.* Mimeographed. Sacramento: Sacramento City College, 1965.

"In the Good Old Summertime." *The Shape of Education for 1965–66.* Washington: National School Public Relations Association, 1965.

Kanun, Clara; Ziebarth, E. W.; and Abrahams, Norman. "Comparisons of Student Achievement in the Summer Term and Regular Quarter." *Journal of Experimental Education,* Fall 1963.

Knutson, Howard. *Report on the 11-week Summer Session.* Mimeographed. Cedar Falls: State College of Iowa, 1964.

Lins, L. J. *Comparison of Use of Time During 1961 Summer by Undergraduate Students Registered at Madison and Milwaukee During 1961 Fall Semester.* Mimeographed. Madison: University of Wisconsin Office of Institutional Studies, 1962.

Lins, L. J., and Abell, Allan P. *Attendance Patterns of Fall 1958 New Freshmen for Twelve Semesters After Entrance: The University of Wisconsin, Madison Campus.* Mimeographed. Madison: University of Wisconsin Office of Institutional Studies, 1965.

Lins, L. J.; Abell, Allan P.; and Kegel, Paul L. *Comparison of Summer Session and Fall New Freshmen: The University of Wisconsin, Madison Campus.* Mimeographed. Madison: University of Wisconsin Office of Institutional Studies, 1963.

Lins, L. J.; Abell, Allan P.; and Stucki, David R. *Student Evaluations of the 1964 Summer Sessions with Special Reference to the Twelve-Week Session.* Mimeographed. Madison: University of Wisconsin Office of Institutional Studies, 1964.

Lins, L. J.; Schoenfeld, C. A.; Rees, Robert A.; and Abell, Allan P. *Student Reactions to 1961 Summer Sessions: The University of Wisconsin, Madison Campus.* Mimeographed. Madison: University of Wisconsin Office of Institutional Studies, 1962.

Little, John R. "Organizations for Summer Administrators: Development, Current Status and Possibilities." Speech to the North Central Conference of Summer Schools, March 29, 1965.

Little, John R. "Problems, Trends, and Implications of the Year-Round Program." Speech to the North Central Conference of Summer Schools, March 17, 1963.

McFadden, H. B. *Summary of Summer Faculty Salary Questionnaire.* Mimeographed. Laramie: University of Wyoming Summer School, 1966.

Miller, Howard S. *The University of Wisconsin Summer Sessions, 1885–1960.* Madison: University of Wisconsin Office of Summer Sessions, 1960.

Morton, John R. *University Extension in the United States.* Birmingham: University of Alabama Press, 1953.

Moyer, James H. *Report on the 1964 Summer Session at Heidelberg College.* Mimeographed. Tiffin, Ohio: Heidelberg College, 1964.

Munster, Joe H., and Smith, Justin C. "A Second Look at Government-Supported Research." *Educational Record,* Spring 1965.

Owens, William A. *Summer Study and Higher Education.* New York: Columbia University Office of Summer Sessions, 1961.

*Proceedings of the First Annual Meeting of the National Association of College and University Summer Sessions, 1964.*

*Proceedings of the Third Annual Meeting of the National Association of College and University Summer Sessions, 1966.*

*Proposed Policy Statement and Working Paper on Strengthening the University of Wisconsin Summer Sessions, 1961.* Mimeographed.

Madison: University of Wisconsin Office of Summer Sessions, 1961.

*A Report by a Special Committee of the Ford Foundation to the University of Pittsburgh.* New York: The Ford Foundation, January 1966.

Richey, Robert, and Dressel, Fred. *A Study of Salaries and Fringe Benefits for Resident Faculty in 115 Major Colleges and Universities in the United States.* Mimeographed. Bloomington: Indiana University, 1963. Revised 1965.

Richey, Robert, and Gwaltney, Bernita. *The Development of Summer Study at Indiana University.* Bloomington: Indiana University Office of Summer Sessions, 1965.

Richey, Robert; Sinks, Ralph W.; Burrin, Frank K.; and Ried, Harold O. "A Study of Newer Policies and Procedures in the 1964 Summer Sessions." Report to the Association of Summer Session Deans and Directors, 1964.

Richey, Robert W.; Sinks, Ralph W.; and Chase, Clifton I. *A Comparison of the Academic Achievement of Students Enrolled in Nine Courses in the Intersession of 1963 and that of Students Enrolled in the Same Courses in the Spring Semester of 1962–1963.* Mimeographed. Bloomington: Indiana University Office of Summer Sessions, 1965.

Richey, Robert; Yaple, Graydon; and Utley, William. *North Central Conference of Summer Schools Comparison of Characteristics.* Mimeographed. North Central Conference of Summer Schools, 1963, 1964, 1965.

Sanford, Nevitt, ed. *The American College.* New York: John Wiley and Sons, 1962.

Sanford, Nevitt, ed. *College and Character.* New York: John Wiley and Sons, 1964.

Saupe, Joe L. *A Survey of Summer School Students, Summer, 1960.* Mimeographed. East Lansing: Michigan State University Office of Institutional Research, 1961.

Schoenfeld, Clarence A., ed. *The Shape of Summer Sessions to Come.* Madison: University of Wisconsin Office of Summer Sessions, 1961.

Schoenfeld, Clarence A. *The University and Its Publics.* New York: Harper, 1954.

Schoenfeld, Clarence A., and Schmitz, Neil. *Year-Round Education.* Madison: Dembar Educational Research Services, 1964.

Schoenfeld, Clarence A., and Shannon, Theodore J. *University Ex-*

*tension.* New York: Center for Applied Research in Education, 1965.

Sharp, Harry. *Students View the 1962 Summer Session at the University of Utah.* Mimeographed. Madison: Wisconsin Survey Research Laboratory, 1962.

Sinks, Ralph; Allen, Donovan; Burrin, Frank; Ried, Harold; and Richey, Robert. "A Study of Financial Assistance Granted in 1963–64 to Undergraduate and Graduate Students in Member Colleges and Universities of the Association of Deans and Directors of Summer Sessions." Report to the Association of University Summer Sessions, October 1965.

Smith, Clodus R. *The University of Maryland Summer School, 1963.* Mimeographed. College Park: University of Maryland Summer School, 1963.

*Standards for the Evaluation of Summer Schools.* Mimeographed. Chicago: North Central Conference of Summer Schools, 1962.

Stecklein, John E.; Corcoran, Mary; and Ziebarth, E. W. *The Summer Session: Its Role in the University of Minnesota Program.* Minneapolis: University of Minnesota Bureau of Institutional Research, 1958.

Stirton, William E. "The Summer Session in University Relations." Speech to the Association of Summer Session Deans and Directors, October 19, 1956.

*Summer Session Questionnaire 1963.* Mimeographed. Kalamazoo: Western Michigan University, 1963.

Valaske, John M. *A Report on the Summer Student at the Kenosha Extension Center of the University of Wisconsin.* Mimeographed. Kenosha, Wisconsin, 1962.

Veysey, Laurence R. *The Emergence of the American University.* Chicago: University of Chicago Press, 1965.

Wallace, Donald G. *Is Summer School the Way to "Fatten-up" a Grade Average?* Mimeographed. Des Moines: Drake University Office of the Summer Session and Institutional Research, 1964.

Warner, Donald F.; Retzlaff, Bernice R.; and Haswell, Harold A. *Summer Sessions in Colleges and Universities of the United States, 1960.* Washington: U.S. Office of Education, 1963.

Whan, Forest L. Report to the North Central Conference of Summer Schools, 1964.

Whan, Forest L. "Report of the Personnel Committee, 1965." Report to the North Central Conference of Summer Schools, 1965.

*Year-Around Operation in American Universities.* Mimeographed.

SELECTED BIBLIOGRAPHY

Boulder, Colorado: Association of Summer Session Deans and
Directors, 1963.

*Year-round Calendar Patterns and Plans in 116 Selected Universities.*
Mimeographed. Compiled by the Association of University Summer Sessions, 1963, 1964, 1965. Revised October 1966 in a
report of an ad hoc committee of the Association.

Ziebarth, E. W. "The Summer Session: Still an Appendage? Or, a
Research View!" Speech to the North Central Conference of
Summer Schools, March 18, 1963.

# Index